FAITH
MADE
PERFECT

FAITH MADE PERFECT

Commentary on James

HERMAN HANKO

REFORMED
FREE PUBLISHING
ASSOCIATION
Jenison, Michigan

Scripture cited is taken from the King James (Authorized) Version

Cover design by Christopher Tobias/www.tobiasdesign.com
Interior design by Katherine Lloyd, The DESK/www.theDESKonline.com

Reformed Free Publishing Association
1894 Georgetown Center Drive
Jenison, Michigan 49428
616-457-5970
www.rfpa.org

ISBN 978-1-936054-86-2
ISBN ebook 978-1-936054-87-9
LCCN 2015936711

To the memory of Herman Hoeksema,
a superb exegete, from whom I learned all I know
concerning how to interpret sacred scripture

Seest thou how faith wrought with his works, and by works was faith made perfect?

—James 2:22

CONTENTS

PREFACE

I had just finished preaching a series of sermons on Galatians in the pulpit of Hope Protestant Reformed Church. I was enthralled with the glory of the gospel of justification by faith. It was doctrine that fed the hungry soul, comforted the heart of one burdened with sin, and directed us to the one great goal of all our lives, the glory of God alone.

I am aware of Rome's denial of this grand truth and that it formed the sharp dividing line between Rome's apostasy and the gospel of the Reformation. I also am aware of the dreadful error of those who teach what they call the federal vision and their open and often contemptuous denial of justification by faith alone and promotion of salvation by faith and the works of the law. My study of Paul's epistle to the Galatians gave me opportunity to weigh these errors in the glowing light of Paul's epistle.

Rome appeals to James to defend its doctrine of justification by faith and works, and the proponents of the federal vision follow Rome. The argument is simple. James says, "Was not Abraham our father justified by works, when he had offered Isaac his son upon the altar?" (2:21). Rome's appeal to James in support of a doctrine that apparently flatly contradicts Paul requires an answer.

The answer is not to be satisfied with a reassertion of Paul's statements in his letter to the Galatians, nor is the answer an appeal to Paul's glorious letter to the Romans, which teaches emphatically the truth of justification by faith alone without the works of the law. An answer has to include an explanation of James' epistle and his words in James 2:21.

This required a careful study of James that proved to be extremely valuable because it clearly demonstrated not only how the epistle in no way contradicts or amends Paul's writings, but also that the epistle is a necessary and important addition to what Paul fiercely defended in the arena of Judaistic errors in the churches of Galatia.

It is not surprising that no contradiction exists, for that is in keeping with scripture, which is not a collection of the writings of individual men from Moses to the apostle John. But scripture has one author, the Holy Spirit. God the Holy Spirit wrote Galatians. He knew what he was writing. God the Holy Spirit wrote James. He knew what he was writing. Both are part of the gospel of God's sovereign grace through the work of Christ and are given to the church through Christ's Spirit poured out on Pentecost.

James does not contradict Paul, for the Holy Spirit does not contradict himself. Nor does James make a necessary amendment to what Paul wrote, for the Holy Spirit does not need to amend his writing. James is a wonderful and necessary implication and development of the truth of justification by faith alone without the works of the law. What James teaches is found in Paul's epistles to the Romans and the Galatians. Paul could and did say amen to what James writes. James develops what Paul wrote, for the Holy Spirit develops his theology in this part of his writings.

Some commentators seem reluctant to find contradictions in scripture, but they want to maintain their heresy of justification by faith and works. Their way of achieving this goal is to reinterpret Paul's writings in Romans and Galatians in such a way that Paul's condemnation of justification by faith and works applies only to the self-righteous Jews of his day and is not a fundamental truth of the saints' confession.

There is an answer to this type of argumentation that is almost as strong as any proof can be: an appeal to common sense that is impossible to refute. To deny justification by faith alone without the works of the law is to repudiate the validity of Martin Luther's agonizing and soul-wrenching experience in the monastery as he searched for peace with God. It is to repudiate Luther's overwhelming joy that came from heaven when the truth of justification came into his heart. It is to turn one's back on almost five hundred years of Luther's scholarship, all of which is united in affirming that justification by faith alone was the one doctrine that forced his break with Rome and became the pillar of the entire sixteenth-century Reformation.

Besides, to give Paul an interpretation that the scriptures cannot possibly sustain is to scorn the Westminster divines and the fathers at Dordrecht as being sadly mistaken, when their scholarship and spirituality make today's theologians look like pygmies. It is to take from the grasp of countless saints a treasure to which they clung when they faced death by torture.

Anyone who values and understands his own salvation would not dare to trust his salvation to his own keeping of the law and his righteousness to his own works. He brings nothing for his salvation but simply clings to the cross of Christ. Without that truth he would despair.

To follow the proud claims of those who support the federal vision it is necessary to do violence to scripture in the interest of retaining the shattered remnants of one's sinful pride. Pride alone puts man in conflict with scripture's scathing denunciation of man, the sinner. Pride lies smashed at the foot of the cross.

Heretics in Paul's day claimed that justification by faith alone without the works of the law had a necessary consequence: the complete destruction of the law. Paul battled them and wrote in answer to their objections, "What shall we say then? Shall we continue in sin, that grace may abound?" (Rom. 6:1). The church throughout the ages has been plagued by these pests who attempt to destroy the gospel of grace by similar whining complaints. Luther fought those enemies of the truth when his close friend Agricola turned against him and pleaded for the crucifixion of Moses and the need to throw the law in the dump.[1]

Similarly, the truth of justification by faith alone has been criticized for denying the responsibility of man. This is more subtle because those who make this criticism imply that by itself the truth of justification by faith is unbalanced and incomplete. It needs additional definition so that man can be responsible for what he does. This is the claim of those who hold to conditional salvation and want to make justification conditional as well.

James does not cater to their complaints. Neither does the Holy Spirit. James asks in defense of the truth of justification by faith alone, "Was not Abraham justified by works?" Then he writes immediately, "Seest thou how faith wrought with his works, and by works was faith made perfect?" (2:21–22). That is the clearest statement of justification by faith alone one can find in all of scripture—justification by faith that produces works, not justification by a faith that needs works added to it. God forbid!

The Heidelberg Catechism teaches the following regarding justification and the necessity of doing good works:

Since, then, we are redeemed from our misery by grace through Christ, without any merit of ours, why must we still do good works?

---

1 For further information on the controversy see Herman Hanko, *Contending for the Faith: The Rise of Heresy and the Development of the Truth* (Jenison, MI: Reformed Free Publishing Association, 2010), 171–78.

Because Christ, having redeemed us by his blood, renews us also by his holy Spirit after his own image, that with our whole life we may show ourselves thankful to God for his blessing, and that he may be glorified through us; then, also, that we ourselves may be assured of our faith by the fruits thereof, and by our godly walk may win our neighbors also to Christ.[2]

---

2 Heidelberg Catechism Q&A 86 in Philip Schaff, ed., *The Creeds of Christendom with a History and Critical Notes,* 6th ed., 3 vols. (New York: Harper and Row, 1931; repr., Grand Rapids, MI: Baker Books, 2007), 3:338.

INTRODUCTION

Authorship

Conservative scholars generally agree that the author of this epistle is James, the brother of Jesus.[1] Roman Catholic scholars deny this and claim that Mary remained a virgin after the birth of Christ. Rome has adopted this false doctrine in connection with its worship and adoration of Mary.

We know that James was the half brother of Jesus because Joseph was not the father of Jesus, but Joseph was the father of James. Scripture teaches clearly that Jesus was a member of a family with many children, both girls and boys (Matt. 12:46; 13:55–56; Mark 6:3; John 2:12; Acts 1:14). That Christ was a part of a family is in keeping with the general truth of scripture that our Lord was like us in all things except sin.

Our Lord came into the world to form a new family. Earthly family ties had to be subordinate to higher, spiritual ties of a heavenly family. In this heavenly family, the triune God is father, Christ is the elder brother, and all God's people are brothers and sisters of Christ and sons and daughters of God (Matt. 12:47–50; 2 Cor. 6:18).

---

1 For a lengthy discussion of authorship, see D. A. Carson, Douglas J. Moo, and Leon Morris, *An Introduction to the New Testament* (Grand Rapids, MI: Zondervan Publishing House, 1992), 410–13. The authors conclude that James, the half brother of the Lord, was the author.

James and other members of the family did not believe in Christ during his earthly ministry (John 7:5). We cannot be sure when the other members of Christ's earthly family were brought to faith in Christ, but they were present with the church after the ascension as they awaited the outpouring of the Holy Spirit (Acts 1:14). James was probably converted by an appearance of the Lord in the forty days between Christ's resurrection and ascension (1 Cor. 15:7).

After Pentecost James became an influential elder in the church of Jerusalem. He represented the Jerusalem church at the synod that considered the question of whether the Gentile converts had to be circumcised. He offered his advice on the matter, and it was essentially his advice that was adopted (Acts 15:13–22). He is referred to as an apostle in Galatians 1:19, where "apostle" is used in the broad sense. It is believed that James suffered a martyr's death about 62 AD.[2]

Date and Purpose of the Epistle

The date of the writing of this epistle is uncertain, but it was likely written prior to the Jerusalem Council, the history of which is recorded in Acts 15. Most commentaries place the date very early in the history of the church, perhaps around 40 AD.[3]

The epistle was written primarily to Jewish converts throughout the Roman Empire. After the martyrdom of Stephen, the saints in Jerusalem were scattered throughout Judea and Samaria. They also spread throughout the Mediterranean world. On his missionary journeys Paul went first to synagogues (Acts 13:5, 14;

---

2 Simon J. Kistemaker, *Exposition of the Epistle of James and the Epistles of John* (Grand Rapids, MI: Baker Book House, 1986), 18.

3 Carson, *Introduction to the New Testament*, 414.

14:1; 17:1, 10; 19:8), where mainly Jewish converts worshiped, for the church until Stephen's death was composed primarily of Jews (Acts 8:1). These Jews had been brought up in the traditions of legal works-righteousness and salvation through the keeping of the law. Such teachings were strong in the church, and many references are found in scripture to the struggles brought about by those who held these views.

Another danger arose among these Jewish converts. There was a tendency among some to go to the opposite extreme of works-righteousness and to abandon the importance of the law. Denying the usefulness and validity of the law, they denied also the necessity of good works. They claimed to have faith in Christ but opposed the doing of good works, because good works would detract from justification by faith alone.

James writes his epistle to counteract this mistaken idea and to define the correct relationship between faith in Jesus Christ and good works. James considers the mistaken position that opposes the necessity of good works to be as dangerous as the errors of those who clung to the Old Testament laws as the means of salvation.

The epistle occupies an important place in the canon of scripture. Many times in the history of the church the saints have battled against the error of what has become known as antinomianism, which comes from the two Greek words *anti* (against) and *nomos* (law). Antinomians are against the law. An outstanding historical example of an antinomian against whom Luther battled is Georgius Agricola, who carried Luther's emphasis on justification by faith alone to a denial of the necessity of good works.

This danger is always present in the church. If theoretical antinomians are scarce, the church is often plagued by those who live wicked lives and justify their conduct on the grounds that they adhere to the doctrines of the church and faithfully attend divine worship services. But their lives reveal quite the opposite. They are practical antinomians. Against such James directs his epistle.

Outstanding Characteristics

The epistle of James is often used to prove that scripture teaches justification by works and that James directly opposes Paul.

The Roman Catholic Church in the days of the Lutheran Reformation almost continuously threw James in the face of the great reformer of Wittenberg. Luther himself, before he came to understand this epistle and its teaching, called it "a right strawy epistle."[4] Schaff wrote, "He [Luther] disliked, most of all, the Epistle of James because he could not harmonize it with Paul's teaching on justification by faith without works, and he called it an epistle of straw as compared with the genuine apostolic writings."[5] Later in his ministry Luther came to see that one could not charge either Paul or James with contradicting the other. As so many since have seen, he saw that James also teaches firmly and clearly the doctrine of justification by faith alone without the works of the law.

Because James fights the deadly error of antinomianism, the epistle is extremely practical. Almost the entire epistle consists of admonitions. Its emphasis is on the works of a child of God and the necessity of good works. It is clear from the epistle that James condemns those who think good works are unnecessary for the Christian and encourages those with true faith to demonstrate their faith by doing good works.

Because of his condemnation of those who deny good works,

---

4 Martin Luther, *Luther's Works*, ed. E. Theodore Bachmann (Philadelphia: Muhlenberg Press, 1960), 35:362.

5 Philip Schaff, *History of the Christian Church* (Grand Rapids, MI: Eerdmans, 1950), 7:35.

his epistle is sometimes very sharp. James can get angry with those who want no part of good works. He is not at all averse to calling them "adulterers and adulteresses." Such language includes all those to whom James writes, but especially those who trouble the congregations by their insistence that works are not necessary. The sharpness of these angry words warns God's people of the seriousness of the whole matter and calls them to live new and holy lives.

The epistle has sometimes been criticized as being without Christ. It is true that on the surface not much explicit mention is made of Christ and his work. But we must not be misled by this, for when James asserts that he is a servant of God and the Lord Jesus Christ (1:1), he says as it were, "What I have to say is Christ's word, and as such it is part of Christ's work of saving his people."

Another outstanding characteristic of the book is James' references and allusions to the Old Testament scriptures. Fully aware that the Jews to whom he writes were thoroughly acquainted with the Old Testament, he couches his writing in the familiar (to the Jews) language of the Old Testament. Thus James shows how the essence of the old dispensation is preserved in the new, while the form of the gospel used in the old dispensation has fallen away.

It is also characteristic of James to use many concrete and specific illustrations to drive home his point. This makes his writings particularly vivid and easily applicable to our lives in the twenty-first century. His illustrations deal with both people who have only dead faith and with people who have true and living faith. The epistle has much to teach us about a life of faith as it is and must be manifested in us.

JAMES 1

Salutation

1. James, a servant of God and of the Lord Jesus Christ, to the twelve tribes which are scattered abroad, greeting.

James, a servant of God and the Lord Jesus Christ (1:1)

James introduces himself as the writer in the usual way by putting his name at the beginning of the letter rather than at the end, as we do. "Servant" can be better translated as "slave." It is somewhat startling that James, a half brother of Christ, should call himself a slave of Christ, but the word is significantly used. James is not ashamed to emphasize that the relationship in which he stands to Christ is not primarily a natural relationship of brothers, but a spiritual relationship of master and slave. The natural fades to make room for the spiritual and heavenly reality.

Because of its position in the sentence, the phrase "of God and of the Lord Jesus Christ" receives the emphasis. Translated literally the sentence reads, "James, of God and of the Lord Jesus Christ, a slave." As Paul was pleased, so James is greatly pleased that he can give himself this designation. Paul ended his controversy with the Judaizers in Galatia by appealing to his position in relation to Christ as being that of a slave who bore in his body the brand marks (his scars of beatings and stonings) that show him to be Christ's slave. James does not look on the Lord as a relative in the flesh, but as his Lord and master, to whom he belongs with body and soul, and whose will is his delight. He writes as a servant of his heavenly Lord and thus writes what he is commanded to write. God and Christ own him. He has been purchased by the blood of Christ shed on the cross. He has been made a slave by a wonder of grace. His only joy is found in obedience to his master.

By the expression "of God and of the Lord Jesus Christ" James does not mean that he has two masters: God and Christ. By belonging to Christ and serving Christ he belongs to God. Christ is God's eternal Son through whom God accomplishes all his purpose.

The use of these three names of our Lord is intended to emphasize at the beginning of the epistle that Jesus is the promised Messiah (the anointed one, the Christ) and that this Christ is Lord of all. Hence James' emphasis on the works of true faith is not a denial of Christ's all-sufficient work, but is an important part of Christ's salvation.

To the twelve tribes which are scattered abroad (1:1)

It is impossible to interpret "twelve tribes" as referring to the twelve tribes of old dispensational times. The nation of Israel had long ceased to exist as twelve separate tribes. But the church in the old dispensation, limited to the Jews, was called Israel, and sometimes specific tribes were mentioned. This is also true in the New Testament church. The tribes of Israel are mentioned in the sealing of the one hundred forty-four thousand (Rev. 7:4–8). Paul also spoke of the "Israel of God" (Gal. 6:16). In these two passages the church of God gathered from Jews and Gentiles is referred to as Israel of the twelve tribes. Revelation 7:4–8 mentions twelve tribes and excludes Ephraim but includes Joseph.

In fact, Israel was composed of thirteen tribes, because Joseph's two sons were separate tribes, and although Levi was scattered it was also a tribe. The apostles also numbered thirteen. Judas Iscariot was not numbered among the twelve, but Matthias and Paul were. We might call these numbers "the imperfect twelve," indicating that the church on earth, represented by the number twelve, is imperfect. It is possible that James refers to the national Jews as part of the New Testament church, so that the reference is not to the national Jews *per se*, but only as they are a part of the church of Christ.

The Jews were scattered throughout many lands bordering the Mediterranean Sea. Although James' letter was probably prior to Paul's first missionary journey, the scattering of the Jews was wide (Acts 8:1, 4; 9:1–2; 11:19).

Greeting (1:1)

The verb *chairo* means to rejoice or to be glad. Here it is used in the present active infinitive as a word of greeting. It has the implication of saying, "I hope all is well with you."

Joy in Trials

2. My brethren, count it all joy when ye fall into divers temptations;
3. Knowing this, that the trying of your faith worketh patience.
4. But let patience have her perfect work, that ye may be perfect and entire, wanting nothing.

My brethren, count it all joy when ye fall into divers temptations (1:2)

Although James at times castigates in fierce language those to whom he writes, he nevertheless intersperses his denunciations with the assurance that he loves them in the Lord as fellow members of the family of God and that his sharp criticisms of their actions are meant for their salvation. They are together in God's family, and it is his calling to bring to them God's word.

The translation of "temptations" in the text is incorrect. It ought to be translated as "trials," as it is translated by most commentators.[1] The Greek uses the same word for both temptations and trials, and that leaves open the possibility that temptations are referred to here, especially because James speaks of falling into temptations. Nevertheless, the translation "temptations" does not work. To fall into temptation means to succumb to temptation. It is impossible to count it all joy when we give in to temptation and commit the sin by which we were tempted.

There are three differences between trials and temptations. First, the author of temptations is Satan and never God. The author of trials is God. James assures us of this in 1:13. Second, the purpose of each is different. Satan tempts to persuade one to sin; his motives are always evil. God's purposes are always good. God sends trials to bring out the good in a man and to purify him. God strengthens faith through trials. Peter spoke of this in 1 Peter 1:7. Third, the result is different in each trial. If one falls into temptation, he has committed sin and needs to confess his sins to God. If one endures trials, he emerges stronger and with a strengthened trust in God.

Although there are differences in meaning, trials and temptations are closely related. That close relation is the reason scripture uses the same word for both. Trials always carry with them a certain temptation. If God sends serious illness to a child of God,

---

1 Kistemaker, *Exposition of the Epistle of James*, 30–31; John Calvin, *Catholic Epistles*, trans. and ed. John Owen (Grand Rapids, MI: Wm. B. Eerdmans Publishing Company, 1959), 278–79.

the illness can be and must be a trial for him, but it can also be a temptation. It can tempt him to question God's ways, criticize him, and be querulous toward him. It is our calling to humble ourselves beneath the mighty hand of God (1 Pet. 5:6) and count it all joy when we are tried. Temptations can well be and ought to be trials. They are trials when we are tempted and resist the temptation and seek the path of righteousness. Such overcoming of temptation also strengthens our faith, and God's grace in resisting temptation has a purifying effect on us.

Although temptations and trials are closely related, James emphasizes trials. This is evident from verse 3, where the text makes clear that trials are a trying of our faith.

The Jews to whom James writes were subject to many trials. It is possible that the persecution that had begun in Jerusalem forced many of the saints to flee to other parts of the empire where persecution was particularly severe at the time James writes his epistle. The Jewish converts were hated by their fellow Jews in whatever country they settled. They went everywhere preaching the word (Acts 11:19–20). Their preaching of Christ crucified would naturally infuriate the unconverted Jews.

Trials are "divers," that is, of many different kinds. For Jewish Christians they included persecution, sickness, suffering, pain, disappointment, problems in life, poverty, and the like. The lot of the child of God in this world is cross-bearing and self-denial. God promises trials because they are the means he uses to sanctify his people. The psalmist complains, "Many are the afflictions of the righteous" (Ps. 34:19). He means that the righteous suffer many more afflictions than the wicked do. Asaph had the same complaint and very nearly lost his faith because of the problem it presented to him (Ps. 73).

The way to deal with our many afflictions, whatever kind they may be, is to consider these afflictions "all joy." This comes as a shock to us. We are not very often advised to consider our afflictions reasons for joy, and we are tempted to do quite differently. We may do as the world does and drown our sorrows in the mad pursuit of pleasure. We may attempt to escape them by alcohol or drugs. We may complain about them and let them destroy our serenity and peace of mind. We may, as we are often taught to do, be stoical about them, make the best of them, steel ourselves to bear them without too much complaint, or in desperation seek the help of a psychiatrist.

James calls the saints to something much loftier: consider your trials a reason for joy, he urges. If that is not enough, consider your trials as a reason for "all" joy. Look at your trials not as joy mixed with sorrow and bitterness, but as reasons for pure and unadulterated joy, for that is the meaning of "all joy." The admonition is in keeping with other scriptures. James speaks especially of persecution, just as Jesus counts them blessed who are persecuted and admonishes them to rejoice (Matt. 5:10–12).

Joy is the opposite of sorrow. It is the freedom from all worry, anxiety, fear, and distress. Joy manifests itself in happiness, singing a doxology of praise to God, and being thankful—thankful not in spite of our trials but because of them.

Such joy is possible only if in the midst of our sorrows we lay hold on the promises of the scriptures that affliction is for our profit, that God saves us through trials, and that all trials put us in closer communion with Christ so that we suffer with him. If we suffer with him, we will also be glorified with him in heaven (Rom. 8:17).

This joy is very difficult for us, and sometimes the only way to attain it is humbly to seek God's grace to enable us to count it all joy when we fall into trials.

The text speaks of a "fall" into trials. This seems to be a strange way to express the way in which trials are our lot. This term is intended to emphasize that we do not actively seek trials in our lives. They come unbidden. God, who governs all the pathways of our lives, sends trials. Frequently they come unexpectedly. They are like holes in the pathway of our pilgrimage that we cannot see because we cannot see the road ahead. They make our pilgrimage harder and our walk difficult. We fall into these trials, but they all come from the hand of our God.

The teaching of James is consistent with the rest of scripture. Paul wrote in Ephesians 5:20, "Giving thanks always for all things unto God and the Father in the name of our Lord Jesus Christ." The emphasis is on "all things," which include trials. For all things we are to give thanks (see also Phil. 3:8; 4:6–7).

Knowing this, that the trying of your faith worketh patience (1:3)

The connection between verses 2 and 3 is clear. James gives the reason we ought to consider trials as occasions for joy. Trials bring joy because the fruit of them is the wonderful Christian virtue of patience. The subordinate participle "knowing" is causal: we are joyful in trials *because* the trial of our faith works patience.

The Holy Spirit put this explanation of trials in the scriptures because he is very merciful, and he knows how difficult it is for us to rejoice in trials. In boundless mercy he gives us God's reason for trials. The reason, as described in this verse and the following, is completely adequate to be an incentive to count trials as reasons for joy.

Although the word translated as "trying" refers to the trials spoken of in verse 2, a different word is used.[2] The difference

---

2 "Trials" in verse 2 is *peirasmois,* while "trying" in verse 3 is *dokimion.* Both words are used in 2 Corinthians 13:5: "Examine [*peirazo,* the verb of the same word used in James 1:2] yourselves, whether ye be in the faith; prove [*dokimazo,* the verb form of the word used in James 1:3] your own selves. Know ye not your own selves, how that Jesus Christ is in you, except ye be reprobates [*adokimoi,* the adjective of *dokimazo* with the alpha privans—the prefix of negation]."

between the words is not great. Both can refer to the testing of anything, but the one (*peirazo*) emphasizes a favorable result of the test: something is proved to be genuine. Raw gold mixed with many impurities will be purified by fire because the pure gold will be separated from the useless material to which it is attached.

In James' day coins were made of gold or silver, and their value was determined by the amount of gold or silver in them. Sometimes cheats would mix other, less costly substances with the gold or silver, hoping no one would notice and that the coin would be considered pure gold. To test the purity of a gold coin, one would bite it. Because gold is softer than other metals, teeth marks would appear in the coin if it was genuine. The biting would be the test, and if the result was favorable, the coin would be genuine and unalloyed gold.

According to the figure of the verse faith is put to the test by the trials of life, and faith is both purified and found genuine by the trial. This figure is beautiful and is also found in 1 Peter 1:7. Faith is mixed with many impurities. It is weak and mixed with doubts and fears and is not the strong faith it ought to be. Trials act like fire on gold: they burn away the impurities and make the gold of faith pure and strong.

The faith of the believer is a gift of God, but it operates through our sinful natures. God sends trials to purify that faith, but the purification also is God's work through the instrumentality of afflictions. Faith always has as its object Christ. When faith is tried, the believer seeks closer union with Christ.

The main theme of James' letter is the difference between genuine faith that produces works and counterfeit faith that does not. Already in the early part of the epistle, James talks about genuine faith and how it is purified by fiery trials. Counterfeit faith would be devoured by the fire of trials. But trials, in burning away the impurities of our faith, make faith stronger. The faithful man, when tried, clings more strongly to Christ. The faith of a believer is like the roots of a small cedar tree on a rocky cliff near a mountain summit. In that high country fierce winds blow and terrible storms rage. Snow and ice, cold and tempests blow against that tree, but forced by the raging weather the tree sinks its roots more deeply into the soil. So the believer sinks the roots of his faith more deeply into Christ when the trials of life batter his soul. That is true because faith lays hold on the scriptures and the promises of God; and laying hold on the scriptures, the believer lays hold on Christ. The more fiercely the storms of trouble beat against him, the more fiercely he clings to Christ, his only hope. In this way his faith is tested, purified, and found genuine.

The trying of faith works patience, which is an important and blessed virtue. It is the gift of God, and it is merited for God's people by the suffering of Jesus on the cross. It is worked in the believer through the Spirit and God's word by the instrument of afflictions or trials. It is next to impossible for us to learn patience except by means of trials, and God is wise in sending these trials upon us.

The Greek word for patience means to abide under or to bear up under. It is a figurative word that depicts trials as heavy burdens placed on us, which we are required to bear as we walk our earthly pilgrimages to heaven. We cannot shuck off these burdens and drop them along the way. We must carry them, for God places them on our shoulders, and only he can take them away. Our inclinations are to groan under their weight, complain about the difficulty of walking with them, and refuse to go another step unless we are relieved of them. Patience means that we bear up under them and continue on our way.

Patience includes, first, knowledge that our trials come not by chance but from the hand of our heavenly Father; second, humble submission to his will and a refusal to force our wills on him; third, assurance that even if we cannot see the good of it, God's purpose is good and right because it leads to our salvation; fourth, waiting on Jehovah for him to remove the burden we carry or waiting for Jehovah to show us his reason for placing such a load on our shoulders. One who has patience sings the last verse of Psalm 27: "Wait on the LORD: be of good courage, and he shall strengthen thine heart: wait, I say, on the LORD." Patience is sometimes only waiting on the Lord.

Because of our sinful natures we are inclined to take a wicked attitude toward our trials, but God uses trials to save us. If it were left to us, we would never have patience. But God works powerfully within us by his word and the Spirit to destroy all our doubts and fears and to sanctify us.

That is abundant reason to count it all joy when we fall into divers trials.

The word "worketh" is used because trials work patience. There is a divine power in the trials that the believer is called to endure, which, because it is divine, brings about the fruit of patience. The power lies in the trials, but only because of the supreme power of the cross of Christ. In trials we are united to his suffering and death. He endured to the end when he bore the heavy load of the wrath of God. Our trials connect us to him and have the fruit of patience because he bore with patience the wrath of God.

The believer with genuine faith knows beyond a doubt that trials work patience. He knows this from the word of God, which points him in many ways to this truth. He also knows this from his experience, for the Holy Spirit seals the truth on his consciousness in connection with the trials he undergoes. It is the knowledge of personal certainty.

The difficulty for us is not ignorance of this fundamental truth, but the spiritual inability to apply it to our lives in such a way that it indeed brings us joy.

But let patience have her perfect work (1:4)

By an admonition James demonstrates the value of patience. Trials work patience. But patience must have its perfect work. It is possible that patience does not have its perfect work in our lives because of the sin that still characterizes us in everything we do. Hence there is a great need for the admonition. We are called not to obstruct the progress of patience that trials work but to give room to patience to accomplish its goal.

The word translated as "perfect" comes from a root similar to the Greek word that means end or goal, that is, something that is considered from the viewpoint of the goal attained or the purpose accomplished. The word does not mean end in the sense of the end of a road in a cul-de-sac but the end of a war when the purpose of fighting is achieved: the enemy is defeated.

Patience may be present in our lives, but it is an imperfect patience that barely holds its own against doubts and fears, worries and anxieties. When patience achieves its goal, the child of God in whom patience works knows complete submission to God's will, a walk with calmness and serenity in the storms of life, a confident and quiet reliance upon God, and a patient waiting upon his will.

The expression may leave the wrong impression that patience is a power within us that tries to accomplish a certain task, but we impede its progress. The admonition warns us against impeding the progress of patience. Rather than being impatient, it is our calling to cultivate patience and exercise ourselves in it. However, patience is not a power in its own right. It is a virtue given us by the work of God in our salvation.

The tense of the verb is present, indicating that we must continuously strive to exercise patience.[3] The work of patience is

---

3 The verb is *echetō*, the present active imperative third person singular of *echō*.

"perfect." Taking into account the meaning of perfect, the saints are admonished to cultivate patience so that this Christian virtue attains its goal in their lives.

That ye may be perfect and entire, wanting nothing (1:4)

The goal of our patience is sanctification. This is a remarkable importance given to patience; if patience attains its goal, the person in whom patience has worked is also sanctified, that is, without sin. Patience, if it performs its perfect work, can transform a regenerated child of God into a sinless saint.

How does God work this miracle? The answer lies in the meaning of patience. Patience attains its end when we are completely and joyfully submissive to God's will. To be completely and joyfully submissive to God's will is to walk every moment of our lives in the consciousness of our dependence upon God and in the awareness that all that we have comes to us from him. It is a glad recognition that he, even through trials, draws us closer to heaven. Thus patience means to walk in perfect, uninterrupted covenantal fellowship with God, praising him and giving glory to his name.[4]

Hence the goal of the working out of the Christian virtue of patience is the sinless child of God, sanctified and cleansed from sin. The word translated as "entire" is a synonym of "perfect," and it literally means in every part. It comes from two words (*holos* [entire] and *kleros* [lot], as in casting the lot). Thus the word means the entire lot.

The phrase "perfect and entire" forms a hendiadys in which the conjunction "and" ties the two words it connects to form one

---

4 The construction is a *hina* clause with the verb *ete*, the present active subjunctive of *eimi*, the verb of being. This is a purpose clause that tells the reader what the purpose of the action of the verb is. It is also possible that the *hina* clause is a clause of conceived result, but this construction is rare in the New Testament.

idea. The perfect work of patience is perfection in the entire man and in every circumstance of life. No matter what trial the believer faces, he walks blissfully conscious that he walks with God.

The perfect work of patience is described negatively as "wanting nothing." The clause adds negatively what has already been said: the perfect work of patience is so complete that there is nothing lacking in the life of one who has it. No troubles can upset him; no burdens can crush him; no trials can bring him to his knees in despair; no troubles can rob him of his joy. There is nothing lacking in his confident and joyful walk with God.

Perfection is unattainable in this life, but the admonition gives us a goal for which to strive and a glimpse of our perfection in heaven. In heaven we will no longer experience trials, because patience in trials will have attained its goal.

The Prayer for Wisdom

5. If any of you lack wisdom, let him ask of God, that giveth to all men liberally, and upbraideth not; and it shall be given him.
6. But let him ask in faith, nothing wavering. For he that wavereth is like a wave of the sea driven with the wind and tossed.
7. For let not that man think that he shall receive any thing of the Lord.
8. A double-minded man is unstable in all his ways.

The connection between verses 5 and 4 is unclear. There are two possibilities. One is that James begins a new thought with verse 5 and no connection exists. The other is that James is aware that it requires wisdom to be able to count trials as all joy, so now he points to the source of wisdom.

There is no reason that both ideas cannot be true. James' first thought is that wisdom is necessary to keep the admonition he has just made. We need wisdom so that patience may have its perfect work in our lives and so that we count it all joy when we fall into trials. This connection does not preclude that the principle has a much broader application than dealing with trials. Wisdom is also an essential attribute of the Christian, and one entire book of the Bible, Proverbs, is devoted to defining wisdom and explaining how wisdom is applied to life.

If any of you lack wisdom (1:5)

Everyone lacks wisdom, for wisdom is a spiritual gift.[5] There is a natural wisdom found also among wicked men, but James characterizes that as "earthly, sensual, devilish" (3:15). It is the kind of wisdom frequently found in Ann Landers' advice columns or worldly books on childrearing. True wisdom is a gift of God earned for his people in the cross of Jesus Christ and given by grace through the operation of the Holy Spirit. This is evident from Proverbs 8, which tells us that Christ is the wisdom of God.

What is this virtue called wisdom? It is the spiritual ability to apply the abiding truths of God's word to all of life, including its problems and difficulties. Although knowledge is surely necessary for wisdom, knowledge is not in itself wisdom. This is true even on a natural level. A man may have an advanced degree in mechanical engineering, but have no idea how to fix his car when it won't run. It is possible to graduate from an accredited agricultural school, but to have no idea at all about how to operate a farm.

---

5 Everyone's total lack of wisdom is indicated by the construction of the clause. It is a first class condition in which the if-clause is a statement of a fact: if any of you lacks wisdom and you all do.

This obvious truth is also applicable to the spiritual life of a man. A man may have a vast knowledge of theology and be able to teach in the chair of dogmatics in the seminary, but he may have no idea of how to apply the truths of the Reformed faith to his own daily walk. Everyone is acquainted with an example of someone who lacks wisdom.

Wisdom is very practical. Wisdom presupposes knowledge. Woe to the man who is always pleading for practical preaching and expresses vehemently his distaste for and impatience with doctrine and the knowledge of the truth. One cannot entrust one's car to a man who has never done anything else but fix people's teeth. He must have some knowledge of what makes a car run. Woe to the man who knows no doctrine and yet thinks he can live the Christian life. Woe to the man who tries to cope with the trials of life without any awareness of all the detailed instruction scripture gives concerning suffering.

But mere knowledge of scripture is not enough. One must believe scripture to be the word of God and love God's word as a lamp to his feet and a light on his pathway (Ps. 119:105).

Concerning this important attribute of wisdom scripture says, first, that God alone is wise (1 Tim. 1:17). As an attribute of God, wisdom is God's determination to attain the highest goal for himself, namely, the glory of his name. Further, wisdom is the knowledge that God has the best means of attaining that goal. The best means of attaining that goal is to reveal himself in Christ Jesus, the eternal Son of God in our flesh, and through Christ to save a people who can live with him in covenantal fellowship.

Second, Christ is the full revelation of the wisdom of God, for Christ is the highest means for God to attain his glory. This is why Christ is in himself the wisdom of God. His name is Wisdom (Prov. 8:1); he is before all things (Prov. 8:22–36; John 1:1–3; Col. 1:15–19; Heb. 1:1–3); all things are for his sake.

Third, wisdom is earned for God's people by Christ's suffering and death.

Fourth, wisdom is freely given to those who ask God for it, and in receiving wisdom they receive Christ himself and his Spirit: "But of him are ye in Christ Jesus, who of God is made unto us wisdom, and righteousness, and sanctification, and redemption" (1 Cor. 1:30). Apart from the gift of wisdom, we are fools who know the difference between right and wrong and the terrible consequences of sin but foolishly commit sin anyway.

Fifth, by wisdom, knowing the truths of scripture, the child of God can choose the highest goal of his life, fellowship with God through Christ in the new heavens and the new earth. By that same wisdom the child of God can apply God's truth to every aspect of his calling and live and count it all joy when he falls into trials.

Let him ask of God (1:5)

The wisdom to know the best possible way in this life to gain the highest possible good is something we totally lack. Where will we find it? Let him ask God.

The verb is in the present tense, which indicates that we are admonished to do this as a continuous activity. We are always lacking wisdom; we need always to seek it at God's throne. We constantly face new problems, temptations, trials, and experiences in our lives for which we need wisdom. The need is constant; the praying is continuous.

God is the source of all wisdom. We may read books on how to have a happy marriage or how to bring up children. We may read books written by learned psychiatrists on how to cope with troubles. But when all is said and done, the source of all wisdom is God alone. No wisdom is to be found outside of him. People sometimes leave the impression that the reason they read all kinds of self-help books on how to have a happy marriage, to discipline children, to get out of credit card debt, or to find the key to happiness is that they do not want to practice the clear injunctions of scripture. They want a short cut, an easy way, to solve life's problems. They want deliverance from trouble, but they also want to live in pleasure. Scripture tells us that the only way to true happiness is by self-denial and cross-bearing and daily struggles against the sins in our corrupt natures. Scripture is the one book that contains everything we need to know. A prayer for wisdom will teach us how to apply scripture to our lives and callings.

That giveth to all men liberally, and upbraideth not (1:5)

The construction here is important. Literally the text reads, "Let him ask of the liberally giving and not upbraiding God." The point of the Greek is to underscore that God is a giving God. His nature is to give. He cannot receive, for all things are his. He created them, and he upholds them. There is nothing that is not his. Thus he can only give. We cannot give anything to him, for we have nothing. We are always empty. All we have comes to us as a gift. We can only wait with outstretched arms to be filled from the overflowing fountain of all good.

God gives to "all men." "Men" is not in the Greek text. God gives to all who ask not to all men head for head. God gives to adults and children, to men and women, to rich and poor, to Americans and Chinese, to kings and garbage collectors, to healthy and sick, to working people and dying people, to great sinners and moderate sinners, to grateful people and ungrateful people, and to murderers and philanthropists. It makes no difference: whoever asks, receives. Asking is itself the guarantee of receiving.

God gives liberally. This passage is the only place in the scriptures where this word is used. Its basic meaning is that God gives simply, openly, frankly, and sincerely. He gives out of no ulterior motive, but only because it is his pleasure to give. He expects nothing back, as we so often do. His delight is in giving.

And he does not upbraid. He never sternly rebukes for past faults those who ask wisdom of him. A parent may say to a child who has squandered his monthly allowance, "I am not going to give you your allowance this month because you wasted last month's allowance. Until you learn how to use your money properly, you are getting no more." It is a good thing God never does that with us. We are unappreciative of his gifts and barely aware of them most of the time. We pursue earthly wisdom and scorn the wisdom from on high. We deserve reproach, but God does not reproach us and remind us of our sins and refuse to give us wisdom when we seek it. His gifts of wisdom flow from his great grace revealed to us in Christ, freely giving to undeserving people as proof of his unmerited favor.

And it shall be given him (1:5)

This is God's promise to those who ask him for wisdom. There are no qualifications, no conditions, and no small print at the bottom of a signed and sealed promise. It is God's own word. "And I say unto you, Ask, and it shall be given you; seek, and ye shall find; knock and it shall be opened unto you. For every one that asketh receiveth; and he that seeketh findeth; and to him that knocketh it shall be opened." (Luke 11:9–10).

How foolish it is then when we put our trust in human wisdom and scorn the wisdom of God.

But let him ask in faith, nothing wavering. For he that wavereth is like a wave of the sea driven with the wind and tossed (1:6)

A strong qualification is described here. God gives to all those who ask, but their asking must be sincere. They must ask in faith. Faith is the bond that unites us to Christ. Faith's object is Christ's perfect sacrifice for sin as revealed in the sacred scriptures. To ask in faith means that we are confident that God will give us what we ask for Christ's sake. This faith may not always be present with us. We may doubt whether God will give us wisdom because we are overwhelmed by our sins and unworthiness. We may not ask in faith because we seek the solutions to life's trials in human wisdom and not at the throne of grace. We only tip our hats to God as a gesture of piety. It can be true also that our earlier prayers for wisdom were answered unexpectedly, and the answers were not always appreciated. Thus we are not sure that we want to ask God for wisdom, for we could receive something we do not expect.

But faith says that God is very wise, and he answers our prayers according to a greater wisdom than we can ever have.

Faith clings to Christ and believes God's promises for Christ's sake.

Wavering must not characterize our prayers. Wavering is the opposite of faith. Wavering is halting between two opinions: God or Dr. Spock, scripture or the latest book on child-rearing, the word of scripture or the psychiatrist's advice. We are not quite sure. We are not even quite sure that we want wisdom, because wisdom may require us to forsake our wicked ways, and we are not prepared to do that. The price is too high.

"Wavering" comes from a Greek word that means to be divided against oneself. It is to have one part of us wanting God's wisdom and another part unsure that God's wisdom is our real desire. Anyone who has struggled with the doubts of his sinful nature knows exactly what this is all about.

The figure is powerful. If one has ever been in a storm on the ocean or in one of the Great Lakes on the northern boundary of the United States, one will appreciate the figure. On a stormy sea where the wind blows fiercely, the waves are not even and predictable swells that come one after the other against the shore, but they are high, boisterous, and choppy waves that form whitecaps in every direction and are tossed first in one direction and then in another. They are totally unpredictable and dangerous.

A wavering man is like that sort of wave. One never knows what such a man wants, or whether he really wants what he asks. He is influenced by every passing event, tossed by every wave of doubt and fear, and unable to direct himself or his prayers to a specific goal and purpose.

For let not that man think that he shall receive any thing of the Lord. A double-minded man is unstable in all his ways (1:7–8)

James places heavy emphasis on how *not* to ask. The positive instruction is to ask in faith, but many different expressions are necessary to tell us how not to pray for wisdom. Undoubtedly the negative is stressed, as in the ten commandments, because of our strong inclinations to ask wrongly.

James reminds his readers that if they waver in their prayers they will never receive an answer from the Lord, for they might ask with wavering inclinations and desires and still think that God will give them what they ask. A man may want desperately to escape the trials of life and may ask for wisdom to escape them but refrain from asking for wisdom that will enable him to be joyful in life's trials. He wants his cancer to be cured and is not satisfied in finding joy and peace in having terminal cancer. Thus he is hesitant and even hypocritical. God will never answer such a prayer.

Hebrews 11:6, in connection with the faith of Abel, says, "Without faith it is impossible to please him: for he that cometh to God must believe that he is, and that he is a rewarder of them that diligently seek him." We must see the seriousness of this warning. If we do not ask in faith that recognizes that everything that happens to us in this life, including trials, is sent by the hand of our heavenly Father and that all things work together for good to those who love God and are called according to his purpose, but if we want our own way, we will not receive the wisdom we need. We will be left in our agitated state, tossed about like the waves on a stormy sea and without the spiritual ability to cope with what God is pleased in his wisdom to send us.

The wavering man is a double-minded man who is unstable in his ways.

"Is" does not appear in the Greek. The translation can therefore be, "A double-minded man, unstable in all his ways." However, it is common in Greek to omit the word *is*, and it can be added. The difference between the presence or absence of *is* is very minor and need not detain us, however I prefer omitting it.

The words "double-minded" and "unstable" define a man who wavers. A double-minded man is literally a "two-souled" man. He has two minds and two wills, and the two are always in conflict with each other. He is a man who wants two opposing things at the same time or a man who cannot make up his mind about what he wants. He is always uncertain, always hesitant, always wishy-washy, having a kind of spiritual schizophrenia. Such a man is also unstable in all his ways. He is unreliable and untrustworthy. What he says on one occasion may be different from what he says on another occasion. What he promises to do cannot be considered a firm commitment, because he may regret his promise a moment later. He is spiritually like Israel in Elijah's day, a nation that halted between Baal and Jehovah. That man receives nothing from God.

Wisdom comes to those who ask, but let their asking be in faith. Thus the emphasis in James' epistle continues to be on faith.

Poverty and Riches

9. Let the brother of low degree rejoice in that he is exalted:
10. But the rich, in that he is made low: because as the flower of the grass he shall pass away.

11. For the sun is no sooner risen with a burning heat, but it
    withereth the grass, and the flower thereof falleth, and the
    grace of the fashion of it perisheth: so also shall the rich
    man fade away in his ways.

Let the brother of low degree (1:9)

Although the Authorized Version does not include a conjunction, the Greek uses a weak conjunction (*de*) usually translated
as "but, in distinction from the strong adversative *alla*. The conjunction connects the admonition of verse 9 to the foregoing
verses. Most probably the connection goes back to verse 2, for
verse 9 refers to poverty, which certainly is a trial.

The idea of trials is dominant throughout the entire first
chapter. In a sense the verses immediately preceding verse 9 are
a digression, especially the apostle's relatively long description of
the man who prays for wisdom while he doubts.

The admonition is addressed to the poor members of the
church. Literally the text reads, "Let the brother, the lowly one."
That the lowly one is poor is clear from the contrast between him
and the rich who are addressed in verse 10.

The contrast between wealth and poverty is a relative one. In
the most basic sense, anyone who has more than his daily bread
is rich. In the world there are the very wealthy and the very poor:
millionaires and people who die of starvation. The same is true,
although to a lesser degree, in the church, especially if one considers
the church worldwide. There are wealthy people in the church and
there are poor saints who have difficulty obtaining their daily bread.

Generally, the contrast between rich and poor is between the
wicked and the righteous. And this James has in mind. The people James addresses included many poor in their fellowship. This
ought not to surprise us. The Jews who professed faith in Christ
were hated by their compatriots. They were mocked, slandered,

ostracized, and deprived of work. In a broader sense the presence of poor people in the church is not a surprise because this is the way it always is in the church. The law from Sinai repeatedly made provisions for the poor. Asaph found in his relative poverty a reason to doubt God's favor (Ps. 73). Jesus promised the church that it will have the poor with it always (Matt. 26:11; Mark 14:7; John 12:8).

Believers are generally on the lowest rung of the social ladder. They are peaceful men who do not incite violence even when they are denied their rights. Yet they are the despised, the ostracized, the ignored, and the overlooked. They are called to suffer for Christ's sake. They are deprived of the best jobs, cannot receive the benefits the world receives, and are not even interested in accumulating vast earthly wealth. Covenantal responsibilities demand them to give large parts of their incomes to the causes of God's kingdom and covenant.

The word translated as "low degree" can also mean "humble." Undoubtedly that meaning is implied here. Paul wrote in 1 Corinthians 1:26–29:

26. Ye see your calling, brethren, how that not many wise men after the flesh, not many mighty, not many noble, are called:
27. But God hath chosen the foolish things of the world to confound the wise; and God hath chosen the weak things of the world to confound the things which are mighty;
28. And base things of the world, and things which are despised, hath God chosen, yea, and things which are not, to bring to nought the things that are:
29. That no flesh should glory in his presence.

God's people are required to be humble. Humility is the Christian virtue that manifests itself in never boasting, always trusting in God, clinging to the cross, and in not seeking self but God and his glory. Humility is born out of a profound sense of unworthiness.

Rejoice in that he is exalted (1:9)

These poor and humble people are admonished to rejoice in their exaltation. This admonition is based on a general principle of scripture: God resists the proud but gives grace to the humble. The proud are brought low, but the humble are exalted (Eccl. 7:8; Isa. 57:15; James 4:6; 1 Pet. 5:5).

Always in scripture humility stands over against pride. The two are opposites and mutually exclusive. The people of God are always in principle humble, while the ungodly are always proud. The humility of the people of God is evident in their confession of sin. But the wicked are always lifted up in pride against God.

Because poverty and its humbling power are undesirable, this admonition is necessary. Sometimes we covet the wealth of the wicked, as Asaph did. More often we are dissatisfied with our lowly estate and complain bitterly about it. Especially when we are poor and lowly because we are persecuted, the temptation is strong to assume a rebellious spirit against God for the way he treats us. How important the admonition is!

This word of God is strongly expressed. It is strong because the admonition uses a word (*kauchaomai*) that means boast. To boast about our poor estate is to consider it to be more prominent, beneficial, noble, and superior to wealth. There is a wrong kind of boasting of one's poverty. It is boasting that has a tinge of bitterness and really means to say, "I in my poverty show clearly that I have no desire to be wealthy; hence I am above mundane things." That sort of boasting was frequently found among ascetics of old, who took vows of poverty and considered themselves on a higher plane of holiness than others.

The child of God does not boast in his poverty, but he boasts that "he is exalted." To be exalted is not to be made rich or to boast of about poverty as if boasting will guarantee wealth from God. The exaltation of which the text speaks is profoundly spiritual. Isaiah puts it wonderfully: "For thus saith the high and lofty One that inhabiteth eternity, whose name is Holy; I dwell in the high and holy place, with him also that is of a contrite and humble spirit, to revive the spirit of the humble, and to revive the heart of the contrite ones" (Isa. 57:15). Those who are lowly may expect that God will dwell with them. Although he inhabits a high and lofty dwelling place, he comes to dwell with the lowly.

A lowly man's exaltation is a reality in this life. It consists in God's making him his friend and the lowly man's knowing the nearness and presence of God with all its accompanying blessings. A humble man's exaltation takes place also at the second coming of Christ. The poor and humble will be exalted in the judgment day to the great glory of heaven where Christ is, while the proud will be told, "I never knew you. Depart from me."

But the rich, in that he is made low (1:10)

The admonition with which verse 9 began is operative also in this clause. The rich man must boast about being made low, just as the lowly must boast of being exalted.

Commentators argue about whether "the rich" refers to a believer or an unbeliever. In support of the latter position some argue that the rest of verse 10 and verse 11 speak of the rich man's perishing and a believer cannot perish. The argument is specious, however, for these verses speak only about the swift passage of life and the obvious fact that the rich are unable to take their riches with them when they die. This is true of believers as well as of unbelievers.

The church of Christ, while composed for the most part of poor and lowly people, nevertheless has rich members also. So it has been in all the ages and so it is today. It is not in itself wrong or sinful to be rich. God gives the things of this world in different measures to different people. To some he gives much and to others he gives little. Neither riches nor poverty has any virtue in itself. They are never something about which to boast.

The Authorized Version is somewhat misleading when it translates the text as, "But the rich, in that he is made low." That translation implies that somewhere in the life of a rich man, God humbles him. But that is not quite the idea. The admonition in full and literally is, "Let not the rich man boast in his humiliation." The idea is that the rich man, even though he is rich, is nevertheless a lowly man. He is a lowly man because he is a believer. A believer is a humble man. Thus the rich man's humility or lowliness is not that God humbles him by taking away all his wealth and reducing him to poverty. It is rather the humility or lowliness that is characteristic of a believer who knows his own sin and unworthiness before God and seeks his salvation in the cross of his Savior.

This does not deny the need for the admonition. It is true that the admonition actually urges the poor to boast in their exaltation and the rich to boast in their humility, but surely implied is the admonition to the poor to refrain from grumbling about their poverty and to lay hold of the glory of their exaltation. The same is true of the rich. Implied is a stern warning against boasting of one's riches and being lifted up in pride because he has a large house, two or three cars, a motor home, or a summer house on the lake. True humility must be his inner spiritual frame of mind. James says to the rich, "Boast in your humility not in your riches." It is better by far to boast in one's spiritual blessedness in the cross than in the wealth of fruitful investments.

Because as the flower of the grass he shall pass away. For the sun is no sooner risen with a burning heat, but it withereth the grass, and the flower thereof falleth, and the grace of the fashion of it perisheth: so also shall the rich man fade away in his ways (1:10–11)

The figure of plant life is used to underscore the reality of wealth in its passing attractiveness. A flower is very pretty and glorious in its outward appearance. It is clothed with color in delicate hues and is rich in fragrance and strength. The rich man is like this. From outward appearances, wealth is attractive and the rich man lives a glorious life. He has a magnificent house and his yard is impeccable in its landscaping. Others ride past the home to see its beauty and to ponder what wealth can bring. It all looks like something to be coveted.

In my front yard I had a star magnolia, which is a small tree with beautiful white blossoms in the spring. When these blossoms are all fully developed, the tree looks beautiful, arrayed in the whiteness of holiness. During a very cool spring, the tree will continue to show its white blossoms for as long as two weeks. But one spring, the day after the tree bloomed, a heat wave brought temperatures into the high eighties. By the end of the day the blossoms were gone. One day! That is as long as their beauty lasted.

James makes this comparison between the plant life we enjoy and the wealth of a rich man. The word translated as "sun" can also refer to the dry, hot sirocco, a wind that withers everything in its path, or to the heat of a blazing sun that burns everything on which it shines. The plants droop and wither. Their beauty, color, texture, and structure perish. What a moment before was bright and beautiful is now ugly and useless.

So is the wealth of a rich man. This creation with its wealth and man in it are under the curse of sin. The curse of sin means

death. When a man is stripped by death of all his earthly possessions, the glory and glitter of his wealth cannot make his corpse
appealing. No one is jealous of him; no one claims to see any
beauty in him. His body is best put away where it cannot be seen
at all, for its appearance will only get worse with the passing of
the days. Where he goes, no treasures can be taken.

Although it is not wrong to be rich, the warning of James
is that it is foolishness to boast or glory in riches, for when a
man dies his riches pass away as a flower that withers beneath the
scorching sun, and he too withers as the flower of the field if he
boasts in riches. Let him rather boast in his inner humility and
consequent hope of the salvation God has promised in the cross
of Christ. Let him not brag about his possessions to others, but
rather point his fellow saints to the way of the cross. Let him say
with Paul and with all God's people, "God forbid that I should
glory, save in the cross of our Lord Jesus Christ" (Gal. 6:14).

Thus the entire passage reminds us that whether we have
much or little, it makes no real difference: the treasures of heaven
are all that count. Let the rich not look down in disdain on the
poor, and let not the poor covet what God has not been pleased
to give them. Let the rich use their wealth for the advancement
of the kingdom, and let the poor glory in their God. Let them be
content with what God has given them.

Enduring Temptation

12. Blessed is the man that endureth temptation: for when he
    is tried, he shall receive the crown of life, which the Lord
    hath promised to them that love him.
13. Let no man say when he is tempted, I am tempted of
    God: for God cannot be tempted with evil, neither temp-
    teth he any man:

14. But every man is tempted, when he is drawn away of his own lust, and enticed.
15. Then when lust hath conceived, it bringeth forth sin: and sin, when it is finished, bringeth forth death.
16. Do not err, my beloved brethren.

Blessed is the man that endureth temptation (1:12)

The connection of verse 12 to verse 2 is obvious. In verse 2 James urged his readers to rejoice when they fall into trials. Here James expands the thought by adding that our calling is to endure in the midst of trials in order to receive the reward that comes to those who do endure.

I have established that scripture uses the same word for trial and for temptation. It is a difficult choice between the translation trial or temptation in this verse. We are admonished to endure trials, but we must also endure temptations. In favor of translating the Greek word as "trials" is that endure means literally to bear up under, as under a very heavy load. One can hardly deny that temptations are heavy loads to bear, especially when we are commanded by our Lord to pray, "Lead us not into temptation." Because this verse is connected to verse 2 (where trials is the better translation) one would tend to think in terms of trials here as well. However, in favor of translating the word as "temptations" is the reference to temptations in verse 13.

My judgment is that the Holy Spirit has both meanings in mind. Temptations can be trials when by grace they are successfully resisted. We emerge from temptations stronger and better equipped to resist further temptations. Yet trials can surely be temptations when in the agony of them our inclinations are to rebel against God, criticize the ways through which he leads us, and become angry with him for what he does. Then a trial is not only a temptation, but we have also fallen by temptation into sin.

David faced this when in the throes of a great trial he did not dare to speak, lest he say something evil of God. (Ps. 39:1–3, 9).

If it is true that the Holy Spirit has both meanings in mind, the admonition to endure applies equally to both trials and temptations. God calls us to endure both. The text implies the figure of a man who carries a heavy load that makes him bend over and stagger. Such is true of both trials and temptations. Trials are very difficult experiences in life. Afflictions, which bring these trials, are heavy loads. They are even referred to in scripture as crosses that we must bear, with obvious reference to the cross of Christ. We are called to take up our crosses and to follow our Savior (Mark 10:21; Luke 9:23). To bear trials is to say with Job, "Though he would slay me, yet will I trust in him" (Job 13:15).

Temptations are burdens. Each person has his own character sins that are the fruit of weaknesses in his depraved nature. Against these sins he battles all his life and they become grievous burdens to him, for the struggle is deadly. A young man or woman whose spouse has left him or her and who knows that remarriage is wrong faces daily the burden of temptation.

In all our trials and temptations we are called to endure, that is, to remain steadfast in our faith, to be implacably unmoved by temptations to sin, and to be firm and calm in our trust in God. Endurance requires patience, for the Lord does not deliver us from our burdens at the same moment we cry out to him for relief and deliverance. To endure necessarily implies also that we wait on Jehovah, for his deliverance comes in his way and at his time.

It is striking and altogether fitting that verse 13 uses a word translated as "tried." The word (*dokimazō*) means to try something to determine if it is genuine, and it has the connotation of finding it genuine. Perhaps it would be better to translate it as "to find something to be genuine by testing it."

The reference is to God's people who are admonished to

endure trials and temptations and who do indeed endure. Literally the clause reads, "Blessed the man who endures trial [temptation] because, having been approved by trial…" The trials show that the Christian is a genuine believer. Especially in the context of the epistle, in which James warns against counterfeit faith, the Christian's faith has proved to be genuine. It is truly a saving faith that engrafts one into Christ.

James puts his finger on an important part of our lives and tells us how we are to conduct ourselves in trials. When the Lord sends trials of any kind to us, we are to receive them at his hand, although they sometimes are almost unbearably heavy. We could easily be crushed by them. We could cry out that God is unkind and takes pleasure in our suffering. We could even say, as the wicked so often do, "We can't do anything about it; we had better make the best of it and keep a stiff upper lip," but this would mean only that the trials have become temptations to which we succumb. We fall into sin and refuse to take up our crosses and follow Christ.

When these trials are temptations, we are to resist temptation of every kind, for to succumb to temptations means that we have given way to the devil. We are rather to resist the natural inclinations of our wicked natures to complain and rebel, and we are to submit to God's hand in humility and reverence before him.

For when he is tried, he shall receive the crown of life, which the Lord hath promised to them that love him (1:12)

This verse adds another dimension to our calling to endure: the reward of a crown of life is promised to those who love God. Part of enduring is loving God. We cannot submit utterly to him who sends trials unless we love him, knowing that he loves us and seeks our good in all things. If we love him, we will believe that he loves us. He loves us so much that whatever he may be pleased to call us to endure he sends for our spiritual good.

The crown of life is the reward. Scripture uses one word (*diadem*) for a king's crown and another word (*stephanos*) for the wreath of entwined laurel leaves given to the victor of an athletic contest. The latter is referred to here and is appropriate, for the one who endures has finished a very difficult course and has emerged victorious.

The wreath of laurel leaves is identified as eternal life. The figure is amazing. We will wear eternal life as a wreath of victory. Eternal life, God's triune life, earned for us and given to Christ at his resurrection, is now our possession. It is a transforming crown, and its transforming nature carries with it the aura of victory. Eternal life is the knowledge of God in Jesus Christ (John 17:3). It is not only to know God in the sense of mastering a dogmatics tome, but it is to know God as a man knows his wife (Gen. 4:1) in the intimacy of covenantal fellowship. It is the reward of grace. It is to know God as our husband and friend.

Verse 12 calls us to a seemingly impossible obligation. Nowhere in scripture is it even suggested that endurance in trials is easy. The anxiety, grief and struggle; the failing and falling, the picking up of oneself and continuing under the load; and the daily weariness of seeking peace and joy in bitter suffering—all this is known to God alone. To encourage the weary saints, God gives a wonderful promise. Part of the incentive to faithfulness is the promise of God himself. His promise cannot fail; it is as certain as God himself. It is an unquenchable light at the end of a dreary and troubling way that spurs us onward and upward and urges us to be faithful. It is the reward as the weary saint staggers the last mile on his difficult journey.

Let no man say when he is tempted, I am tempted of God (1:13)

That this warning immediately follows the admonition to endure indicates that James is fully aware of how easily we blame

God when we are tempted, especially when we stumble and fall in the struggle with temptation.

Several points of grammar enforce the seriousness of the admonition. The words "no man" stand first in the text. No man! No one! The second point is that "tempted of God" is literally "tempted from God" or temptation that proceeds from God.

The admonition does not deny that God is sovereign over temptation. He surely is; he is sovereign in everything he does, and he determines and controls all the circumstances of our lives. If God were not sovereign over temptation, prayers that God will not lead us into temptation would make no sense. Why ask God not to lead us into temptation, if he can do nothing about temptation?

However, God's sovereignty over temptation does not make him the source of temptation. Not only is God sovereign over temptation, but he is also sovereign over sin. Yet he works his sovereignty over sin in such a way that man's will is never violated and man's sin always remains his own, for which he is accountable before God.

The tendency to blame God for the temptations to which we succumb is strong. Adam did this in paradise when he shifted the blame for his transgression to Eve and thereby subtly shifted the blame to God, who had given Eve to Adam as his wife. Eve pointed to the serpent as the one responsible for her sin and thought she was quite cleverly blaming God, who had made the serpent.

While justifying ourselves for what we know to be sin, we may blame our transgressions on God's providence. God placed us in situations that almost guaranteed that we would fall. As antinomians, we may claim that all things work together for good to those who love God, and thus even our sin works our salvation, so let us sin that grace may abound (Rom. 6:1). In times of sinful courage, we may appeal to God's sovereignty over all things, including sin, as our excuse. We may even blame our failure to fulfill our covenantal responsibilities on God's control of our lives that makes fulfillment impossible: "We do not earn enough to pay our Christian school tuition," we say. As a result God makes it impossible to fulfill our covenantal obligations. Or someone becomes a member of an ungodly labor union because he needs the job to feed his family, and perhaps God does not provide him with a different job.

And so the sad litany of excuses rolls on its dreary way.

For God cannot be tempted with evil, neither tempteth he any man (1:13)

This verse presupposes not only the fact of temptation, but also falling into it. God's nature, in which holiness is an essential attribute, precludes the possibility of his being tempted. God cannot be tempted so that he sins. The same is true of the eternal Son of God, the second person of the Trinity. The triune God cannot be tempted as Christ was tempted. Although God's knowledge is all-encompassing, the subjective knowledge of temptation, as Christ experienced it, cannot be ascribed to the triune God.

Christ was tempted in all things as we are tempted (Heb. 4:15–16). The possibility of temptation for Christ lay in his human nature. He could be tempted because he was fully man, like us in all things except sin. But he could not sin, not even in his human nature, for God cannot sin.

Here is an important point concerning temptation: temptation itself is not sin. Even when we recognize the alluring character of a temptation and understand why it is enticing, we do not sin. Surely when our Lord was tempted in all points as we are tempted, he understood why the temptations were attractive. When Satan tempted the Lord to make stones into bread, Christ could see that to do this would lead to the adoration and acclaim of the people and would be a step toward his being made king in a way that would make the cross unnecessary.

Although we are able to understand the attractiveness of a certain course of action, our wills abhor it because it is a transgression of God's law. The sin lies in the willing.

Although the verse concludes with the statement of fact—"neither tempteth he any man"—it is connected with what precedes in the same verse. Because the infinitely holy God is beyond temptation, he cannot tempt man. To tempt is to try to persuade someone to commit a sin. God cannot and does not do anything of this sort. His holiness makes it impossible.

But every man is tempted, when he is drawn away of his own lust, and enticed (1:14)

Although in modern usage "lust" generally refers to illicit sexual desires, it has a variety of meanings in the New Testament. It is the general word for any strong desire. It can be used in the good sense, as Paul used it in 1 Thessalonians 2:17: "We...endeavoured the more abundantly to see your face with great desire." The word can also be used to describe all sinful objects of one's desires, as in 1 John 2:17: "And the world passeth away, and the lust thereof." It can also mean man's sinful and depraved nature, which is the emphasis in James 1:14. It is the same as what Augustine meant by *concupiscence*, which was central to Augustine's thinking and which he identified with original sin.[6] Man's sinful nature is characterized by lust for everything evil.

The words "his own" are added to emphasize, especially in contrast with the previous verse, that every man is responsible for

---

6 Allan D. Fitzgerald, *Augustine through the Ages: An Encyclopedia* (Grand Rapids, MI: Wm. B. Eerdmans Publishing Co., 1999), 224.

his own sin because his nature is lustful. What may be a temptation for one is not necessarily a temptation for another. We are all different people with different personality sins and different circumstances of living, but the phenomenon that temptation is due to men's lustful natures is universal.

Temptation is used here in the sense of falling into temptation. The reference obviously cannot be to objective temptation. When one succumbs to temptation, the sin of falling is no one's fault but his own.

Two participles are added to emphasize the reference to the lustful nature: "drawn away" and "enticed." The sentence reads literally, "But each is tempted by his own lusts, being drawn away and enticed." The words are nearly synonymous. To be drawn away is to be lured out as a lion is lured out of its cave by a chunk of raw meat, or a fish is lured to a hook by the bait. To be enticed means more the deception of the bait: a fish is lured to the hook only to be caught and killed.

Both participles may be causal: every man is tempted, because he is drawn away of his own lust and enticed. Temptation is always deceitful. Temptation promises happiness and pleasure to the one who falls into the temptation, but it actually destroys him. Riches may seem to be the way to true happiness and pleasure, freeing us to acquire anything we want, but in fact, as Paul says, "They that will be rich fall into temptation and a snare, and into many foolish and hurtful lusts, which drown men in destruction and perdition" (1 Tim. 6:9). But objective temptation cannot lure us into sin, unless our natures are (to fall back on the figure used above) like hungry fish. Food, though dangling from a hook, creates lust within us.

Thus the blame is not to be ascribed to God, but to the depravity of our lustful natures. It could be argued that we are not responsible for our sinful natures with which we were born, but scripture teaches that our sinful natures are God's punishment for our sin in Adam of eating of the forbidden tree in paradise. This is the doctrine of original guilt.

While this fearful picture of the effect on our sinful natures is true of the unbeliever in the absolute sense, it is also true of the believer. Even then, the meaning is not that the unbeliever always commits the overt act of sin to which temptation entices him: he is capable, even apart from grace, to resist committing the outward act. If, for example, he is tempted to commit adultery, the thoughts of how adultery would hurt his wife and destroy his family can be sufficient to prevent him from committing the act. However, such restraint is not a good work that merits God's approval, but self-interest. God knows and judges the heart.

When a believer succumbs to the enticement of temptation, whether in his thoughts or in fact, he does not lose his status as a believer, for there can be no falling away from and loss of faith. Even when he sins, he hates his sin. Paul described this anomaly in Romans 7:20: "Now if I do that I would not, it is no more I that do it, but sin that dwelleth in me." That unwillingness to sin (even if the believer commits the sin) is the work of grace that brings him to the cross seeking forgiveness and pardon, thus conquering sin through the cross of Jesus Christ.

Then when lust hath conceived, it bringeth forth sin: and sin, when it is finished, bringeth forth death (1:15)

The connection of verse 15 with verse 14 is established by "then." The idea is next, after a man is drawn away by his lust; after this, as the next event that happens in the process of sin's development; or furthermore, in addition to what has been said. Either translation captures the idea.

In verses 14–15 James gives a remarkable psychological and spiritual analysis of temptation. I say that it is "psychological and spiritual" because the truly psychological is also spiritual.

In verse 14 the figure was of a hungry fish lured to a hook by the dangling bait. In verse 15 the figure changes radically to conception and childbirth. Our evil natures are like a womb fertilized by an objective temptation. The result is conception. That is, the depraved nature impregnated by a temptation produces sin. The union of the temptation and the depraved nature begets sin.

There is an added step to this process. James uses the words "when it is finished" and a brutally powerful illustration. The figure is of a baby conceived but not born, because it has not yet reached full development. After full development the baby is born. The word translated as "finished" means the goal is achieved, the purpose is accomplished. But horror of horrors, the goal, the end of the process, is not a healthy or mature baby, but death, a baby that has begun to rot.

This is temptation when one's depraved nature is aroused. Sin is the result: sin either in one's thoughts and desires or in words and deeds. Sin can produce nothing but death. This death is complete alienation from God and everlasting hell if it is not confessed and forgiven.

Do not err, my beloved brethren (1:16)

James uses the tender address "my beloved brethren," which reminds God's people that although they do sin frequently when temptation has its way with them, nevertheless they are still of the family of God, brothers with the apostle, and thus have hope even in the dire circumstances of a melancholy fall.

This is a transition verse that connects the previous verses to what follows. On the one hand, we are faced with two alternatives: endure trials and, insofar as they constitute temptations, resist them or succumb to trials and bring forth death as the result. On the other hand, we are not to blame God when we fall into sin, for God, the Father of lights, gives only good gifts.

When we stand before the choices of enduring trials by resisting temptation or succumbing to temptation, we must not deceive ourselves into thinking that James' description of the process of temptation is exaggerated in any way. We can easily think along those lines. We can argue that a little sin is not so bad: a bottle of beer at a beach party, a puff of a marijuana cigarette, a white lie, or one visit to a pornographic site on the Internet. What harm can that do? We can also argue that although temptation has consequences, we can break the process by our will power. Even worse, we might say that God does not mean what he says that the end result is really hell.

When we use this line of argumentation we are deceived.

There is some question about the words "do not err," which is better translated as "be not deceived." This can be translated as "you are not deceived" or as "do not deceive yourselves." Almost certainly the first translation is incorrect, for the use of a command rather than a statement of fact fits into the line of thought. Whether someone else deceives us or we deceive ourselves makes very little difference. In fact, to allow ourselves to be deceived by another is actually self-deception.

Self-deception mocks God. We are reminded of Paul's words in Galatians 6:7–8: "Be not deceived; God is not mocked: for whatsoever a man soweth, that shall he also reap. For he that soweth to his flesh shall of the flesh reap corruption; but he that soweth to the Spirit shall of the Spirit reap life everlasting." God is mocked by such self-deception because we do not really believe that what God says is true.

This is much like Satan's ploy in paradise, "Ye shall not surely die: For God doth know that in the day ye eat thereof, then your eyes shall be opened, and ye shall be as gods, knowing good and evil" (Gen. 3:4–5). If God does not mean what he says, he is a deceiver who threatens us with empty threats. What a dreadful thing to say.

Rather than to succumb to temptation, we are to endure the trials God sends upon us. The child of God, though he carries with him his wicked and sinful flesh, is regenerated and possesses the life of Christ. In principle he hates sin and has the spiritual power in Christ to resist sin. We must never say in the face of temptation, "I am too sinful to resist successfully this temptation. I, being the kind of man I am, cannot do anything but let the temptation have its way with me." This too is slander of God's work.

A believer's power to resist sin, to fight a good fight against temptation, and to stand in the evil day is the power of the cross of Christ. He must not rely on himself but face temptation in the power of his victorious Christ. The child of God is always victorious. After his soul-wrenching description of his struggle with sin and his cry, "O wretched man that I am!" Paul confidently shouted, "I thank God through Jesus Christ our Lord" (Rom. 7:24–25). With each victory the child of God grows stronger in the battle, for temptations overcome become trials that purify his faith.

All this does not mean that the believer will never fall. He will. But he will never find pleasure in sin, and he always comes to repentance at the foot of the cross. Repentance delivers him from the horrible process that ends in death. The baby of sin is aborted by repentance. When he is almost overcome with remorse and despair, God's unfailing promises come to him to shine as a light in his darkness, for they reveal God's faithfulness and everlasting love through Christ.

God's Good Gifts

17. Every good gift and every perfect gift is from above, and cometh down from the Father of lights, with whom is no variableness, neither shadow of turning.
18. Of his own will begat he us with the word of truth, that we should be a kind of firstfruits of his creatures.

The connection between these verses and the foregoing context is not established grammatically or by a conjunction. The connection must be learned from the thought. This is a common occurrence in James, and this is a propitious time to say a few things about this characteristic of the epistle.

James frequently seems to change the thought abruptly from one section to another. On the surface, this makes it difficult to follow his thoughts and to understand why a new subject is suddenly introduced without warning. Such is the case here. James has been discussing what I call the psychology of temptation. Now, with a disconcerting abruptness, the apostle begins to discuss God's good gifts. How can one jump so quickly from this subject to that subject without leaving his readers behind?

It would be a serious mistake to think that James is simply handing his readers a long list of unrelated thoughts and admonitions, as if he wanders from one idea to another as a bee flits from one flower to another in search of nectar. This is not characteristic of scripture, nor must it be said to characterize James' epistle. If we look at the book as a series of unrelated ideas, we will lose important insights into the meaning.

However, James' epistle is not like Paul's epistles, for James is not Paul. Paul was the supreme logician. His letters are exercises in logical reasoning. He presented his thoughts in the form of syllogisms and made abundant use of *therefore*. Not all of the New Testament books do this. John's writings, for example, are marked by an intuitive sense of meaning that is somewhat baffling to the logical mind. James is much like John in this respect, although without the intuitive insights into things that John possessed. God used many different men with many different gifts to write his scriptures. Although God is the sole author of scripture, he preserved the characteristics of the men he used to write scripture.

James' connectives are subtle and sometimes not made explicit by grammatical constructions or conjunctions. They are internal and must be ascertained by a clear understanding of James' thought. For that reason the connections are very powerful, and once having understood them, new vistas of thought emerge to enrich our understanding of God's works.

So it is here between verses 16 and 17 and between verses 17 and 18.

Verse 16 is connected with the broader context. We have been warned to endure our trials and to rejoice in them. This is still the dominant thought. To endure the trials God sends we must have wisdom, which we are to seek from God alone, the only one who can explain properly the significance of the trials we face. However, we must not blame God when we do not endure our trials. When they become temptations to which we succumb, we have only ourselves to blame, for our melancholy falls are because of our weak and sinful natures.

In verse 17 James stresses that God cannot be blamed for our wicked sins because he only ever gives good gifts. He cannot give bad gifts. Even the trials we endure are good gifts. That they are good gifts is the reason we must rejoice in the midst of them. It is in God's nature to give only good gifts, for in him is no variableness or shadow of turning.

Every good gift and every perfect gift is from above (1:17)

The two words translated in this verse as "gift" are two different words, although they may have the same root (*didōmi* [to give]). The first word (*dosis*) emphasizes the act of giving, and the second (*dōrēma*) stresses the gift. Together they make clear that everything we receive in this life comes from God. We have nothing of ourselves, nor have we acquired anything by our strength or efforts. We may think that we acquire our weekly wages by our diligence and hard work, but although God may use work to give us wages, even our strength and health that enable us to work are gifts from him. We may exercise so that we strengthen our hearts, but the beat of our hearts is a gift. Even our breath is given us by God.

The first word describing God's gifts is "good." God's gifts are morally good. They are never defective, and they are certainly never in any respect conducive to our sinning and falling into temptation. The second word is "perfect, and it means that these gifts are complete, without deception, never partial, always fully what God says they will be, and totally sufficient for us to serve God without sin.

Thus we live in a world that God has created and in which he has placed us as the representatives of his cause in the world and as those called to use the gifts he gives to the praise and glory of his name.

And cometh down from the Father of lights, with whom is no variableness, neither shadow of turning (1:17)

It is somewhat difficult to know the meaning of this expression, but most commentators agree that it has a double reference. This is correct. It refers first to God as the creator of all the heavenly bodies; second, it means that God's nature is essentially light.[7] That God as creator can be called Father of the creation ought not to disturb us, for the Apostles' Creed speaks of our faith in God the Father almighty, maker of heaven and earth. He is the Father of his creation because he made all things by the word of his

---

7 Kistemaker, *Exposition of the Epistle of James*, 53; Alexander Ross, *The Epistles of James and John* (Grand Rapids, MI: Wm. B. Eerdmans Publishing Co., 1954), 35; D. Edmond Hiebert, *Exposition of James* (Chicago: Moody Press, 1979), 113; Calvin, *Catholic Epistles*, 291. Calvin does not say in so many words that he gives to the expression a double reference, but he does hint at this idea. If the reference is first to the celestial sphere and thus to the heavenly bodies, the genitive of the word "lights" is a genitive of the object. If the meaning is that God's very essence is light, the genitive is a genitive of description. It is certainly possible that both ideas are meant.

power, and he continues to uphold all things by that same word.

Genesis 1:14 informs us that the celestial lights are for signs. They reveal to us the wonder of God's being, which is light and no darkness at all (1 John 1:5). He is the source and fountain of all light, whether it is the physical light of the sun, moon, and stars or the spiritual light that shines in Christ and through Christ into all his people.

Scripture equates light with holiness. Just as darkness is sin and unbelief, so light is holiness and a reflection of God. Thus James' double use of "Father of lights" is eminently appropriate, for he says that every gift of God is good, that is, morally perfect. It is therefore a reflection of God's essential holiness. God's holiness is a blazing light before which the seraphim cover their faces with their wings and cry, "Holy, holy, holy, is the LORD of hosts: the whole earth is full of his glory" (Isa. 6:2–3).

The question remains, why does James refer to the holiness of God by referring to the heavenly bodies? The answer is undoubtedly that God's infinite holiness is revealed in the lights in the sky, which God set in the firmament of the heavens. It is impossible to look at the light of the sun without burning our eyes. The same would be true of the uncountable planets, stars, and galaxies if they were not so far distant that we are able to look at them without injury to our eyes. They remind us in earthly terms that the essence of God is so bright that he is beyond seeing (Ps. 19:1–3).

The lights in the heavens vary in the strength and intensity of the light they give. From an earthly perspective they vary in clarity, intensity, heat, and the light they emit. They also vary in light in themselves, for stars diminish in power and can burn out. "Variableness" and "turning" indicate that the heavenly bodies also vary in light according to the revolutions they make in harmony with their positions in relation to the earth and the rest of the heavens. The moon is not always equally bright, and the seasons make a difference in the strength of the sun. The turning of the heavenly bodies has an effect on the light they give.

Such is not the case with God, the fountain and source of all light. In him is not this variableness and shadow of turning that characterizes heavenly bodies. Hence his giving of every gift will necessarily be perfect. He is the eternally unchangeable one without any variation, faithful to himself and without alteration. He never changes his mind nor alters his plan. He is not a god who reacts in different ways to situations on earth. He is eternal and unchangeable in all his counsel and in all his works.

The nature of God is to give. He never receives, for there is nothing that is not his. We can bring nothing to God; we cannot enrich him; we cannot add to his happiness or make his glory greater than it is. Our works never provide God with something that is not his. He gives and gives and gives again. And because he is holy, what he gives is good and perfect.

In contrast, man's nature is to receive. He cannot give anything. His being, dependent for its existence and functions upon God, is never capable of giving anything to the Father of lights. It is always possible only to stand before him, the great giver, and wait to be filled out of his fullness. What shall I render to the Lord for all his benefits to me? Nothing! Nothing, ever! All I can do (and even that is of him) is to say, "Thanks, Lord" and then ask for more (Ps. 116:12–13).

Let no man say when he is tempted, "I am tempted of God." To be tempted of God is impossible, for God gives only good gifts. Even God's gifts to the wicked are always good and perfect. God does not give evil or spoiled gifts to the ungodly. The controversy with the defenders of common grace does not lie in the nature of God's gifts. God's gifts are always good—even rain and sunshine. Rather, the controversy with the defenders of common grace is that God's gifts to the reprobate are said to be grace, that is, evidences of his favor and love. Against this notion the whole of scripture is an abundant and consistent testimony.

That God's gifts are always good makes the sins of the wicked more heinous. The ungodly take what they receive from God and use it to destroy God and to blot out his name in the world. They turn God's gifts against him and make war with him. They are worthy of the worst of all punishments.

James still has our trials in mind, and we may well ask whether our trials are good gifts. We must, however, evaluate them from the viewpoint of God's purpose. If we do that, we can conclude that even our trials are good gifts to us from God. They are surely not good gifts in themselves and are reasons for suffering and grief. As these afflictions come over the wicked, they are God's fierce punishment for the sins of which they are guilty. But James is talking here about what God sends to his people. These afflictions are good gifts for which they ought to be thankful. God uses all the afflictions that he sends for their good, that is, to save them (Rom. 8:28).

Of his own will begat he us with the word of truth, that we should be a kind of firstfruits of his creatures (1:18)

It is clear that this verse is one instance of the good and perfect gifts God gives to his people. Why is the particular gift of regeneration mentioned in distinction from other gifts? The answer is undoubtedly that regeneration contrasts with blaming God for our falls into temptation. God does not tempt us. Quite the contrary, God gives us the good gift of regeneration, a gift that enables us to resist temptations and to endure in trials. That this contrast is in James' mind is evident from the play on words between this verse and verse 15. Verse 15 says that sin brings forth death; verse 18 says that God brings us forth as saints: "of his own will begat he us." The two words are the same in Greek. In us sin brings forth death; in God's work his word brings forth life.

We are begotten again of God's will. The Greek word (*bou-lomai*) for will used in this verse is different from another word (*thelō*) that means the living will of God by which all his counsel is carried out. "Will" here refers to the counsel of God. The use of the word that means God's counsel emphasizes that the regeneration of his people is a wonder of God, a gift of his love that he has ordained from all eternity as a special gift for his people. The regeneration of the elect is according to God's eternal and unchangeable counsel and the realization of that counsel in time. Because God has eternally determined to beget us as his children, he loves us with an eternal love, and his divine and sovereign purpose is to save us.

To be begotten by God is to be regenerated, to be born again. To be born again is a spiritual necessity because our first and natural birth from our parents was a spiritual stillbirth. We were conceived and born in sin. But our rebirth is from above, worked by the Spirit of Christ by whom we are given a heavenly and everlasting life. It is the life of Christ's resurrection imparted to us by a wonder of grace.

The question is, does this passage speak of regeneration in the broad sense of including sanctification, which is worked by God through the preaching of the gospel, or of regeneration in the narrow sense as the first work of God in the heart of the elect and yet dead sinner, which takes place by a direct act of God through the Spirit apart from the preaching.[8]

Verse 18 refers to regeneration as the whole work of God that brings the full life of Christ to his elect children. Regeneration begins with the first work of the implanting of the new life of

---

8 For a more detailed explanation of mediate and immediate regeneration, see Herman Hanko, *A Pilgrim's Manual: Commentary on 1 Peter* (Jenison, MI: Reformed Free Publishing Association, 2012), 23–25.

Christ; it continues as that new life of Christ comes to consciousness in believing; it manifests itself in the holy walk of the saints; it is perfected in the soul at death when the soul goes to glory; and its full perfection takes place when our corrupt bodies are also raised from the dead at the return of Christ and conformed to the likeness of the body of Christ (Phil. 3:21). The regeneration that results in a sanctified life of faith while we are in this world is worked in the elect sinner by the preaching of the word. That the result of regeneration is called "a kind of firstfruits of his creatures" is evidence that regeneration in the broad sense is referred to. Still more clearly, verse 19 refers to the preaching, which admonishes us to be slow to speak and swift to hear when we come under the preaching.

This regeneration is worked in us "by the word of truth."[9] The expression most likely refers to the content of the preaching.[10] The preached word proclaims the truth and makes it known. The truth is God himself. He is, in his own being, truth. There is no truth anywhere except it is an expression about God; all else is the lie. That truth is revealed in Jesus Christ, who proclaimed, "I am the way, the truth, and the life" (John 14:6).[11] Thus the preaching is always and only the preaching of Christ: his crucifixion, death, resurrection, and ascension into heaven. The preaching has as its sole content Christ crucified (1 Cor. 1:23). The preaching works

---

9 "Word" is in the dative case and is a dative of means. It explains the means God uses to regenerate us.

10 "Truth" is in the genitive case. It can be a genitive of description, which could be translated as "true word." Or it could be a genitive of content, which means that the truth is the content of the spoken word, that is, the word reveals the truth. While the last two usages are similar, I prefer to take this as a genitive of content, which means that the content of the word is the truth.

11 The construction is a hendiadys. The meaning is that Christ is the way (to the Father), because he is the truth, and he is the way and the truth because he is the life.

faith in the hearts of regenerated sinners by the work of the Holy Spirit, and faith's sole object is the Christ of the scriptures. Faith lays hold of and appropriates Christ and believes that from Christ they receive all things for time and for eternity.

"That we should be a kind of firstfruits of his creatures" is a purpose clause that depends on "begat he us" in verse 18. It expresses the purpose of God's regeneration in our hearts.[12] The figure is taken from the Old Testament and the law that stipulated the need for Israel to bring the firstfruits of the harvest to the tabernacle or temple (Ex. 23:16, 19; 34:22, 26 and similar passages in Leviticus and Deuteronomy). Their bringing the firstfruits of the harvest was the Israelites' confession that they had received their harvest from God, that the rest of the harvest was sure to follow, and that because God gave it, all they possessed belonged to God and had to be used in his service.

Christ is the firstborn in the realization of God's purpose. He is the firstborn of every creature and the firstborn from the dead (Col. 1:15, 18). The firstborn children of the Israelites had to be given to God as well as the firstfruits of the harvest (Ex. 13:2, 13, and many other passages in the law). The tribe of Levi, however, took the place of the firstborn sons of Israel, for the Levites were dedicated to God in his service in the tabernacle and temple. Israel is called God's firstborn in Exodus 4:22.

---

12 The construction is *eis* with the infinitive. Most commentators make the expression a purpose clause, but Lenski is the exception. He takes issue with most commentators, including Meyer's commentary (Joh. Ed. Huther, *Critical and Exegetical Handbook to the General Epistles of James, Peter, John, and Jude*, trans. Paton J. Gloag, D. B. Croom, C. H. Irwin, Timothy Dwight [New York: Funk & Wagnalls, 1887], 58). Lenski makes this a result clause on the grounds that if it were a purpose clause the promise of a kind of firstfruits would be put too far into the future (R. C. H. Lenski, *Interpretation of the Epistle to the Hebrews and of the Epistle of James* [Columbus, OH: Lutheran Book Concern, 1938], 556). Lenski is wrong because we need not wait until the judgment day to be firstfruits. God can and does make us that already in this life.

Christ is called the firstfruits from the dead in 1 Corinthians 15:20–23. The resurrection of Christ as the firstfruits guarantees that all who belong to Christ will follow him in the resurrection and receive the power of their own resurrection from Christ, for the life of regeneration in them is the life of Christ's resurrection (John 11:25–26; 1 Pet. 1:3).

Our regeneration makes us the firstfruits of all the creation, that is, the regeneration of the elect is the guarantee that the entire creation of God will also be regenerated and made new. The creation is God's creation. He never relinquished his claim on it. He made man the head of it, with the result that when man fell the creation came under the curse. Wicked man took over the creation and determined to use it in the service of Satan, who tempted man to be his ally in his nefarious scheme. But God maintained his cause. Christ died for the world and accomplished reconciliation for all the creation by his death (Col. 1:20). Thus the creation as well as the church will be brought to the full perfection of heaven when Christ returns. Romans 8:21–23 teaches this truth clearly: "The creature itself also shall be delivered from the bondage of corruption into the glorious liberty of the children of God. For we know that the whole creation groaneth and travaileth in pain together until now. And not only they, but ourselves also, which have the firstfruits of the Spirit, even we ourselves groan within ourselves, waiting for the adoption, to wit, the redemption of our body."

Because this glorious truth is our possession, let us endure trials, fight a good fight against temptations, and be faithful to the end.

The Responsibilities of Regeneration

19. Wherefore, my beloved brethren, let every man be swift to hear, slow to speak, slow to wrath:

20. For the wrath of man worketh not the righteousness of God.
21. Wherefore lay apart all filthiness and superfluity of naughtiness, and receive with meekness the engrafted word, which is able to save your souls.
22. But be ye doers of the word, and not hearers only, deceiving your own selves.
23. For if any be a hearer of the word, and not a doer, he is like unto a man beholding his natural face in a glass:
24. For he beholdeth himself, and goeth his way, and straightway forgetteth what manner of man he was.
25. But whoso looketh into the perfect law of liberty, and continueth therein, he being not a forgetful hearer, but a doer of the work, this man shall be blessed in his deed.

Verses 19–25 are introduced by the conjunction "wherefore," which makes these verses the conclusion of the truth of regeneration. Because we are regenerated and thus children of God with the life of Christ in our hearts, we are to give attention to the following admonitions. The admonitions are directed to God's regenerated people who are commanded to do what God has enabled them to do not to become what they are not.

The passage has an important place in the entire epistle. James is intent on combating those who have only counterfeit faith—faith in outward confession but faith that produces no good works.

In the preceding verses James has reminded us that faith is given in regeneration. Faith unites us to Christ and regeneration brings to us the life of Christ. Faith is the bond through which the life of Christ comes to us. Hence the admonitions that follow are admonitions that the people of God must do out of living faith.

The first admonition has to do with our attention to the preaching of the word. That James begins with our calling with respect to the preaching ought not to surprise us, because he has just said that our ongoing regeneration (our faith and sanctification) takes place by the preaching. Such would never be the fruit of the preaching if we paid no attention to what the minister says. We must be careful how we hear.

At the same time, this admonition and the following admonitions begin to pave the way for the doctrinal heart of the epistle in 2:14–26, which deals with the great truth of justification by faith manifested in our works. If we are to understand that doctrinal section correctly, and not as some who make the text a ground for justification by faith and works, we must understand these verses that lead up to that important discussion.

There are hints already in this passage of what the apostle will say later. Foremost among these hints is the emphatic truth that the good works by which we fulfill these many admonitions are not in any sense the ground of justification. These good works are the fruit of regeneration, a work so obviously God's work that only the crassest Arminian can ascribe it to man. No more than we had anything to say about our first birth, which ended in a spiritual stillbirth, do we have anything to say about our second birth. While we were dead in trespasses and sins, God quickened us (Eph. 2:1).

Immediately the apostle slams the door in the face of all Arminians and those who teach justification by faith and works by pointing out that *because* we are regenerated, we are to perform these good works, which good works are what these admonitions require. James also closes the door to the antinomians, who claim that good works are unnecessary. He says, "You are regenerated, therefore God has given you the spiritual power to do these good works. Be what God has made you. You are justified by faith and faith produces good works."

Wherefore, my beloved brethren, let every man be swift to hear (1:19)

One's attitude when he enters the house of God and listens to the preaching makes all the difference between being blessed by the preaching and receiving no benefit from the preaching. James gives instruction in what our attitude ought to be.

Once again those to whom James writes are addressed as "my beloved brethren." They are national brethren, for James writes primarily to Jewish converts, but above all they are spiritual brethren. When James addresses those to whom he writes in anger in chapters 4 and 5, he drops this address. But here he refers to his readers as his beloved brethren, and they remain that even when he chastises them with hard words.

Although the text does not give any instruction on scripture's teachings concerning the preaching, various truths concerning the preaching are presupposed. We ought briefly to mention the most important. Preaching is the calling of the church of Christ in the world. For this reason the church is organized into an institution with membership rolls and officers. It is an organization established by Christ so that it can perform its one calling to preach the gospel. It is organized for this task because the preaching of the gospel is the most important event that takes place in the history of the world. It is more important than the rise and fall of empires, than the wars of nations, than the activities of the world's great powers. It is most important because by the preaching Christ himself gathers, defends, and preserves his church.[13] The church is the sole reason for all that transpires in the history of the world from the first moment of creation to the end of time.

---

13 Heidelberg Catechism Q&A 54, in Schaff, *Creeds of Christendom*, 3:324–25.

Preaching is performed by the church through the called and ordained ministry. When that moment of preaching takes place, Christ speaks through the preacher to his church (Rom. 10:13–17). When Christ speaks to his church through the preaching, the Holy Spirit efficaciously calls his people out of the darkness of sin into the light of the kingdom of heaven. By Christ's word through the preacher and the work of the Spirit, faith is quickened, strengthened, and made a power in the lives of the children of God. Thus all the spiritual benefits of Christ's atoning sacrifice are made the possession of Christ's people by the preaching.

For this reason James admonishes God's people how they are to listen to the preaching. They are to be swift to hear. The Greek makes it emphatic: be swift with a view to hearing. There is a tradition that claims that when the Jews made their way to the temple or synagogue to worship, they were commanded to walk as swiftly as they were able, while on their return from the synagogue they were to walk very slowly. The first was indicative of their eagerness to hear the word; the latter, their reluctance to leave it. This was obviously outward, but it is possible that James refers to this practice.

In the hearts of God's people there must be the same eagerness to hear the preaching of the word as characterizes a newborn baby who hungers for its mother's milk (1 Pet. 2:2). The preaching is the food of their souls, able to nourish them unto everlasting life. Forbidden is a reluctance to go to church. Some sleep in on Sunday morning, only to throw on their clothes hastily and dash off to church wholly unprepared to worship. Some go to church out of a sense of obligation: the elders require us to be there and will inquire of us why we are not there if we do not come. Some carry into church such a heavy load of the cares of life that their feet drag as they make their way to the house of God, and these cares keep them from attentiveness to the preaching.

Swift to hear the word means that God's people assemble for worship and listen with hearing mixed with faith (Heb. 4:1–3). Believing that Christ is speaking to them, they lay hold on Christ and his word and eagerly appropriate the word and carry it with them throughout the week.

Preaching has an aura of the miraculous. Paul called it "the foolishness of preaching" (1 Cor. 1:21). So it seems to anyone who does not believe the scriptures. A man, weak and frail, himself a great sinner, stands before an audience and talks. That preaching has in it a greater power than the world's worst earthquake, the most powerful volcanic eruption, or twenty powerful nuclear bombs. Who can believe that?

Yet, as Paul said, preaching is the power and wisdom of God (Rom. 1:16; 1 Cor. 1:24). It is the power to make saints out of sinners, inhabitants of heaven out of hell-bound fools, and friends of God out of those who shake their fists in his face.

No wonder James admonishes us to be swift to hear. The preaching is, after all, our life! Listening to the preaching is done with the zest and eagerness that a hungry man shows when he comes to the dinner table. The man who eats with enthusiasm is aware of his need for bodily nourishment. So the believer, aware of the need for his soul to be fed with spiritual food, eagerly devours that word and applies it to himself, so that his spiritual life may be fed and strengthened.

Slow to speak, slow to wrath (1:19)

The two admonitions belong together: the second explains the first more fully. The apostle certainly does not object to pious and edifying discussions among the saints about sermons. Such reactions to the preaching are necessary, required, and of great benefit.

But there is another kind of speaking that is made in anger against preaching. There may be reasons for anger, although that is not an excuse. The preaching of the word is like a sharp surgeon's knife (Heb. 4:12) that cuts into our deepest being and exposes the sin that lies there. It does this because it is quick and powerful and sharper than a two-edged sword. Sometimes people complain that the preaching has hurt them, but that is exactly what it is supposed to do. They become angry because the minister spoke against their pet sins and exposed them for what they really are. The preaching has a way of tearing off our masks of hypocrisy and exposing our inward thoughts and desires. It should make us squirm in our pews.

In today's churches the minister thinks it is his calling to make people feel good and to help them have a positive self-image, as it is called. The result of such preaching will never be that believers run with all possible speed to the cross. They are at ease in Zion (Amos 6:1).

True preaching is necessary if the preaching is to accomplish its God-given purpose. In its exposure of sin, it will drive God's people to the cross of Christ, in whom alone is the hope of salvation; but it will also anger people who complain that all they hear from the pulpit is sin, sin, sin, and all that the minister does is send people on guilt trips.

Against this reaction to the preaching the text warns. In such people who become angry at the preaching and with the preacher, the word of God has no beneficial results, but simply hardens them in their sins. We all need to be warned against such folly.

For the wrath of man worketh not the righteousness of God (1:20)

If one becomes angry with the preaching, the preaching also accomplishes God's purpose. Refusing to apply the word to his own life, a listener becomes angry, and in his anger he hardens his heart. Thus James explains more fully the reason for his warning to be slow to speak and slow to wrath. There is no spiritual benefit to be gained by that kind of listening, but only condemnation.

One can also speak angrily against the preaching if he considers the preaching to be too doctrinal. I mention this because this is a great danger in our day, and it shows how proper listening does bring about the righteousness of God.

Doctrinal preaching does not have a very good reputation in today's church world. It is said to be divisive, especially when it necessarily condemns false doctrines and exposes their unbiblical character. Doctrinal preaching is criticized as being "over the heads" of people—a criticism that comes from those who never read solid biblical material and who are not accustomed to thinking of spiritual things. Quickly they clamor for "practical preaching" and become angry when the minister fails to listen to them.

There is a certain irony here, however. It is my experience that in many instances, when a minister preaches an intensely practical sermon, these are the first to become angry at that preaching as well and to complain that there is altogether too much emphasis in the preaching on sin and its consequences.

Wrath against the preaching does not work the righteousness of God. It has the opposite effect: it hardens the listener in his sin.

The positive is also true.

The righteousness of God is the perfect righteousness appropriated by faith that assures the sinner that he is without sin before the face of God because of the complete sacrifice of Christ on the cross. Such righteousness is called the righteousness of God because it is God's essential attribute freely given to the sinner and because it becomes the sinner's possession by appropriating Christ, who accomplished the righteousness of God for his people.

Being swift to hear works the righteousness of God. The sinner who hears the preaching hears with faith—hearing mixed with faith. Every sermon preached that is according to the will of God is the preaching of Christ crucified. Paul gave the main theme of every sermon he ever preached and hoped to preach in the words, "We preach Christ crucified" (1 Cor. 1:23). When preaching leads to the cross, as it always must, it leads to Christ crucified. When hearing is mixed with faith, the listener lays hold on Christ crucified as the only ground of his salvation and thus appropriates by faith the righteousness of God revealed in Christ. Preaching, arousing faith by the work of the Holy Spirit, carries one to Calvary, for there alone is God's righteousness revealed.

It may be that James also has in mind the righteousness of a godly walk in keeping with God's commandments and will. Righteousness in scripture is sometimes used in that sense (Matt. 5:20), but the imputed righteousness of God received by faith is certainly the primary meaning here. It is the basis for sanctification, which is the work of actually making us righteous in our walk.

Wherefore lay apart all filthiness and superfluity of naughtiness (1:21)

To heed the command of God to be swift to hear and slow to wrath is possible only when we lay aside all filthiness and superfluity of naughtiness. "Filthiness" refers to immoral conduct and moral uncleanness. Undoubtedly the word in this context refers not only to physical fornication, but includes spiritual fornication. It includes departure from the will of God, our husband, by us, his bride. Such spiritual fornication includes any illicit attachment to and interest in the world around us. James is not hesitant to call those to whom he writes "adulterers and adulteresses" because they have made friends of the world. (4:4). Every thought, word, deed, and desire must be put aside and thrown from us if we are to hear the preached word properly. If we do not heed this admonition, the word will fall on hearts too full of the world to make room for the word of God. How often we need to hear this admonition. Jesus speaks of such people in Matthew 13:7, 22: "Some [seed] fell among thorns; and the thorns sprung up, and choked them. He also that received seed among the thorns is he that heareth the word; and the care of this world, and the deceitfulness of riches, choke the word, and he becometh unfruitful."

"Superfluity of naughtiness" is a clumsy but striking expression, which literally means remnants of evil. It modifies "all filthiness" and defines more fully the meaning of filthiness. It also presupposes that those to whom the epistle is directed are regenerated. Regeneration is a principle work of God that gives the elect sinner the true life of Christ. It is the creation of a new man in the center of man's being, which is without sin, is destined to grow in influence on the entire nature of man, and will someday make him perfect. But as long as the regenerated sinner is in this life he retains remnants of evil in his nature against which he is called to fight. These remnants prevent him from hearing properly and savingly the word of God and hence must be laid aside.

The believer is never successful in accomplishing this while in this world, for the life of regeneration remains only a principle, and his nature remains depraved. The perfection of that principle takes place only at death when his soul is cleansed and at the coming of Christ when his body is changed into a body like the glorious body of Christ. Nevertheless, that principle is dominant in his life, influences everything he does, and gives him the victory over sin by bringing him to confession of sin and the desire to escape completely from the bondage of sin. Indeed, even the believer's daily struggles against the power of sin in him is the victory over that sin.

And receive with meekness the engrafted word, which is able to save your souls (1:21)

The scriptures use many figures to describe the word of God. The word translated as "engrafted" means implanted, so here the word is compared to a seed planted in the ground. The seed is regeneration, which is the life of Christ that grows throughout a person's lifetime and develops by the power of the preaching. It grows until it produces an entirely new man. That seed of regeneration is a living seed because it grows by the power of the word. The seed is planted in the heart. The word is like the rain and warmth of the sun that causes a seed to germinate and grow as it becomes a part of the seed itself. So that word that is preached and causes the seed to grow is what saves us (Isa. 55:10–11; Matt. 13:3–8; 18–23, Heb. 6:7–8).

We are therefore to receive into our hearts the preaching as the powerful word of Christ. We are to receive it by being swift to hear and slow to wrath. And we are to receive it as the word, "which is able to save [our] souls."

The figure breaks down here. The soil where the seed is lodged and receives the rain and sunshine is passive. The soil of our hearts is passive in the initial work of God when he implants the seed of regeneration, but our hearts are then made active. The responsibility is ours to see to it that that seed grows, and we fulfill our responsibility when we receive that word.

The reception of the implanted word is not a work we perform by our own strength and ability, for it always remains true that God works in us both to will and to do of his good pleasure (Phil. 2:13). Nevertheless, God works his salvation in us consciously, and we have our calling in that work.

We are to receive that word with meekness. Some commentators put "with meekness" with the previous expression, "lay apart all filthiness and superfluity of naughtiness with meekness." This is a mistake. The Christian virtue of meekness is the way in which we are to receive the word implanted in our hearts in regeneration. Meekness is much the same as humility. It is the gift of grace given to the elect by which they submit themselves entirely to the preached word by confessing their unworthiness, acknowledging their total dependence on Christ and his grace, and realizing with profound awareness their total need for the word of Christ to live a life pleasing to him.

But be ye doers of the word, and not hearers only, deceiving your own selves (1:22)

The connection between this verse and the preceding is made by the use of the mild adversative (*de*), usually translated as "but." It means that the following admonition does not necessarily give something opposite to or conflicting with the preceding admonition. Rather, it indicates that a new aspect of the preceding will be further defined and explained.

The text leads us to the heart of the epistle and anticipates the main thought.

Because of the danger of antinomianism among those to whom the apostle writes and because antinomianism is a great evil that hides dead faith and shows no evidence of living faith, we must by living faith be *doers* of the word and not *hearers* only. Those who only hear and never do are antinomians and a cancer in the body of believers.

It is possible to be only a hearer of the preached word in the church. One is a hearer only when he is conscious of what the minister says, but it makes no impact on him. He may fully understand the sermon, even marvel at the minister's skill in exegesis and be caught up in the dramatic presentation of the sermon. He may be able to give a complete summary of the sermon to those who ask him what the minister preached. Worst of all, he may compliment the minister on the message, "Good sermon, Reverend." But the preached word has not changed his life nor altered his normal and worldly way of living.

How easy it is for us to do the same. We listen intently to the sermon, enjoy the preaching, and even recognize what was said as the word of God. But we find many excuses why we do not need to do what the word commands. We say, "It is too hard to change; it is beyond our capabilities to obey. It is not necessary for my salvation, but I hope Mr. Van pays attention. While the word ought to be applied to many in the congregation, it is a word that I need not obey, for I have good reason for not doing what the word commands."

Hearing the word is important. We cannot be doers without first being hearers. That is why James adds the word "only." But hearing is not enough. To do the word is something much more than merely hearing it. Doing the word means that we submit ourselves to the authority of God in humble willingness to obey him. In a way this admonition is redundant, because to receive the implanted word is surely to do the word and not only to hear it. Nevertheless, it is good that James spells this out, for we are slow in hearing and need to be reminded repeatedly of our calling with regard to the word. To do the word is to be obedient to it.

Obedience to the preached word does not include only outward obedience to it. We can easily conform our lives outwardly to what Christ has commanded. We will then be on a par with the rich man who confessed concerning the commandments, and no doubt truthfully, "All these have I kept from my youth up" (Luke 18:21). Obedience also involves the whole of our lives. Obedience means to heed God's commands, to confess our sins, flee to Christ, trust in him alone, love our neighbors as ourselves, walk in humility and in the fear of the Lord, and daily to fight against the sins that so easily beset us. To do these things and many more is to be a doer of the word and not a hearer only.

If we are hearers only, we deceive ourselves. One who is a hearer only takes pride in his careful attention to the preaching and in his ability to remember what was said. He deceives himself, however, for he argues that hearing is all that needs to be done, and doing what the word says is unimportant. He may even argue this as a point of theology and assert to anyone who criticizes him that because of his depravity he is incapable of doing what the word requires. I had that in my own ministry. After a service one of the parishioners said to me, "That was a fine sermon, Reverend, but you know we can't do it."

Antinomianism lurks around the corner for those who hold to sovereign and particular grace.

For if any be a hearer of the word, and not a doer, he is like unto a man beholding his natural face in a glass (1:23)

The conjunction "for" indicates that the text and context give a reason for the importance of our being doers of the word as well as hearers. The reason is that unless we are doers of the word, the word does not profit us in any way, for the doer of the word is blessed in his deed (v. 25). We may very well hear the word, but if we are not doers of the word, we accomplish nothing and hearing is useless.

A man who is only a hearer of the word is like one who sees the reflection of his face in the mirror. This is a striking figure, for James compares the word of God to a mirror. This figure is used in 1 Corinthians 13:12: "Now we see through a glass, darkly; but then face to face." The preaching of the word is a mirror held up before us. Paul's figure implies that preaching makes Christ known to us, although Christ, as it were, stands behind and is reflected in the mirror, but we do not see him clearly. The mirror is only a reflection, so we know only in part. When we are in heaven, we will turn around and see Christ face to face. Then we will know as we are known.

The Heidelberg Catechism speaks of the law as a mirror of our misery, that is, a mirror in which we see that the true reason for our misery is our sin.[14] That the law is also referred to as a mirror is evident from verse 25, where the law is identified with "the perfect law of liberty."

Theologians usually distinguish between the law and the gospel: the law belongs to the Old Testament, the gospel to the New. The law belongs to the covenant of works, the gospel to the covenant of grace. The law condemns, the gospel saves.

While there is an element of truth in the distinction, we must beware because it is misleading. It is true that the moral law was given as a part of the creation ordinance. It is also true that the law as God gave it at Sinai, taken by itself, could only curse, for the principle of the law was that the one who kept the law would have life, while the one who broke the law would be cursed (Deut. 27–28.) It remains true always that those who do not keep the law are cursed.

When God gave the law to Israel it was given as the gospel. In an important way law and gospel are identical. There is no difference between them, and they are connected by an unbreakable bond. The ten commandments given from Mount Sinai preached the gospel, for the entire law was introduced by the words, "I am the LORD thy God, which hath brought thee out of the land of Egypt, out of the house of bondage" (Ex. 20:2). God told Israel that he had delivered them from Egypt's slavery (a type of sin), and they were to keep the law because they were God's people delivered from sin and death.

This awareness caused the psalmist to ascribe wonderful powers to the law. Psalm 19 says that the law converts the soul, makes the simple wise, rejoices the heart, and enlightens the eyes (vv. 7–8). These powers ascribed to the law are blessings of salvation. Psalm 119 is a long paean of praise to the law for all it meant to the psalmist.

---

14 Heidelberg Catechism, Q&A 3–5, in Schaff, *Creeds of Christendom*, 3:308–9.

Christ spoke of the law and the prophets as constituting the Old Testament scriptures, and these scriptures, including the law of Moses, spoke of Christ (John 1:45; 5:45). The point is that the law can only curse, but Christ fulfilled the law. He kept the law perfectly and loved the Lord his God with all his being. Christ fulfilled the law, because while he suffered all the curses of the law that rightfully belonged to his people, he loved his God. When the curses of the law pushed him into the deepest parts of hell, where he knew only wrath, and even when the suffering was so intense that he cried out for an explanation of the great agony of his soul, he said, "Though I do not know why God has forsaken me, yet I will love him perfectly. Though it destroys me, I love him." So, being sinless, yet suffering for our sins, he fulfilled the law. By his Spirit he writes that law on our hearts and minds, so that we are able by his death to keep the law ourselves. That is gospel indeed! There is essentially no difference between the law of God and the gospel. The law becomes the gospel because Christ fulfilled the law.

In the way of Christ's fulfillment of the law for us, God showed that his law is never cancelled. It is always the principle of man's relation to God: keep the law and live; break the law and die. The gospel enables us to keep the law and live.

For he beholdeth himself, and goeth his way, and straightway forgetteth what manner of man he was (1:24)

Most people look into a mirror to shave, fix their hair, or examine blemishes on their faces. But having looked for a while into the mirror and observed their natural faces, they walk away and become involved in the occupations of the day. They forget their reflections in the mirror. So a man who hears the preaching may understand what kind of a man he is, but leaving the mirror, that is, leaving the church after the service, he forgets what he has heard and simply goes on with his everyday life.

A man who is only a hearer of the law is a man who listens to the preaching, even gives careful attention to it, but he never does what scripture requires. Thus he sees only his natural face.

The man who comes under the preaching with dead faith is like one who forgets what he has seen of his reflection in the mirror of the preaching. The preaching of the word of God is always a mirror held up before a person, in which he sees himself as he truly is. Every man, believer or unbeliever, sees himself as he is. All see themselves as great sinners, wholly incapable of keeping the law and wholly guilty of breaking it. The preaching of the law rips away any mask a man may wear. Even the Pharisees under Jesus' preaching saw themselves as smug self-righteous sinners when they used the scriptures as tools to flatter themselves and to earn the flattery of others. They hated Christ for doing this to them and finally crucified him.

James says that a man without faith or with fake faith does not like what he sees in the mirror, so he justifies himself, finds fault with the mirror, and turns away from it to forget everything he has seen of himself. His pride refuses to allow him to admit that the reflection is valid and true in all respects.

When the text describes his reaction to what it sees, it describes the man as going his way. The perfect tense of the verb is used here and the force of the perfect is that from the outset the man is determined not to allow himself to be exposed as a sinner.[15] He sees in the mirror who he truly is but prefers to ignore what he sees. So the man forgets what he saw. He is too preoccupied with other interests and too intent on preserving his favorable self-image. Thus the mirror has no significant effect on him at all.

---

15 The perfect tense in Greek indicates a past action completed with a result that lasts into the present.

But whoso looketh into the perfect law of liberty, and continueth therein, he being not a forgetful hearer, but a doer of the work, this man shall be blessed in his deed (1:25)

The law is called "the perfect law of liberty." In the keeping of it is found true liberty. Americans boast that the United States is a country of liberty, but increasingly liberty is defined as the right of a man to live and do as he pleases, provided his freedom does not encroach on the freedom of others. Such a definition of liberty is really the definition Satan used in persuading Eve to eat of the forbidden tree: "You shall be as God, knowing good and evil." That is, you will be able to decide for yourself what is good and evil, and no longer will God be able to determine this for you. Such exercise of liberty is the cruelest bondage and slavery imaginable.

True freedom comes through the law. God is the creator of heaven and earth and all they contain. Therefore, he alone is the only lawgiver, and he alone has the right to determine for all his creatures the laws that governs their lives. It is the law that defines their place in the creation, whether bird, fish, animal, or man. It is the law that expresses how each creature must serve God's purpose and glorify him. But deny that God is the creator of all creatures, and morality exists no more.

The slavery that results from transgression of God's law is the curse of his anger that drives man, who will not serve God's purpose, out of his creation. It is the slavery of death and of hell. It is slavery to sin so that sin is his master, and in his hopeless sin he is destroyed by God's just anger.

The law is a law of liberty because Christ fulfilled the law when he bore the burden of the sin and guilt of his people on the cross and endured the wrath of God against sin in the place of his elect people. He fulfilled the law by keeping the law, loving the Lord his God even when he knew only wrath and abandonment. By his Spirit he writes the law on the hearts of the elect, enabling them to keep it by the power of his grace. The law of liberty is therefore the law that saves and purifies, that restores and renews, that enables the sinner, in himself a slave of sin, to keep the law and thus to live in perfect liberty.

There are a couple of difficult phrases in the text. For the words "whoso looketh" the Greek has a participle that means one who has stooped down (to look into) the law of liberty. It is somewhat difficult to know what James means with this word, but it is possible that he means that one assumes an attitude of humility in order to peer into this mirror. Before he even looks into it, he comes before the mirror in a proper attitude, knowing that he is a sinner. To put it a bit differently, only one who is already the heir of the grace of Christ and has been humbled by it can see into the law properly and in such a way that the mirror of the law gives a correct reflection.

The second difficult phrase is "and continueth therein." It is possible that the meaning is that this man continues to look into the law so that he knows truly what sort of a man he is. But it is also possible that the meaning is that learning from the law of liberty his true spiritual state, he does not forget what he has learned. This meaning seems more likely. Then "and continueth therein" would contrast with the expression in verse 24 "and goeth his way, and straightway forgetteth what manner of man he was."

In other words, looking into the law of liberty, one sees not just the bare demands of the law and the threatening principle of the law, "cursed is everyone who abideth not in all the words of the law to do them," but he also sees Christ emerge from that mirror as the one who has fulfilled the law for him. And he sees himself reflected in Christ's cross as one who is able to keep the law by the power of the cross.

He is not a forgetful hearer but a doer of the law. He loves that law, and his delight is keeping it. It is the guide he needs on his pathway in life, for it shines as a lamp unto his feet and a light upon his path (Ps. 119:105). When he breaks that law, he flees in great sorrow to the cross, where his Savior died, to find forgiveness and mercy.

The only way to see that glorious reflection of himself is first to see himself as he truly is apart from Christ. Thus the law is a mirror that shows him his misery. He must see this first, for he cannot see the cross without knowing his wretched state. Only when he looks into that mirror with tear-blurred eyes can he see the cross. The way to the cross can be found only by those who know their sins and their helpless and hopeless condition. Strange, but true: the mirror is a law of liberty for those who have tears of sorrow rolling down their cheeks and eyes swollen with grief, and when it is hard to see anything else.

True Religion

26. If any man among you seem to be religious, and bridleth not his tongue, but deceiveth his own heart, this man's religion is vain.
27. Pure religion and undefiled before God and the Father is this, To visit the fatherless and widows in their affliction, and to keep himself unspotted from the world.

If any man among you seem to be religious (1:26)

There are some questions of translation in connection with this clause. First, the clause is the protasis of a first class condition.[16] It is characteristic of a first class condition that it affirms the truth of the if-clause. The meaning is that there were people in the

---

16 A conditional sentence contains two clauses. The first is the protasis and is conditional (the if-clause). The second is the apodosis and is conclusive.

congregations who did seem to be religious. They claimed to have faith, but they did not manifest their faith in good works.

"Seem" (*dokeō*) can mean think or consider, in which case the point is that some in the congregations to which James writes considered themselves to be religious. This is the emphasis of the text. This interpretation is supported by the clause "but deceiveth his own heart."

The meaning of "religious" is very difficult and cannot be determined with certainty. The difficulty is that this is the only place in the Greek scriptures where this word (*threskos*) is used, and one therefore cannot apply the principle that scripture interprets scripture to learn the meaning. Further, the word is not even found in any known secular Greek writings, which, if it were, could perhaps help in an understanding of it. The word is an adjective, and its noun cognate (*threskeia*) is found in the next verse. This noun form is also found in Acts 26:5 and is rare in secular Greek. The result is that the lexicographers give the word a variety of meanings. Thayer claims that the idea of fear stands on the foreground.[17] Robertson claims that the word likely comes from another Greek word (*threomai*) that means to mutter prayers.[18] Trench distinguishes between the adjective and the noun and claims that the adjective refers to the outward service of God and the noun refers to the ceremonial aspect of religion.[19]

Paul said to Agrippa, "After the straitest sect of our religion I lived a Pharisee (Acts 26:5). By "religion" he referred to the external rites and ceremonies of the Jewish religion. Therefore, I prefer

---

17 Joseph Henry Thayer, *A Greek-English Lexicon of the New Testament, being Grimm's Wilke's Clavis Novi Testamenti* (New York: American Book Company, 1886), 292.

18 A. T. Robertson, *Word Pictures in the New Testament* (Nashville, TN: Broadman Press, 1933), 6:24–25.

19 R. C. Trench, *Synonyms of the New Testament* (London: Macmillan and Co., 1880), 175.

to interpret "religious" in James 1:26 as referring to the outward expression of one's religion in the broadest sense, that is, the entire cultus of one's religion.

Some in the churches to whom James writes were content to attend church regularly, to celebrate the Lord's supper, to witness holy baptism, to pay the budget, to support various kingdom causes, and in general to walk according to the precepts of the scriptures. They were confident that they were doing everything necessary for a believer to do. But such outward observance is not enough.

Not only are there many such people in the church today, but there are also true people of God who are content with the mere outward forms of religion.

And bridleth not his tongue, but deceiveth his own heart, this man's religion is vain (1:26)

One naturally wonders why the use of an unbridled tongue is set apart as the one sin that demonstrates the falsity of a man's religion. As illustrations of empty religion we might be inclined to select desecration of the Sabbath or failing to control one's sinful lusts in his thoughts and desires. But the reference to the tongue is entirely appropriate. "Those things which proceed out of the mouth come forth from the heart; and they defile the man" (Matt. 15:18). James may well have had this saying of the Lord in mind when he penned these words, for he talks about deceiving one's heart. Further, James emphasizes the importance of one's use of the tongue: "For in many things we offend all. If a man offend not in word, the same is a perfect man, and able also to bridle the whole body" (3:2). The reference to one's use of the tongue is appropriate, for its misuse is a grave sin that affects all of life.

"Bridleth" is the right word to use, for it comes from a noun that is used for the reins by which a horse is guided. If a man's tongue is bridled, he is in control of everything that proceeds from his mouth. His regenerated heart is the one "sitting in the saddle" and guiding the tongue to say only good things. In the context of a true religion, he is one whose tongue is used to give praise to God in everything he says.

An unbridled tongue runs rampant like a runaway horse. A man with an unbridled tongue talks too much, and much of what he says is nonsense and foolishness. He may use filthy language or take God's name in vain, but more than likely he is guilty of backbiting and even slander.

Examining ourselves, let us hear what the scriptures say to us, "[He] deceiveth his own heart, this man's religion is vain."

It is striking that verse 26 uses a different word for "deceiveth his own heart" from that used in verse 22 for "deceiving your own selves. Both verses uses a form of deceive. In verse 22 the word has the connotation of deception through intellectual dishonesty, that is, to raise a host of arguments to convince yourself that, although you are not a doer of the word, you are nevertheless righteous in hearing that word. The word used in verse 26 means to play a trick on yourself, to engage in a sort of spiritual sleight of hand. The spiritual sleight of hand is an ambiguous use of religion.

Many people today do the same. They say they are religious, but they bridle not their tongues. Bridling one's tongue is therefore evidence that a man's religion is genuine.

A man who does not bridle his tongue deceives his own heart. He convinces himself that he is religious and is content in his self-deception. He is, so he persuades himself, a religious man— while his tongue runs off without any restraint. Such a man's religion is vain.

The word translated as "vain" is not *kenos,* which means empty, but *mataios,* which means aimless. It refers to a religion that is without purpose, without fruit, without any goal, when the goal of one's life ought to be the glory of God and praise to him who is alone worthy of it. Everything he does in the practice of religion is purposeless. His singing in church, his giving alms, and his careful attention to religious practices—all are without purpose, for they are only outward. God is not praised; nothing that man does is of any benefit to himself or to God, all because he does not know how to bridle his tongue. That is a devastating indictment.

One can see how James prepares the way for a severe condemnation of those who claim to have faith, but their faith is without works.

Pure religion and undefiled before God and the Father is this, To visit the fatherless and widows in their affliction, and to keep himself unspotted from the world (1:27)

This description of true religion sharply contrasts with the religion of a man who does not bridle his tongue and whose religion is consequently vain. The contrast is therefore between a pure and undefiled religion and a religion corrupted by the tongue.

"Pure" and "undefiled" are nearly synonymous. Pure means to be morally and ethically clean and not contaminated with any sin. It is the term from which we get the word *catharsis*. The word "undefiled" comes from a word that means dyed or stained.[20]

Pure and unstained religion appears as such before God. It meets with God's approval, is acceptable to him, and serves his intended purpose: to praise and magnify God.

The addition of "Father" is remarkable. It immediately puts all worship in the context of a father-son relationship. Worship

---

20 The word has attached to it the alpha privans, the Greek letter *alpha*, which negates or reverses the meaning of the word that it precedes: undyed or unstained.

is family fellowship—fellowship between a Father and his children. It is a relationship of love and mutual joy. It is a confession, with all that is implied, that worship is conversation between our Father in heaven and his children. It is a conversation between our Father in heaven and his children on earth. Thus true religion before the Father is also religion that preserves the proper "space" between the almighty and eternal God and creatures who are very, very sinful children. True religion is praise to God for his love for us in Christ.

True religion is further defined as this: "to visit the fatherless and widows in their affliction, and to keep himself unspotted from the world."

Religion is a matter of the heart. Jesus reminds the Samaritan woman of this. "God is a Spirit: and they that worship him must worship him in spirit and in truth" (John 4:24). Even though true religion is a matter of the heart, it manifests itself in conduct. That James should so define the reality of true religion from the heart in terms of its outward manifestation ought not to surprise us, because that is what this epistle is all about.

We may not think much of visiting the fatherless and widows, for not only are they fairly few in number, relatively speaking, but they are abundantly cared for by the state and the church. But it was not so when James wrote his epistle. Among the heathen, widows and orphans were often forced to fend for themselves. Widows had no husbands to care for them, and they suffered greatly.

Although it is the responsibility of the church to care for the widows and orphans, in Israel this was not done as it should have been. Jesus spoke of the self-righteous and law-abiding Pharisees as those who devoured widows' houses (Matt. 23:14). The parable of the unjust judge who would not give a widow her just due was a picture from everyday life in the nation (Luke 18:1–8).

Because of the neglect of the widows, part of the blessedness of Christ's ascension is that he is a father of the fatherless and a judge of the widows (Ps. 68:5).

Social Security and other government programs are available and often used, so that widows and orphans have no financial needs, but the tender mercies of the wicked are always cruel (Prov. 12:10). And the afflictions of the fatherless and widows are often more than financial needs. Hence the church must take care of the fatherless and widows and comfort them in their loneliness and vulnerability. We do not know what a visit from fellow saints means to a lonely widow or orphan.

True religion is also to keep yourself "unspotted from the world."

"World" can have many different meanings in scripture. James uses it here and in 4:4 in the same sense in which John used it in 1 John 2:15–17. It is the world of wicked men who are enemies of God, and it includes all God's world that men take as their own to corrupt. God's world is his creation, which is good in itself, and everything in it is good (1 Tim. 4:4). When wicked men take God's world and use it for sinful purposes, they corrupt that world and make it as corrupt as Jericho, all of which had to be burned with fire, except for what was to be dedicated to God in the service of the tabernacle. Those who touch these things are corrupted themselves.

The implied figure is of a man who is clothed in a spotlessly white robe, but who must walk down a very wet and muddy path. He must keep his robe from picking up the mire through which he walks. So the people of God wear the white robes of the righteousness of Christ as they walk through a sinful and corrupt world, their own flesh being a part of this world. They are to walk so that their garments remain clean (Rev. 3:4, 18; 19:14; 21:2). One who has pure and undefiled religion keeps himself from the wicked and from their wickedness.

Why does James use these two examples as true religion when many other Christian virtues could be mentioned? At first glance it seems strange that true religion consists of these two activities in distinction from so many others, such as the fruit of the Spirit in Galatians 5:22–23.

However, the purpose of these two illustrations is to point to the inner demands of the law of liberty: love for God and love for one's neighbor. Love for God is expressed in true worship and hatred of the world: "Know ye not that the friendship of the world is enmity with God? whosoever therefore will be a friend of the world is the enemy of God" (James 4:4). Love for God reveals itself also in love of the neighbor. What greater way to manifest true religion than by loving the neighbor by visiting the weak and helpless who can give nothing in return?

True religion is rooted in a faith that works. An outward faith is no religion at all. A genuine faith loves God and the neighbor.

JAMES 2

The Warning against Respect of Persons

1. My brethren, have not the faith of our Lord Jesus Christ, the Lord of glory, with respect of persons.
2. For if there come unto your assembly a man with a gold ring, in goodly apparel, and there come in also a poor man in vile raiment;
3. And ye have respect to him that weareth the gay clothing, and say unto him, Sit thou here in a good place; and say to the poor, Stand thou there, or sit here under my footstool:
4. Are ye not then partial in yourselves, and are become judges of evil thoughts?
5. Hearken, my beloved brethren, Hath not God chosen the poor of this world rich in faith, and heirs of the kingdom which he hath promised to them that love him?
6. But ye have despised the poor. Do not rich men oppress you, and draw you before the judgment seats?
7. Do not they blaspheme that worthy name by the which ye are called?

James gradually leads up to his main theme of the characteristics of a true and living faith. He has stated clearly in 1:26–27 that a true and undefiled religion of which God approves is a religion of the heart. It begins with a heart that loves God and the neighbor and thus fulfills the law of liberty.

Carrying on the theme of true religion, James now applies the importance of true religion to one's faith. He introduces the concept of faith immediately with the words "my brethren, have not the faith of our Lord Jesus Christ." James will explain faith further when he discusses the real point of the entire letter. He wants to expose and correct the vain and empty faith that claims to be a true faith but is in reality dead faith because it does not manifest itself in works.

As James introduces the subject of living faith that manifests itself in works, he does not do so in an objectively doctrinal way, but in a practical and down-to-earth way. He deals with attitudes toward visitors in the congregations and the danger of letting the outward appearances of visitors determine how they are treated.

We cannot determine with certainty why James chooses this particular example, but it is possible that the warning is directly related to weaknesses in the church life of those to whom he writes and that incidents such he describes actually took place from time to time in these churches.

My brethren (2:1)

It is striking how the apostle in the same letter addresses his audience with warm and friendly terms, and then turns about and addresses the same people in scathing terminology. Here James calls those to whom he writes his brethren. And so they are. In chapter 4:4 he turns upon them in anger and calls them "adulterers and adulteresses." Few ministers would dare to do the same in their congregations.

The reason is obvious. Those to whom James writes constitute the church of Christ, of which James is a part. They belong to Christ and are purchased with his blood. Christ instituted them as congregations in which Christ dwells. They are James' dear brethren. At the same time they are still in the world, and they carry with them their wicked natures. They do not always understand the truth properly, nor do they live that truth. Much sin, sometimes very serious, is found in them. Their sins cannot be overlooked or treated lightly, because they jeopardize their salvation. These sins must be rebuked in the sharpest terms. Such rebukes are the rebukes of Christ himself, and they are necessary for their salvation.

Some ministers refrain from rebuking the flock out of fear that they will offend people, with unhappy consequences for the minister. This is wrong. Others fear to rebuke the congregation because they recognize themselves as sinners in need of the same rebuke they are preaching. This too is wrong. The minister does not speak from a morally superior position, but he speaks as the mouthpiece of Christ. He does not exclude himself from the preaching, but hears what Christ says to the church as something he too needs to hear. A faithful pastor is faithful to Christ.

Have not the faith of our Lord Jesus Christ, the Lord of glory (2:1)

The introduction of the concept of faith here is important. Faith will be the apostle's main concern throughout this pivotal chapter. It is well to understand what the scriptures say about faith, for this will determine in large measure the meaning of James' insistence that we are justified by works (2:24).

Faith is essentially the graft that unites us to Christ. In John 15:1–7 the people of God are said to be with Christ a vine and its branches. Our Lord's reference to himself as the vine with its many branches is intended to be applied first to the nation of Israel (Ps. 80; Isa. 5). The hypocritical Pharisees are the branches that bore no fruit and must be cut off the vine. The disciples were told to abide in Christ, for only in living connection with Christ will they be able to bear fruit. Each individual member of the church is united to Christ by being engrafted into him so that Christ's life flows into him. Faith itself is the graft between us and Christ. Through that graft Christ's life becomes our life.

Faith as a graft between Christ and his people is given at regeneration, for regeneration is a rebirth that makes the child of God spiritually alive. As that faith is brought into consciousness by the preaching of the word (Rom. 10:17) and the operation of the Spirit, faith comes to consciousness and is that power in the believer that enables him to seek all his salvation from Christ. He believes in Christ as an all-sufficient and faithful savior.

Thus the object of faith is the sacred scriptures and Christ revealed in the scriptures. Faith does not simply receive as truth what the Bible says, but faith lays hold on the Christ of the scriptures as the only savior and redeemer. Faith is always personal. Faith appropriates Christ in such a way that the Christ of the scriptures becomes one's personal possession. Faith believes everything scripture says as the truth of God and faith enables the believer to put complete confidence in Christ revealed in those scriptures.

Faith is the gift of God. This is emphasized in this text by the expression "the faith of our Lord Jesus Christ." The genitive "our Lord Jesus Christ" is a genitive of source. Christ is the author and giver of faith.[1] It is not of ourselves that we believe, but it is a gracious gift (Eph. 2:8). It is a gift not only in its first implanting of life in our hearts, but also in all its activity in our lives (Heb. 12:2).

It is striking that the text adds "the Lord of glory." Here the genitive "of glory" is a descriptive genitive: our Lord Jesus Christ is a glorious Lord. He is glorious because he reveals fully and

---

[1] Technically this could be an objective genitive, and the meaning would be that our Lord Jesus Christ is the object of our faith, the one in whom we believe. This explanation is possible, but the addition of the words "the Lord of glory" in the verse tips the balance toward a genitive of source.

completely the glory of God. Glory in God is the brilliant light before which the angels cover their faces with their wings (Isa. 6:1–3). It is the light of all God's perfections, especially his holiness. This glory of God is revealed in Christ and through Christ in his exalted position at God's right hand and as the savior and head of the church.

James adds this unusual and unique description of Christ in the context of our faith to emphasize the importance of faith in our lives. We are united to the Lord of glory by faith, and the result is that the glory of God's infinite perfections, revealed in Christ, becomes the possession of those who are united to Christ by faith.

With respect of persons (2:1)

The phrase "respect of persons" is one word in the Greek that comes from two words, one of which (*prosōpon*) means face, and the other (*lambanein*) is a verb that means to receive. Hence respect of persons is receiving a person at face value, accepting him by his outward appearance and judging the kind of man he is by how he looks.

We are immediately reminded of the Lord's word to Samuel when he was in the house of Jesse trying to determine who was the Lord's choice to be the next king of Israel, "Look not on his countenance, or on the height of his stature; because I have refused him: for the LORD seeth not as man seeth; for man looketh on the outward appearance, but the LORD looketh on the heart (1 Sam. 16:7). Peter confessed the same truth when he brought the gospel to the Gentile Cornelius and his house, "Of a truth I perceive that God is no respecter of persons" (Acts 10:34).

The figure James uses makes clear that he speaks not of the tendency to form an opinion of a man by looking at his outward demeanor, but of how a man's outward demeanor can influence our attitudes toward him and treatment of him—particularly whether he is treated with fawning deference or with disdain.

Thayer writes about the Greek word used here: "The fault of one who when called on to requite or give judgment has respect to the outward circumstances of men and not to their intrinsic merits, and so prefers, as the more worthy, one who is rich, high born, or powerful, to another who is destitute of such gifts."[2]

For if there come unto your assembly a man with a gold ring, in goodly apparel, and there come in also a poor man in vile raiment; And ye have respect to him that weareth the gay clothing, and say unto him, Sit thou here in a good place; and say to the poor, Stand thou there, or sit here under my footstool (2:2–3)

The picture here is dramatic and colorful.

The entire section from verses 2–4 is a conditional sentence. The if-clause includes verses 2–3, while the main clause is in the form of the rhetorical question in verse 4. The entire conditional sentence is called a third class condition. The meaning is that James does not emphatically state that such incidents take place in churches to which he writes, but he suggests the strong possibility and even a probability that this could happen or has happened. At the same time something very near to this was evidently common practice among the people. James does not pull the circumstances he describes out of the air.

"Assembly" in verse 2 is the translation of the Greek word that means synagogue. It may be that the church met in a synagogue prior to the establishment of a church in a particular place. However, *synagogue* can be used in a broader sense to include any place in which the church meets. The Authorized Version takes the broader meaning of the term in the word "assembly."

The picture in the text is that of a small congregation found

---

2 Thayer, *Greek-English Lexicon of the New Testament,* 551.

in some populous city somewhere in the Mediterranean world. The congregation was small because the number of Christians in the city was not large. It was composed chiefly of Jews, perhaps entirely of Jews. Its small size could be attributed partly to persecution (1:2). The meeting place was small, crowded, dark, and meagerly furnished. There were only a few seats, and some of the congregants had to stand during the service or sit on the floor. It was adequate for worship, but only because the outward furnishings of a sanctuary made no difference in the quality and true spirituality of the worship.

Occasionally the church received visitors, which created a stir among the people, for the congregation was small and not widely known.

A wealthy and prominent figure in the city once visited the congregation for worship. On his hands were gold rings, impressive symbols of wealth, influence, and social standing. His clothing was expensive and tailored from costly linen or silk. The congregation was excited, and he was immediately greeted at the door, shown utmost deference, complimented on his appearance, asked about his welfare, ushered in, and given the most comfortable seat, which required someone already seated to give up his seat and to sit on the floor. The attention paid to to the rich man was in keeping with his lofty status.

At another time or perhaps the same morning the rich man came, a poor man entered the congregation to visit and to attend the worship service. He was obviously the opposite of the rich man in all respects. His clothing was "vile," which literally means unwashed and ragged. He was unshaven, unkempt, and emaciated. The way the congregation treated him was quite different from their treatment of the rich person. The poor man was rudely told that he could either stand during the service or sit on the floor somewhere. He was barely tolerated.

Such conduct was the crassest respect of persons one could imagine. It was directly contrary to the "faith of our Lord Jesus Christ, the Lord of glory." It was paying attention only to outward appearances without any regard to the inner character of the man.

Evil thoughts were behind the conduct of the members. James accuses them of becoming "judges of evil thoughts." The congregation was small and poor and could use the extra money a rich man could put in the collection plate. He may have been an influential man in the city and could use his influence to alleviate the persecution of the saints. He may have operated a large business and could have provided work for some in the congregation who could not find work. It would be beneficial to the members to cultivate the rich man's favor. It is true that there was an element of self-seeking. They were small, poor, and barely able to meet their expenses, and the prospect of a wealthy person's joining the church was enticing.

However, the poor man could give no material assistance for the congregation's welfare. Instead, he would be another drain on the benevolent fund. Besides, his appearance was repulsive and no respectable person would want to sit near him.

Such attitudes manifested a deep, underlying spiritual fault. They revealed what was important to the members of the church who claimed to be believers. They were more interested in being respectable and having a good reputation among those outside the church than they were in bringing the lost into the fellowship of the church.

How close to home James comes with the sword strokes of the word of God. How true it is that we cherish the approval of those outside our churches as being eminently desirable. How easy it is to compromise our faith or at least soften it in the presence of others so they do not become angry and turn against us. How pleased we can be when others who do not teach the truth speak favorably of us. How it would benefit a congregation to have a well-known and wealthy man join the church! Such attitudes can be at the expense of our most fundamental calling to be God's instruments to bring others to salvation.

The conduct James describes reveals that the faith professed by the members was imitation faith. Outwardly professing themselves to be true believers in Christ, they were ready to compromise their faith for earthly advantages. Insofar as their faith had as its object the truth of scripture, including the injunction of the Lord not to be respecters of persons, they did not live out of the principle of faith. They lived out of a willingness to soften the sharp edges of their faith in the interests of being liked.

Are ye not then partial in yourselves, and are become judges of evil thoughts (2:4)

The two clauses "are ye not then partial" and "are [ye] become judges" complete the thought begun in verse 2 and continued in verse 3 ("If there come into your assembly" and "ye have respect"). So the sentence would read, "If there come into your assembly… and ye have respect…are ye not then partial in yourselves, and are become judges of evil thoughts?" James means to say, "If it should happen that these strangers come into your worship services, and ye should show partiality, are ye not in that case partial in yourselves and judges of evil thoughts?"

James asks two rhetorical questions: "Are ye not then partial in yourselves, and are become judges of evil thoughts?" No answers are given to these questions because the answers to the questions are strongly implied: "You are partial in yourselves and judges of evil thoughts, are you not?"

Commentators have many ideas about the meaning of verse 4. Most of the differences of opinion center on the meaning of "partial in yourselves." "Partial" comes from a word that can mean "to judge," and is a slightly different form of the same word in the second part of the verse that is translated as "judge." We need not go into all differences among the commentators, for the solution is relatively simple. The translation "are ye not judgmental in yourselves" captures the meaning precisely, and that translation agrees with the second part of the verse: by being judgmental in this way you have evil thoughts.

If almost obsequious behavior was shown to the rich man and cold indifference to the poor man, is that not being judgmental? Everyone would agree that it is. But the judgment would be on the basis of outward appearances. Thus it would be what true judgment never ought to be.

In the second part of verse 4, James shows the wrongness of this judgmental attitude. The members of such a congregation are in their judgmental attitudes judges of evil thoughts. That is sharp language and is another example of James' ability to put his finger on a raw nerve. Judging by outward appearances only, one becomes a judge of evil thoughts. To capture the idea "judges of evil thoughts" can be translated as "judges with evil thoughts." The word translated as "evil" is the strong word used in scripture and means morally corrupt or deliberately vicious. Further, the word for "thoughts" means those that result from careful thinking, that is, calculated not spur of the moment ideas.

When one is a respecter of persons he makes judgments on the basis of evil considerations, such as how the person can benefit and serve him, be advantageous to him. Never mind what is spiritually good for the church and what will advance the cause of the gospel. How will fawning on the rich and despising the poor bring ease, comfort, financial stability, and a good reputation to the church?

Hearken, my beloved brethren, Hath not God chosen the poor of this world rich in faith, and heirs of the kingdom which he hath promised to them that love him (2:5)

Characteristic of James' writings is his rapid change from sharp reprimands to friendly terms of endearment. So here he says, "Listen, my beloved brethren." These words are followed by a careful and tactful explanation of why those in the church did wrong in showing respect of persons. The carefulness of expression and the patient explanation are born from a conviction that if only the saints would understand the work of God, they would not do what they do.

God is not a respecter of persons and does not choose on the basis of wealth or poverty. He does not prefer the wealthy and overlook the poor. God does not choose on the basis of outward appearances and considerations at all. If one were to speak the truth of the matter, God chooses poor people in preference to wealthy people.

The word translated as "chosen" is the same word used in scripture for election. The clause could be translated as "hath not God elected the poor of this world?" Referring to the divine decree of election, James does not mean to say that being poor is the reason for God's choice of an individual. God's election is not based on anything other than his sovereign good pleasure. Election means that from all eternity God chose a people in Christ for his own possession, to be the objects of his everlasting favor and to be blessed forever by fellowship with him. He chose them not on the basis of works, outward appearances, or anything at all in them, but simply because he creatively and causatively chose those whom he decided to make his own. They are what they are because of sovereign election.

As the decree of election is carried out in history and the

elect are gathered, those who are God's people are not the mighty, the powerful, the influential, and the wealthy, but the poor and downtrodden. There are wealthy people in the church, though they are the exception, not the rule. Those whom God chose are, generally speaking, poor.

This is the rule of scripture. Jesus reminded us that it is easier for a camel to go through the eye of a needle than for a rich man to enter the kingdom of heaven (Matt. 19:23–24). Paul spoke of riches as being grave dangers that threaten the salvation of those who possess them (1 Tim. 6:9–10). Paul wrote to the Corinthians:

26. For ye see your calling, brethren, how that not many wise men after the flesh, not many mighty, not many noble, are called:
27. But God hath chosen the foolish things of the world to confound the wise; and God hath chosen the weak things of the world to confound the things which are mighty;
28. And base things of the world, and things which are despised, hath God chosen, yea, and things which are not, to bring to nought things that are.
29. That no flesh should glory in his presence. (1 Cor. 1:26–29)

Because the gathering of the poor of the world is the rule of God's election, it is wrong to base our judgments of the value of a man on his wealth or lack of it, to regard the wealthy and to despise the poor. Thereby we do just the opposite of what God does.

Yet the poor are only poor "of this world." God's chosen poor are lacking only with respect to the things of this world.[3] The poor are very rich in those things that really count. They are rich

---

3 "World" is in the dative case and is a dative of respect.

in faith. Here faith means the act of believing, by which the elect saint holds Christ before himself as the fullness of all salvation in this life and in the life to come. When he has Christ, as he does when he has faith, he possesses innumerable riches of great value and worth that remain into all eternity. That is wealth indeed.

The faith that makes a person so spiritually wealthy is further defined. The poor are spiritually wealthy because they are the heirs of the kingdom God has promised them.

There is no need to develop here everything scripture says about the kingdom. Briefly, the kingdom is God's kingdom established by the work of Christ. It is a kingdom over which Christ rules in the name of God. It is a kingdom built on the foundation of the perfect righteousness of God earned for his elect on the cross and that pervades the entire kingdom. The kingdom is heavenly not earthly, as so many today claim, and it is realized in the history of this present world. It embraces the new heaven and the new earth, the elect men and the elect angels, and Christ himself, whom we will see face to face. The kingdom is full and complete blessedness for those who inherit it. All sin will forever be banished, and the curse with its terrible consequences will be eradicated.

The heirs of that kingdom are such because God is their Father who gives his great possessions to his children as their inheritance. He loves them through Christ and determines to make them most blessed. The kingdom is an inheritance because it is freely given, for nothing the heirs do can earn what they receive.

The heirs of the kingdom love God. Their love for God is not the basis or ground of God's choice of them, but they manifest themselves in the world as God's elect by loving him. They may be poor and own almost nothing of this world's goods, but they love God. James almost certainly uses this description because love of God is the fundamental command of the law, and God's law will be introduced in verse 8.

One thinks immediately of the rich man and Lazarus. The rich man had everything he could possibly want in this world, but he had no love of God in his heart. He had love only for himself, since love for God would have been manifested in his tender care of the poor beggar outside his front door who had to subsist on crumbs. Yet Lazarus loved God. When both died, the rich man went to hell and the angels carried Lazarus to Abraham's bosom. Who then was rich? Who then was poor?

But ye have despised the poor. Do not rich men oppress you, and draw you before the judgment seats? Do not they blaspheme that worthy name by the which ye are called (2:6–7)

The connection between these verses and the foregoing verses is obvious. As a general rule God loves and saves the poor in this world and not the rich. But frequently the church does the opposite. They favor the rich and despise the poor. Yet they claim to have true faith, while true faith would manifest itself in doing what God does.

The words "but ye have despised the poor" belong with the preceding verse. To despise someone is a strong word, much stronger than to ignore. To despise is to look down on someone with contempt as being inferior to oneself. This despising of the poor by the members of the churches to which James writes is somewhat ironic, for the apostolic churches were often poor. That the members despised the poor clearly indicated their ulterior motives regarding visitors. If they saw the possibility of getting some material gain or advancement from someone, they fawned on such a one. If someone could not be of any earthly advantage to the members, they despised such a person. It would have been bad enough to ignore a poor man, but to despise him was hypocritical in the extreme.

Still more, usually the rich hate the church and use their wealth to persecute the people of God. They oppress the saints. Money is power in this wicked world. A man can do anything he wishes if he has money. Because the rich are never content with what they have and always desire more, they are ruthless in their determinations to increase their wealth, even if their actions are at the expense of the poor. So it was in James' day; so it is today. They build their fortunes from the blood of those whom they oppress. This cruel fact of life explains class struggles, unionism, and socialism in the world. In the Netherlands, in the days of my forebears, the poor were almost starved to death by wealthy land-owners who hired them for meager wages, even though in many cases the rich and the poor went to the same church.

The rich also use their wealth to bring the poor into the courts of law. They use the power of money to escape punishments they deserve and to shift the blame for their misdeeds onto the poor who have no money and no voice in the courts of the land.

The church always struggles to maintain itself in the world when it is faithful to Christ and to Christ's word. As the end of the world comes nearer, this will be increasingly true. Already the threat is here. Publicly to condemn the sin of homosexuality will bring upon the one who speaks this word of Christ the judgment of the courts for hate crimes.

The wicked also blaspheme the worthy name by which the saints are called. This sin is the greatest of all the sins of the rich in the sight of God. Surely such was the case in the apostolic church.

The "worthy name" to which the apostle refers is probably Christian. The disciples of Christ were first called Christians in Antioch of Syria (Acts 11:26). The name Christian was a term of hatred, a way of mocking believers, a cruel taunt of reproach and mockery. It designated those who believed in Christ as belonging to the despised sect of the followers of Christ, a man who was crucified by a combined condemnation of the rulers of the Jews and the Roman governmental officials in Jerusalem.

The Jews who were brought to faith in Christ endured the slander of their compatriots, who called them traitors to the Jewish religion, blasphemers of Moses, and despisers of the temple. The Roman authorities accused them of fornication because of their love feasts, of cannibalism when they celebrated the Lord's supper, and of being enemies of the empire because they claimed Christ as their king. Such charges were blasphemous, because they were made against Christ, whose name Christians bore and for whose sake they suffered. The name Christian became a cherished name for the faithful, and it was with eagerness that the saints took that name for themselves.

Today the unbelieving church blasphemes true believers. Believers are called eccentric, narrow-minded, fossils of a bygone era, condemnatory of others, unloving, and many other scathing names. This is their lot because they confess the name of Christ as he reveals God to the church.

How utterly inconsistent it is when Christians try to gain the approval of the rich and mighty, and do that while they despise the poor!

Fulfilling the Royal Law

8. If ye fulfil the royal law according to the scripture, Thou shalt love thy neighbour as thyself, ye do well.

9. But if ye have respect to persons, ye commit sin, and are convinced of the law as transgressors.

10. For whosoever shall keep the whole law, and yet offend in one point, he is guilty of all.

11. For he that said, Do not commit adultery, said also, Do not kill. Now if thou commit no adultery, yet if thou kill, thou art become a transgressor of the law.

12. So speak ye, and so do, as they that shall be judged by the
law of liberty.

13. For he shall have judgment without mercy, that hath
shewed no mercy; and mercy rejoiceth against judgment.

In the preceding section James pointed out the evil of having respect of persons. In this section James connects the sin of
respect of persons to the law of God, particularly to the fundamental law of the second table: "Thou shalt love thy neighbor as
thyself."

There is a good reason to connect the sin of respecting persons
with the second table of the law. Those in the churches who had
dead faith kept outwardly the basic commands of the first table
of the law. They did not serve other gods, make graven images,
take God's name in vain, or violate the Sabbath. Although the
first table of the law also demands love for God, the second table
of the law is somewhat different: it demands love of the neighbor.
To love one's neighbor is to engage in specific actions of love, and
such love out of true faith is proof that one's faith is genuine. To
love your neighbor as yourself is to refrain from respecting persons and to treat the poor man with the same love with which one
treats the rich man.

James is leading up to verses 14–26, which are the heart of the
epistle. But he is doing this carefully so that the people to whom
he writes may know well the difference between living faith and
dead faith, especially as both are related to the law of God.

Although the Authorized Version does not join verses 7–8
with a conjunction, the Greek text does. It uses a conjunction
(*mentoi*) that is uncommon in scripture and that means nevertheless or rather.

Most commentators agree that the force of this conjunction
in the context is that the apostle anticipates an objection to his
sharp reprimand. He anticipates that many will say that they

showed love for the neighbor by treating the rich man with dignity and respect and that James agrees with them. But he points out that their claims ring hollow, because their treatment of the poor shows them to be false. Thus James lays bare their motives and shows that they certainly do not keep the law of God, especially what he calls "the royal law" or "the law of liberty."

However, the matter is simpler than this explanation. The conjunction is used to state a contrary position from what James has just said. His point is that rather than show respect of persons, one with living faith does the contrary and keeps the law of God, which requires us to love the neighbor as ourselves. James says, "You show respect of persons? You should rather love your neighbor as yourselves, whether he is rich or poor." To love one's neighbor means to seek his salvation no matter who or what he is.

If ye fulfil the royal law according to the scripture (2:8)

"Royal law" is a concept at the heart of verses 8–13. It is a term unique to James, but it is an extremely important term, especially in connection with his condemnation of counterfeit faith.

God is the only lawgiver, for he is the ruler of the universe that he created. The universe is his kingdom. By his law for every creature, God defines how each creature is to serve the glory of his name, that is, the purpose of each creature in God's creation. Each creature has its own law. Man, being a rational and moral creature, lives by the law of love. His purpose in God's world is to love the Lord his God and his neighbor for God's sake.

God's eternal purpose in his whole creation is to glorify his great and holy name through Jesus Christ as the supreme ruler of the new creation, which embraces the new heavens and the new earth. It is the realm of a kingdom established in the cross of Jesus Christ, for that kingdom is a domain of perfect righteousness in which the law of God is fully and perfectly kept. It is a kingdom that is manifested in this earth by the church of Christ and in the lives of the elect saints who are citizens of that kingdom. Although they are still on this sin-cursed earth, they remain citizens of the kingdom of heaven. The elect will inherit the kingdom fully at their death and resurrection. Satan and all those who worked closely with him will be banished into the pit of fire.

The law of that kingdom is a royal law. The objection is sometimes brought against this epistle that it has no gospel in it and little reference to the work of Christ, but this objection is rooted in a serious misunderstanding of the book. Royal law speaks volumes concerning the work of Christ. God's law remains valid for all time and on into eternity. It is as valid in everlasting bliss in heaven as it is on earth. It is always and eternally a valid law. It is the law of the kingdom of heaven.

The law of God is the rule of the kingdom of heaven because Christ fulfilled the law. He who was lawgiver came under the law (Gal. 4:4), so that the obligation of keeping the law was imposed on him. He kept the law perfectly throughout his life, and he also kept the law when he went into hell to bear the awful suffering of God's wrath for the sins of his people. He merited for us the privilege, the right, and the ability to keep the law as citizens of his kingdom. Thus the royal law is the law written upon the tables of our hearts, and the "must" of the law becomes by divine grace the "can," the "will," and the "do" of the law. I must keep the law, but by grace I can keep the law; I will keep the law; I do keep the law. That is the royal law. It is the law of Christ's kingdom. James reminds his readers that they are citizens of the kingdom of heaven and that thus they live under the royal law.

Thou shalt love thy neighbour as thyself, ye do well (2:8)

The law is the same as was given in the creation ordinances and repeated in detail from Mount Sinai. It is the law that requires man to love God with his whole being and for God's sake to love his neighbor as himself. James refers to Leviticus 19:18: "Thou shalt not avenge, nor bear any grudge against the children of thy people, but thou shalt love thy neighbour as thyself: I am the Lord." Jesus reiterated this law when the Pharisees tried to trap him with the question, what is the greatest commandment? (Matt. 22:37–40). Paul quoted this commandment in the context of his discussion of true liberty: "For all the law is fulfilled in one word, even in this; Thou shalt love thy neighbour as thyself" (Gal. 5:14). James does the same and calls it "the law of liberty" (2:12).

Many wrong ideas circulate about the meaning of this commandment. It is even used as a basis for a social gospel according to which we are to help solve the social problems that afflict this sad world. But such is not the meaning of the commandment at all.

Our neighbors are those with whom we come into contact on our pathways in life. They are the persons who brush against us as we make our way and fulfill our callings. Some of our neighbors are close to us, and we brush against them almost constantly. The nearer our neighbors are to us, the more urgent is this command. Our neighbors are always those who need us for whatever reason.

Our nearest neighbors are wives, husbands, children, and parents. How often love for them is neglected. In the interests of solving the world's social problems, we neglect our families, divorce wives or husbands, and let the children go undisciplined. It is impossible to love any neighbor in the street if we do not love our nearest neighbors. Anyone who forsakes his or her spouse or children loses the ability to love any neighbor.

Other neighbors include relatives, fellow church members, acquaintances, and those who are even for a few moments on our pathways in life.

To love our neighbors means to seek their spiritual good. This does not preclude doing what we can to alleviate their suffering: to feed the hungry and clothe the poor; to rescue a drowning man or pull an injured man out of a wrecked automobile. But these acts must always be in the name of Christ and for his sake. They must be done out of love for God manifested in our love for our neighbors.

We love God because he loves us. His love is overwhelming, for he loves us as sinners for Christ's sake. In the consciousness of his love, we are called to love him and our neighbors. To love our neighbors for God's sake is to seek their salvation and to testify to them of God's love for us and our earnest desire to see them love God and join with us in praising his great and holy name.

We do everything in our power to strengthen the spiritual lives of our spouses, children, fellow saints, and all those who need our help. We seek to advance their spiritual lives by helping them in their earthly needs, but for the sake of helping them in their spiritual needs. If they do not love God and go to hell either hungry or well fed, it ultimately makes no difference. But if we feed them and God is pleased to use our testimonies of his love for us to save them, we will live with them now and forever as fellow members of the family of God.

We must love our neighbors as we love ourselves. I once was told by a man with a family that the meaning of this expression is, "I must love myself first, seek my best interests, and then do the same for my family." So he ate steaks, and his wife and children ate wieners. He wore expensive shirts and his wife bought her clothes and the children's clothes in the thrift shop. That is not love for the neighbor, but sheer self-love, because it is not rooted in the love of God.

When we love ourselves, we seek our own spiritual good by fleeing sin, walking in obedience to God, and taking care of ourselves by not putting ourselves in danger with overindulgence, drug use, drunkenness, or dangerous thrills. We love ourselves as those who are image bearers of God, saved by his grace, destined to live with him forever. We love our neighbors as ourselves.

The word translated as "fulfil" is *teleite*, a verb cognate of *telos*, which means goal or purpose. We are called to fulfill the royal law. This means that we are to bring the perfect law of God to its final goal and end in our lives. We are citizens of the kingdom of heaven; the law we obey is the royal law of the kingdom. We are given the Spirit of our King so that we can keep his law. Thus we are to bring that law to its final goal of the love of God and of our neighbors as ourselves. The real law of loving our neighbors is therefore our salvation and the salvation of our neighbors.

Fulfilling the royal law is an activity that must dominate the whole of our lives. It is always a calling throughout our lives because we cannot do anything more than begin to keep the royal law perfectly. In our failures we flee to the cross. In our battle against our sins we look to Jesus, the author and finisher of our faith. In the daily struggles of life, we press forward to our eternal destination, where we will keep the law perfectly.

The text speaks of the breaking of one commandment as a breaking of all the commandments. This sad reality is true because the law is one. Its unity lies in the commandment to love our neighbors for God's sake. Loving our neighbors is possible only by loving God; failing to love God makes loving our neighbors impossible. Breaking any of the commandments means that we do not love our neighbors or our God.

But if ye have respect to persons, ye commit sin, and are convinced of the law as transgressors (2:9)

The whole principle of the royal law must now be applied to the particular sin of being a respecter of persons. The people to whom James writes are citizens of the kingdom of heaven and thus are under the royal law of God. They must compare their calling under God's royal law with their conduct. They may find that the two are incompatible. A respecter of persons does not fulfill the royal law, and one who keeps the royal law is no respecter of persons.

If the people to whom James writes were to apply the royal law to the matter of being a respecter of persons, the saints would have to warn the rich man of his covetousness, of his mistaken notion that his wealth gives him the right to respect, and of his calling to support the causes of God's kingdom and to give to the poor. They would have to remind the rich man of his equality with a poor man in a threadbare coat. They would have to confront the man, be it in love, to repent of his sins and to humble himself before God. When the poor man enters their sanctuary, they are called to give him a place in the company of the rest of the worshipers, to inquire into his needs, to speak to him of the great mercy Christ has shown to them, and to urge him to look to Christ for help in all his needs. To be a respecter of persons is quite the opposite.

The judgment of a respecter of persons is sharp.

James apparently is aware of specific instances of the sort of respect of persons that he addresses in this chapter. "If ye have respect of persons" means that they practice respect of persons. The sentence is a first class condition, which asserts the reality of the protasis either in fact or for the sake of the argument. Given the amount of time the apostle spends on this subject, I am inclined to conclude that the condition affirms the reality of the protasis. Thus this if-clause is stronger than the one in verse 2, where James suggested only the possibility of being a respecter of persons. Now he states fact.

To treat people on the basis of their outward appearances is to "commit sin." The New Testament contains many different words for "sin." The word used here (*hamartia*) is the general word for sin and means to miss the mark. Our calling before God is to shoot the arrows of our lives toward the glory of God. We miss the target. This is not due to poor marksmanship, but our sin is that we know well where the target is, but we turn completely around and deliberately shoot in the opposite direction. We do this because we hate the target toward which we are commanded to shoot.

While the translation "commit" is correct, the Greek word (*ergazomai*) is stronger because it emphasizes the deliberate character of sin. Literally it could be translated as "to work sin." To work something implies to set our minds on it, to concentrate on doing it, and to expend considerable energy in accomplishing it.

When we work the sin of respecting persons, we know that to do so is contrary to God's law, the royal law of Christ's kingdom, but because of ulterior motives, we do the opposite of what God's law requires. We want to curry favor with the rich, but the poor can do nothing for us.

The second clause, "and are convinced of the law as transgressors," might be somewhat difficult to understand because of the meaning of "convinced." The Greek word permits the sentence to be translated as "[we] are convicted of the law as transgressors." The law convicts us of our sins; the law is the means whereby we are convinced that we sin. The law says, "Love thy neighbor for God's sake." We say, "I will love those who can do good to me, but not those who are of no personal value to me." Because we look into the mirror of the royal law as citizens of the kingdom, the realization of our sins leads us to shame and sorrow for them.

That is how serious respect of persons is. James calls respecters of persons "transgressors." Scripture uses this as another word for sinners. In distinction from "sin" in the first part of the verse, a transgression is walking in a path other than the path of God's law. The law defines the path we are called to walk. We reject that path as a way wholly distasteful to us. We choose another path, and it is always a path forbidden us by God. We are transgressors.

For whosoever shall keep the whole law, and yet offend in one point, he is guilty of all. For he that said, Do not commit adultery, said also, Do not kill. Now if thou commit no adultery, yet if thou kill, thou art become a transgressor of the law (2:10–11)

"For" at the beginning of verse 10 indicates that the verse gives a reason for the assertion in verse 9: "ye…are convinced of the law as transgressors." When one commits the sin of respecting persons, he is convinced and convicted that he is a transgressor of the entire law. The reason is that a sin against one commandment is a sin against all the commandments. This is a truth we often forget.

The reason for this bold assertion is that the whole law of God is based on the one great commandment: love God and love thy neighbor for God's sake. To break one commandment is to violate the law of love, and because the law of love underlies all the commandments, to violate one commandment is to violate them all. God, the lawgiver, is one God (Deut. 6:4–5). To sin in one way against God is to sin in every respect against God. This is strongly implied in James 2:11. Every commandment is given by God to define the relationship in which man stands to his Creator. To violate that relationship in one respect is to violate the whole relationship in which man stands to God.

We need to be reminded of this as much as those to whom James writes. To be guilty of the wrong of respecting persons is to commit adultery, to kill, to steal, and to take God's name in vain. That is sharp language to which we do well to give our attention.

So speak ye, and so do, as they that shall be judged by the law of liberty (2:12)

With verse 12 James brings his discussion of the sin of respecting persons to its conclusion.

The verbs "speak" and "do" indicate continuous action. We are to make this admonition a characteristic of the whole of our lives.[4] This is the positive calling given to God's people, who are called to abandon all respect of persons.

The verbs also indicate outward conduct, for speaking and doing are overt actions and not thoughts and desires within. Yet only when we love God and our neighbors are we able also to speak and do according to James' injunction. This is in harmony with James' main theme that living faith manifests itself in works. All our speech and all our actions must be free from the sin of respecting persons. The positive is to love God and our neighbors.

While earlier I discussed the positive of not respecting persons, it is not superfluous to shed a bit more light on this calling. The calling has to do primarily with the second table of the law. When in our speech and actions we do the opposite of respecting persons, we always speak good of our neighbors and always seek their salvation, even in helping them in their needs. When we forsake respecting persons, we so love our neighbors that we would never harm their salvation by any harmful word or deed. We do not make use of bawdy and suggestive language when we speak with them; we do not join them in seeking pornography; we do not do anything that might lead to fornication. We do everything in our power to help them live chaste and upright lives. We give when they are in need and sacrifice our personal possessions and comfort to make their lives easier. Our speech is always kind, thoughtful, and geared to blessing rather than to cursing.

---

4 The verbs are both present active imperatives.

These things characterize our relationships with our neighbors, no matter who they are: wives, husbands, children, fellow saints, rich and poor, wicked and holy, small and great, children and adults—everyone whom the Lord places on our pathways.

The unusual expression is used in verse 12 that we will be "judged by the law of liberty." James compels us to look ahead to the judgment day when Christ will come again and bring all men before his throne. That this is the reference in the text is evident from the expression "shall be judged." Literally, the text reads "about to be judged" (*mellontes krinesthai*).

It is true that God's judgment takes place continuously. It takes place in the consciences of men, when their consciences testify of God's approval or disapproval of our deeds. Judgment also comes through the calamities God sends on the world. Judgment also comes at the moment of death, when the souls of men depart either to heaven or to hell. Scripture often calls our attention also to the final judgment, when all men will be judged according to the deeds done in the body (Gen. 18:25; Ps. 7:8; 75:7; 96:10, 13; Matt. 16:27; Acts 10:42; 2 Cor. 5:10; Heb. 4:13).

We will be judged by means of the law of liberty.

I explained the law of liberty in connection with the explanation of the concept royal law in verse 8 of this chapter. The law of liberty is the law of God, unable to be kept by any man, fulfilled in Christ by his perfect atoning sacrifice for his people, and written on the hearts of God's people, so they can keep God's law as expressions of their gratitude to God for his salvation.

By that law God's people will be judged. The meaning involves two important ideas. First, God's people have the law written on their hearts, and second, while they can keep that law by the power of the inward work of God through Christ, they can to do so only as a beginning in their lives, for as long as they live in the world they retain their depraved natures. But because they are given the power to keep God's law, their responsibility is greater than that of the wicked. The principle of Jesus' words must be applied: "Unto whomsoever much is given, of him shall be much required: and to whom men have committed much, of him they will ask the more" (Luke 12:48).

Nevertheless, the law of liberty is fulfilled in Christ who earned perfect righteousness for the elect. Both now and in the judgment day, God's people will not be judged on the basis of their imperfect keeping of the law, but by the law as Christ kept it for them. Christ, by keeping the law, earned perfect righteousness for his people, a righteousness that is imputed by faith. That righteousness will be the ground of their judgment when they too are summoned before Christ with all who ever lived. The believer is not to fear the judgment, but to look forward to it as the vindication of his righteous cause in the world, which is the cause of Christ.

For he shall have judgment without mercy, that hath shewed no mercy; and mercy rejoiceth against judgment (2:13)

"For" introduces the reason for the admonition in verse 12. It therefore serves as an incentive to us to speak and to do according to the law of liberty. We are to show mercy to others because the judgment of Christ is swift and terrible upon those who do not show mercy: it is merciless.

In the judgment day everyone will appear before the throne of Christ, elect and reprobate alike. Although Christ is the judge, he judges in the name of God as the one who has carried out the whole purpose of God. All men's lives will be fully revealed, so that all that was hidden in life may be made known, all the injustices made right, all the crooked made straight, and God will be vindicated in all his works, especially over against the wicked who opposed him and denied his name.

The text speaks of mercy in connection with that judgment.

Mercy is one of God's communicable attributes, according to which he takes pity on poor sinners, suffers with them in their agony and misery, and longs to deliver them from all their woes to make them happy forever. God's mercy is not like our mercy. We may have pity on someone in deep suffering, but we can do little to ease that suffering. God's mercy is his sovereign will. When he is merciful, that mercy is not merely a desire to rescue from misery, but it is a power that actually accomplishes what it wills. The objects of mercy are delivered from misery.

God's mercy cannot be separated from his judgment, for his judgment is just and righteous and an expression of his infinite holiness. All men are sinners. Sin and death, with their accompanying misery, have come on all men. Because man sinned against the most high majesty of God, man comes under the judgment of God's wrath. From righteous wrath mercy cannot be separated.

Many do this. Many will admit readily that God hates sin. They teach that sin deserves the punishment of God's wrath. But when asked to define the relation between mercy and judgment, they answer that mercy overcomes the wrath of God's judgment so that wrath no longer exists, or at least not during the history of the world. God speaks to man only of his mercy, never of his judgment.

The error of common grace teaches such conflict between judgment and mercy. Although God could punish all men for their sins in his just and holy hatred of sin, he nevertheless allows mercy to overcome his justice and he is kind, benevolent, loving, and merciful to all men.

The Heidelberg Catechism contradicts this claim when it asks the question, "Is, then, God not also merciful?" The answer is, "God is indeed merciful, but he is likewise just; wherefore his justice requires that sin, which is committed against the most high majesty of God, be also punished with extreme, that is, with everlasting punishment of both body and soul."[5]

God's righteous judgment against sin and his attribute of mercy came together in the cross of Jesus Christ. In Christ's suffering and death God carried out his just wrath against sin by punishing his Son. At the same time Christ, by his perfect obedience, earned for all those for whom he died the mercy of God. The cross was the revelation of the confluence of justice and mercy for the elect. Mercy and justice kissed each other.

Merely to overlook sin is not mercy. If a murderer who has killed a mother and her three children is apprehended by the law, brought to trial, and found guilty, the judge is required to sentence him to death. The judge might say to the murderer, "You deserve death, but I will show you mercy and let you go free." That criminal may commit another murder equally as gruesome and be brought again before the same judge. Again, that judge may say, "I will be more merciful and show you my mercy even though you have made yourself doubly worthy of the death penalty." But soon the people will cry out, "Save us from the mercy of that judge. His mercy will end in the murder of us all. We want justice done."

Mercy, because it is God's power to save the miserable, can be and is shown only to his elect. Because mercy was accomplished in the cross of Christ, there is no mercy for anyone except those for whom Christ died. Those who teach a universal mercy to all men are compelled to teach also that Christ died for every man to earn for every man the boundless mercy of God and escape from God's just judgment. But God bestows mercy on whom he will (Rom. 9:15–16).

The objects of God's mercy are called to manifest the mercy

---

5 Heidelberg Catechism Q&A 11, in Schaff, *Creeds of Christendom*, 3:311.

shown to them. God does not save robots. While he by his mercy enables a merciless people to show mercy, he also calls his people to be merciful and judges them, as well as all men, on the basis of the mercy shown or the lack thereof.

Mercy toward those in distress is the one great manifestation of loving our neighbors, and this is why James introduces the subject of mercy here. The calling to be merciful is important. In the absolute sense the unregenerate cannot and never do show mercy, for they know not the mercy of God. "The tender mercies of the wicked are cruel" (Prov. 12:10). There are those in the church who are merciless. They claim to be believers and to have faith, but they show no mercy. In the judgment no mercy will be shown to them. They never were the objects of God's mercy; they never knew what God's mercy is; they show no mercy to others.

There are also those in the church who are truly the objects of God's mercy. They experience that mercy as they come to know the depths of their depravity, the terrible judgment of God that they deserve, as well as the wonderful work of Christ who died for them and earned for them the mercy of God. They are so overcome with the greatness of God's mercy that they are and cannot help but be merciful to other sinners like themselves. They help sinners in their need and do everything they can to bring these sinners to the conscious experience of God's great mercy gained by faith in Christ.

God's people imperfectly show mercy. They are not always as merciful as they are called to be. Hence their sins drive them to the cross where they cry out, "God be merciful to me, a sinner" (Luke 18:13). When by faith they take Christ as their own, they know again the mercy of God, and they find in that cross strength to be merciful in life. They are able to look with good cheer to the judgment day when their mercy will be displayed to all.

But the apostle adds, "Mercy rejoiceth against judgment."[6]

The Greek word (*katachauomai*) translated as "rejoiceth" has various meanings. It can mean to boast against, to glory over, to rejoice over, or to triumph over. The meaning is not that mercy triumphs over justice and justice is not exercised or that mercy obliterates justice. That denies the justice and holiness of God.

It is better to follow the translation of the Authorized Version, which is in harmony with the context. In the cross of Christ, mercy rejoiced over judgment because by Christ's bearing the judgment of God against our sins, mercy was shown to us instead of the judgment we deserved. It is mercy that comes with the law of liberty. The mercy of the law of liberty sets us free because it enables us to keep God's law perfectly, if not in this life, then in the life to come. In the punishment of his Son, God revealed the riches of his infinite mercy to us poor sinners. And in our speaking and acting mercifully we show that mercy was given to us.

The Relation between Faith and Works

14. What doth it profit, my brethren, though a man say he hath faith, and have not works? can faith save him?
15. If a brother or sister be naked, and destitute of daily food,
16. And one of you say unto them, Depart in peace, be ye warmed and filled; notwithstanding ye give them not those things which are needful to the body; what doth it profit?
17. Even so faith, if it hath not works, is dead, being alone.
18. Yea, a man may say, Thou hast faith, and I have works: shew me thy faith without thy works, and I will shew thee my faith by my works.

---

6 There is an alternate reading that makes "rejoiceth" an imperative: "Let mercy rejoice against judgment." But this reading must be rejected. The majority of the textual evidence has the reading of the Authorized Version.

19. Thou believest that there is one God; thou doest well: the devils also believe, and tremble.
20. But wilt thou know, O vain man, that faith without works is dead?

What doth it profit, my brethren, though a man say he hath faith, and have not works? can faith save him (2:14)

James does not connect this passage by a conjunction that defines its relation to the preceding, because he begins a new thought with verse 14. The new thought is the relation between faith and works. Yet the inner connection with respect of persons is still present. Showing respect of persons within the church of Christ is failing to do the works of faith and thus putting in question the genuineness of the faith a man claims to have.

The relation of faith to works involves the question of whether justification is by faith alone or by faith and works. That this is the main question James emphasizes in verses 22–23. Verses 14–26 are the heart of the epistle, the doctrinal basis for all the practical admonitions of the epistle and the main point of the entire letter.

This question was the burning issue during the sixteenth-century Reformation. Rome taught justification by faith and works. Luther insisted that justification is by faith alone. Rome repeatedly brought up the teaching of James and so pestered Luther about James that almost in fury, Luther called James "a right strawy epistle." He was driven to distraction by Rome's incessant clamor.

The controversy has been revived with a vengeance by those who hold to the federal vision view of justification. With hardly a blush that Rome's views are being revived and that Luther's insistent emphasis on justification by faith alone was the spark of the Reformation's fire, the defenders of federal vision theology appeal to James in support of their preposterous doctrine of justification by faith and works. Almost disdainfully they push aside Luther's principle of justification by faith alone and over four hundred years of confessional orthodoxy that followed Luther, and they continue to promote their heresies. They do this with ecclesiastical arrogance almost beyond belief.

It is well to be reminded that the controversy of justification by faith alone versus justification by faith and works also touches on the assurance of the Christian. One can never find solace from the misery of sin in the doctrine of justification by faith and works. True peace and the riches of the joy of salvation are the possession of the one who holds firmly to justification by faith alone. Luther tried desperately to escape his misery by Rome's formulas, but he failed and was filled with despair. When he came to know the truth of Paul and James, he knew peace with God. The reason is simply this: if salvation depends in the smallest measure on our works, salvation is nothing but a mirage in the wasteland of life. Rome wrote in large letters at the entrance of her citadel, "Abandon all hope, ye who enter here." The Reformation wrote, "What is thy only comfort in life and in death? That I belong to my faithful Saviour Jesus Christ."[7] The joy of the justified sinner reverberates in his soul with the words of Psalm 32:1–2: "Blessed is he whose transgression is forgiven, whose sin is covered. Blessed is the man unto whom the LORD imputeth not iniquity, and in whose spirit there is no guile." It is impossible to conceive of singing "Blessed is he who has done enough good works to earn the forgiveness of his sins."

The wording of verse 14 is important. It is clear that the apostle distinguishes between true, saving faith and faith that a man claims to have. What profit does he have? He does not have faith. He only says he has faith. James in this way strongly defines the

---

7 Heidelberg Catechism Q&A 1, in ibid., 3:307.

issue. The issue is not works added to faith. The issue is faith that works.

True faith has several characteristics. It is the gift of a living, God-given bond between the elect sinner and Christ. It is the spiritual power by which one becomes a part of the body of Christ. Scripture uses the figure of the vine and the branches as a picture of Christ's relation to his people. The branches may be cut off, and the command is given to the disciples to abide in Christ (John 15:1–7). In a similar figure in Romans 11, the apostle spoke of the natural branches of the olive tree, which comprise the Jewish nation that was cut out of the olive tree to make room for new branches from a wild olive tree that are grafted into the old olive tree. That grafting in is faith, by means of which the new branches are united with Christ.

With an eye on this figure the Heidelberg Catechism defines faith as a graft: "Are all men, then, saved by Christ, as they have perished in Adam? No; only such as by true faith are ingrafted into him, and receive all his benefits."[8] The means by which new branches are grafted into the old olive tree is a picture of faith that grafts the elect into Christ. They are not grafted into Christ by works. On the cross Christ earned all of salvation for his people as their exalted Lord. He is filled with salvation. Faith so engrafts God's people into Christ that what is in Christ becomes their possession.

Faith as the bond that unites the elect to Christ is the essential and fundamental idea of faith. No aspect of faith as knowledge, confidence, trust, receiving Christ as one's own, or believing him is anything else than the activity of the bond that unites one to Christ.

The bond of faith is given in regeneration. Faith is like the power line between a light and the source of power in the

---

8 Heidelberg Catechism, Q&A 20, in ibid., 3:313.

generating plant. The bulb in the socket is of no use and does not shine except it is connected to the source of power. So a man is lifeless in himself, but he lives by the unending flow of power that becomes his through faith in Christ. Faith is like the pipeline that connects a faucet to the water reservoir. Christ is the reservoir of all salvation that flows into a person, carrying with it all the blessings of salvation. Faith is not man's work, but God's work. We are no more conscious of God's initial work of binding us to Christ by faith than we are of our regeneration.

Further, the Heidelberg Catechism defines faith as "not only a certain knowledge whereby I hold for truth all that God has revealed to us in his Word, but also a hearty trust"[9] Faith as a bond that unites one to Christ becomes conscious and active. That conscious and active faith is the spiritual power to hold for truth what the scriptures say. The object of faith is God's word, and the one with faith receives the scriptures as God's word. Because scripture makes known on every page God's great work of salvation in Jesus Christ, the object of faith becomes Christ revealed in the scriptures. Thus faith in the believer's conscious life lays hold on Christ as the only hope of salvation.

Because the bond of union between Christ and the elect sinner is the essence of faith, it is personal. Faith personally appropriates Christ as his own, and thus he comes to the assurance of his salvation. The salvation earned by Christ becomes the conscious and joyful possession of the believer. That faith is expressed in the believer's confession of the truth and his conduct in his family, his church, his workplace, and in his relations to those about him. He talks and walks as a possessor of Jesus Christ. Faith is like the bond of marriage that unites a man and a woman in one flesh (Eph. 5:28–33).

---

9 Heidelberg Catechism, A 24, in ibid., 3:313.

Because faith manifests itself in speech and life, people can be found who imitate the speech of believers and to a certain extent manifest the life of believers. They are always to be found in the church. They come to church, sing the songs of the church, confess with their mouths the truth of scripture, claim to believe the Bible, and give their tithes in the collection plates. They appear no different from true believers. They claim as well to have faith and even speak of it. They confess that they were purchased as Christ's possession with the price of his blood (2 Pet. 2:1). But they do not have faith as a bond of union with Christ and, consequently, they do not have the life of Christ in their hearts or the blessings Christ earned on the cross. They only *say* they have faith.

While these people claim to have faith, they do not have works. That, James insists, is the difference between true believers and those who only say they have faith. They may have an outward and external conformity to the law, but they do not have the inner life that produces love for their neighbors for Gods' sake.

The works to which scripture refers are not necessarily the works of singing psalms, sitting in the pew on the Lord's day, and making a verbal confession of faith with the congregation. As Israel of old, they may join outwardly in the worship of the church, but they engage in mere lip service, which the Lord abhors (Isa. 1:10–15).

Works that have their source in love for God and for the neighbor are a necessary part of saving faith. When a branch of another tree is grafted onto a parent tree, the graft makes the branch a real part of the new tree. The life of the tree flows through the graft into the branch. That life produces fruit from the branch. So the believer united to Christ produces the fruit of works.

While certainly the doing of works acceptable to God is a conscious appropriation of Christ, the author and finisher of our faith, the good works of the believer are inevitable. Paul expressed this inevitability when he argued against the pernicious error that the doctrine of justification by faith alone produces carnal people. "What shall we say then? Shall we continue in sin, that grace may abound? God forbid. How shall we, that are dead to sin, live any longer therein" (Rom. 6:1–2)? Paul expressed the impossibility of one who is bound to Christ by faith to continue to sin.

Jesus suggested strongly in Matthew 25:31–46 this inevitability of good works by one who possesses the life of Christ. Nearing the end of his public ministry, Christ gave a vivid description of the signs that will precede his return in judgment. He concluded with three parables, the last of which was a description of the final judgment and the Lord's separation of the sheep from the goats. When the Lord sends the wicked off to their eternal punishment, he tells them, "I was an hungered, and ye gave me no meat; I was thirsty, and ye gave me no drink: I was a stranger, and ye took me not in: naked, and ye clothed me not; sick, and in prison, and ye visited me not." The wicked challenge the Lord, for they think they did these things. But the Lord refutes their charge, "Verily I say unto you, Inasmuch as ye did it not to one of the least of these, ye did it not to me" (Matt 25:42–43, 45).

In contrast, when the Lord says to his people, "Come, ye blessed of my Father, inherit the kingdom prepared for you from the foundation of the world" (v. 34), he gives as the reason for this blessedness their willingness to feed him, to quench his thirst, to give him needed clothing, and to visit him in prison. They too protest. Their protest, however, is that they never did these things. They have no recollection of these works. They are astounded that the Lord can say of them that they actually fed and visited him. The point is that they did these things to the Lord when they did these things to one of the least of Christ's brethren, and thus to him (vv. 37–40). They did these good works unconsciously; they were not aware they were doing good works. These works were inevitable because they lived out of Christ by faith. A consciousness of doing these good works would have erased their moral value and made them works done out of a self-congratulatory spirit.

One who does not do works of love, mercy, and obedience does not have true faith. He may say he has faith and conclude that he has faith if he measures by certain external aspects of his conduct. But in reality the faith he claims to have is counterfeit faith, an imitation faith, a fake faith.

If a brother or sister be naked, and destitute of daily food, And one of you say unto them, Depart in peace, be ye warmed and filled; notwithstanding ye give them not those things which are needful to the body; what doth it profit (2:15–16)

James could have chosen different illustrations to prove his point that faith that is not manifested in good works is useless, but he chooses, under the inspiration of the Spirit, an illustration that is particularly appropriate. It must have been appropriate in his day, for the churches he addresses were frequently small and the members were poor. But it remains appropriate for all time, particularly for us, and its character enables us to apply James' teaching not only to this one instance of helping the poor, but to all circumstances in which we are called to love our neighbors.[10]

The text limits the illustration to material and physical needs that a brother or a sister in the church has, which makes the illustration more sharp. When our Lord commanded us to love our

---

10 The text is grammatically a third class condition. A third class condition is hypothetical, but suggests a strong probability that the if-clause (es) is/are true. The protasis contains three conditional clauses: "If a brother or sister be naked, and destitute of daily food"; "[if] one of you say unto them"; "[if] ye give them not those things which are needful to the body." The apodosis is "what doth it profit?"

neighbors as ourselves, he referred to all our neighbors, those within the church and outside the church. Paul also applied that same principle in Galatians 6:10: "As we have therefore opportunity, let us do good unto all men, especially unto them who are of the household of faith." James does not intend to contradict that precept of the gospel when he limits his example to a brother or a sister. But, as Paul also taught, the nearest neighbors whom we are to love are our fellow saints. If we cannot love them as ourselves, we will never have the spiritual ability to love those outside the church "as we have opportunity." The fulfillment of the law begins in the fellowship of believers.

It must not be considered unusual to find poor people in the church. Jesus promised to see to it that the church would always have poor in it (Matt. 26:11; Mark 14:7). The presence of the poor is one of Christ's blessings to the church, for it is more blessed to give (to the poor) than to receive (Acts 20:35). In the office of deacon, Christ is present in his church as its merciful high priest.

The brother or sister to whom James refers has a need. The brother lacks his daily bread. It is not that he has enough for one day, but is concerned about tomorrow. In that case he would have no need. But he does not have enough food for the day. He was ousted from his dwelling in the cold of winter. He does not have winter clothing and cannot keep warm.

His need comes to the attention of someone in the congregation who has enough. He may not be a rich man or have plenty of food; he may himself have only enough for one or two days. How much he has is not the point. We are all rich if we have enough food, shelter, and clothing for more than one day. We are commanded to pray for our daily bread. If the Lord gives us more than that, we are rich, for his promise is to give us only enough for one day. My father often reminded us that in our prayers we had permission from God to ask only for our daily bread. To enforce that he said, "You may pray only for bread but not for peanut butter on the bread."

In James' illustration the fellow saint in the church answers the request of his fellow saint, "Depart in peace. Be ye warmed and filled." That is, he says, "May the blessing of God be upon you and may he supply all your needs." On the surface this answer seems to be pious and godly. He tells the needy person to have faith in God, for after all God cares for the sparrow, and we must not think that he will not care for us. Perhaps he even quotes a few scripture passages. "Trust in the LORD with all thine heart" (Prov. 3:5). "Trust in the LORD, and do good; so shalt thou dwell in the land, and verily thou shalt be fed" (Ps. 37:3). "[God] humbled thee, and suffered thee to hunger, and fed thee with manna…that he might make thee know that man doth not live by bread only, but by every word that proceedeth out of the mouth of the LORD doth man live" (Deut. 8:3).

The answer is pious, scriptural, and very much in keeping with one's calling to admonish one another. But for all that, it is very wicked. It is not the way a man with faith reacts to a brother in need.

We can readily understand the man's reasoning and the thoughts in his heart, for they are found also in each of us. "I barely have enough for today and tomorrow. God surely does not call me to make my children starve. I do not know whether I will have a job tomorrow and be without work for a time. I have a house payment to make tomorrow and a car payment next week, and that will exhaust my resources. My Christian school tuition is unusually high this year, and I can barely pay that." Or even worse, "The man is lazy and could easily find a job if he only looked and was willing to take a lesser paying job. Actually, he is lazy and deserves to go hungry. Maybe the Lord is chastising him to teach him a lesson."

Perhaps we say that this does not happen in the church, but it does. My grandmother told me that the wealthy farmer for whom she worked and who went to the same church as she did never gave her enough to eat. She went to bed at night unable to sleep because of hunger pangs.

The scriptures, in scathing rebuke, brush it all aside with "what doth it profit?"

Certainly there is no profit in it at all for the needy man. He goes away hungry and naked and has no one to supply his needs.

But James refers to a man's faith. If that is the kind of faith the member of the church has when confronted by a hungry and cold person, his faith is of no profit to him. It is dead faith that sounds pious and godly, but is useless. Living faith profits, for it brings to us the blessings of salvation, and it manifests itself in love and mercy toward our brother.

Are we endangering our material positions by helping the poor? Perhaps, but in telling the poor to look to God for his daily bread; let us do that ourselves. A true faith looks to Christ for all things. After all, it is more blessed to give than to receive.

Even so faith, if it hath not works, is dead, being alone (2:17)

This sentence is a third class condition. We must not conclude that "if it hath not works, is dead" suggests the possibility that faith without works is dead. The verse is attached to the previous two verses and carries over the idea that faith without works is always dead. James means that if the above illustration is true of you, your faith is dead. A true faith always produces works. Where works are not present, especially works of love and mercy that keep the law of God, one may be sure that such faith, no matter how pious it seems, is dead. It is no faith at all, but has only the outward appearance of faith.

The words "being alone" have caused some problems. Usually

these two words are interpreted to mean that faith is alone because it is without works. True faith is always accompanied by works. In the case of James' illustration, it is alone.

While this interpretation may be correct, it seems not to do justice to the expression in the Greek (*kath' heautēn*), which translated literally is "according to itself." Thayer claims that the preposition *kata*, which is used here, can also mean *toward*.[11] In that case the meaning is that faith, which a man claims to have but is without works, is toward himself. Although it has the outward appearance of genuine faith, in the final analysis it is self-seeking faith that is concerned only about one's own well-being and thus is not a faith that looks to Christ and produces the works of loving the neighbor. This explanation is surely in keeping with the whole illustration and is probably the meaning here.

Yea, a man may say, Thou hast faith, and I have works: shew me thy faith without thy works, and I will shew thee my faith by my works (2:18)

This passage is difficult, and the opinions of commentators vary.[12] The problem involves the question of who ("a man") is speaking to whom ("thou"). The problem continues with the pronouns in the rest of the verse. Commentators differ on whether these pronouns refer to the same person as in the first clause, or whether they refer to others.

My interpretation is that someone in the congregation (who may be James) agrees with the emphasis James puts on the truth that genuine faith manifests itself in works. He says to one of the antinomians in the congregation who claims that faith alone

---

11 Thayer, *Greek-English Lexicon of the New Testament,* 527.

12 Summaries of the different views and the more reasonable interpretations are found in Robertson, *Word Pictures,* 6:35–36; Kistemaker, *Exposition of the Epistle of James,* 91–94; Lenski, *Interpretation of the...Epistle of James,* 591–93.

is sufficient, "You have faith, and I have works." He continues, "You who claim to have faith and insist that works are unnecessary, show me your faith." Obviously a man cannot show his faith, for faith is of the heart. The speaker stresses that faith that does not manifest itself in good works is a caricature of true faith.

To emphasize this the speaker continues, "I will show you my faith (something you cannot do) by my works." The speaker therefore claims that while an antinomian cannot show his faith because he repudiates the necessity of works, one who has true faith can show his faith by his works.

The point is clear: faith manifests itself as being true by the works that are produced by the one with faith. Again, James stresses the essential and necessary relation between true faith and works.

It is not amiss to point out that the works of faith are not necessarily those that attract the attention of others. It would be wrong to claim that the good works that faith produces are earth-shaking works of philanthropy, powerful deeds that change the course of a city or a nation, or deeds that make the headlines in the daily newspapers. The good works to which James refers are feeding the hungry brother who comes to one's door and clothing the poor sister who has need of protection from the cold. This is surely in keeping with the good works of which Jesus spoke in Matthew 25:34–40. Frequently good works consist of denying self, taking up one's cross, and following Christ. They are the good works of the publican in the temple who cried out, "God be merciful to me, a sinner." They are also the good works of loving one's wife and children and leading them in the ways of the Lord.

The point of this verse is that there is an inseparable connection between living faith and works. When works are not present, faith is absent.

Thou believest that there is one God; thou doest well: the devils also believe, and tremble (2:19)

This verse and the verses in the remainder of the chapter give examples of the truth laid down in verse 18. The first is an example of dead faith. The examples of Rahab and Abraham are of living faith.[13]

The truth that there is only one God is the most fundamental truth of the whole scripture. For this reason James appeals to it. Those who have only faith will certainly insist that they believe this truth. It is basic to Christianity. In confessing this truth they do well. Their confession is true. One can find no fault with it. All of the truth of scripture stands or falls with this confession.

But, says James, the trouble is that "the devils also believe [this truth], and tremble." The confession of this truth in itself and apart from any other consideration does not prove that one has genuine saving faith. Surely no one believes that the devils are saved. In fact, the opposite is true: their faith in this fundamental truth results in their shuddering. The Greek word can be translated as "shudder" better than as "trouble," for the word includes the idea of terrible fear.

That the devils believe this is evident from everything they do. Scripture demonstrates this fear. When the Gadarene demoniac stood face to face with the Lord, the devils that possessed the demoniac were so frightened and aware of Christ's divinity that they cowered in his presence and asked his permission to enter the swine. They knew the Lord controlled their every movement (Luke 8:32). That Satan appeared before God during the

---

13 There are quite a few textual variants of this verse, almost all of which involve the word order and/or the omission of the article *ho*. A slightly different translation is possible, depending on the word order and the question of the presence of the article. Instead of the translation of the Authorized Version, "Thou believest that there is one God," some versions have "Thou believest that God is one," a reference to God's simplicity. I prefer the translation of the Authorized Version.

old dispensation to bring accusations against God's people also demonstrates vividly his "faith" that God is the only God (Job 1:6; 2:1; Rev. 12:10).

James 2:19 does not suggest that those who claim to have faith, but who deny the need for good works are *like* the devils. But the text means that the faith one claims to have, but is lacking works, is as useless as the faith of the devils. It cannot and does not save. It is a caricature.

In theology the distinction is frequently made between true faith and historical faith. The latter is said to be faith that confesses that all the truths of scripture are true, but it is faith that does not save because it does not assure the one who has it that he is actually saved.

In some churches a lack of the assurance of faith is not only condoned, but is also presented as the norm of a church member's life. Such a one can be born and raised in the church, live his whole life in the church, but die without the assurance that Christ is his savior. In some churches it is also sufficient for a person to present his children for baptism without confessing his personal assurance that Christ is his savior, while generally in Reformed churches the father (or mother, in the case of an unbelieving father) must have confessed his faith as not only knowledge and acceptance of the truth, but also as personal assurance that Christ is his savior.

Historical faith means nothing.

James is not directly writing about people who have only historical faith. That seems clear especially from verses 15–16 of chapter 2. James' chief concern is people who deny the necessity of good works and claim that faith without good works can actually save. These same people claim that their faith without works saves them, which prompts James to ask, "What doth it profit, my brethren, though a man say he hath faith, and have not works? can faith save him?" (v. 14)

The faith of the people James addresses was somewhat like historical faith because they claimed to believe the truth of scripture. But it is the same kind of faith that the devils have, even though they are bitter and unrelenting enemies of the cause of God and his Christ. The devils know with certainty deep in their hearts (as every man does) that God alone is God, but they hate this truth (Rom. 1:18–32).

But wilt thou know, O vain man, that faith without works is dead (2:20)

While James emphatically repeats what he said in verses 14 and 17, he adds two important ideas. The first is that faith without works is barren. The translation "barren" is more accurate than "dead." A man with such faith is of no use either to himself or to the congregation of which he is a member. In doing good works a child of God comes to the full assurance of his faith, and in the way of faith that does good works a child of God serves the welfare of the saints.

Further, a man who claims to have faith but does no works is "vain." This strong denunciation of such a man is justified and is the inevitable conclusion of being barren. To be vain means to be empty, to be without any value, to be of no use to anyone, including to himself. Rather than understanding and taking to heart Solomon's description of how a man escapes vanity: to fear God and to keep his commandments (Eccl. 12:13), the vain man comes under Solomon's judgment, "Vanity of vanities; all is vanity" (Eccl. 1:2).

The Examples of Abraham and Rahab

21. Was not Abraham our father justified by works, when he had offered Isaac his son upon the altar?

22. Seest thou how faith wrought with his works, and by works was faith made perfect?

23. And the scripture was fulfilled which saith, Abraham believed God, and it was imputed unto him for righteousness: and he was called the Friend of God.

24. Ye see then how that by works a man is justified, and not by faith only.

25. Likewise also was not Rahab the harlot justified by works, when she had receieved the messengers, and had sent them out another way?

26. For as the body without the spirit is dead, so faith without works is dead also.

Was not Abraham our father justified by works, when he had offered Isaac his son upon the altar (2:21)

The example of Abraham's living faith is particularly appropriate. Abraham is known in scripture as an outstanding man of faith. His whole life was characterized by faith. Paul referred to Abraham's faith in Romans 4:2–5, where he argued for justification by faith alone and not by the works of the law. His example of Abraham is striking: "If Abraham were justified by works, he hath whereof to glory; but not before God. For what saith the scripture? Abraham believed God, and it was counted unto him for righteousness. Now to him that worketh is the reward not reckoned of grace, but of debt. But to him that worketh not, but believeth on him that justifieth the ungodly, his faith is counted for righteousness."

This same emphasis on Abraham as a man of faith is spoken of in Galatians 3:6–9, where Paul argued against the Judaizers in the Galatian churches who taught justification by faith and works. Hebrews 11:8–19 describes Abraham's faith, and his name is high on the honor roll of old dispensational heroes of faith.

This man of outstanding faith was "justified by works." What better example could James use?

The text speaks of Abraham as "our father." The reference is not to Abraham as the father of the Jewish people in the nation of Israel. This idea is a grave misunderstanding of the scriptures. Every text that refers to this subject makes clear that Abraham's place in the unfolding of God's covenant was not as the natural father of a nation, but as the spiritual father of those who believe, whether Jews or Gentiles. This was made clear to Abraham by the change of his name from Abram to Abraham, which means "father of many nations" (Gen. 17:5).

Paul made this truth explicit in Romans 9:7–9, 24–26, where he pointed out that national Israel, the children of the flesh, were never the true seed of Abraham, but "the children of the promise are counted for the seed." In his argument that justification is not of faith and works, but of faith alone, Paul reminded the Galatians that those who are in Christ by faith, whether Jews or Gentiles, are the seed of Abraham (Gal. 3:7–9, 14).

The example James chooses is the sacrifice of Isaac on an altar on Mount Moriah, the spot where the temple of Solomon was later built and the altar of burnt offering was set (Gen. 22; 1 Chron. 22:1). This act of faith (Heb. 11:17–19) was the climax of Abraham's life of faith. By faith he had left his family in Ur and later in Haran to go to an unknown place. By faith he was a stranger in a barren land in which he did not own one square foot of ground. By faith he believed the promise of God that he would have a seed greater in number than the stars and that his seed would inherit the land in which he wandered. By faith he believed that his seed would be Christ, the promised one who would crush the head of the serpent. By faith he believed that he would have a son even though Sarah was ninety years old and barren and he was as dead as a tomb.

Abraham's faith was put to its ultimate test. God gave him and Sarah a son in their old age. But God followed that fulfillment of his promise with the command to Abraham, "Take now thy son, thine only son Isaac, whom thou lovest, and get thee into the land of Moriah, and offer him there for a burnt offering upon one of the mountains which I will tell thee of" (Gen. 22:2). It was a command from God to kill his only son, in whom was locked up the promise of the coming of Christ. Abraham could not expect another son. All of God's promises to Abraham depended for their fulfillment on Isaac.

What would dead faith have done under those circumstances? If Abraham's faith had been dead, he would presumably have convinced himself not to offer his son. He would have reasoned and argued, "I cannot be sure that this is what God really wants. God would not be so cruel as to demand of me that I plunge a knife into the heart of my own flesh and blood. God hates human sacrifices and would not command something that he hates. I am so much convinced that God will fulfill his promise that I need not kill my son to prove it." The point of such reasoning is that obedience to God is too much.

What did Abraham do? Undoubtedly he struggled with the weakness of his faith and his doubts, for he was a man of equal weakness with us. But there can be no doubt that Abraham actually offered his son. We are not permitted to say that Abraham did not actually do it because he was stopped by the angel. James says, "[Abraham] offered his son Isaac upon the altar." Hebrews 11:17 says he did: "By faith Abraham, when he was tried, offered up Isaac; and he that had received the promises offered up his only begotten son." God said that Abraham offered up his son, "By myself have I sworn…for because thou hast done this thing, and hast not withheld thy son, thine only son" (Gen. 22:16). It is true. Abraham did not actually plunge the knife into Isaac's heart, for the angel prevented that from happening. But in his mind and heart Abraham did the deed. He killed his son. He offered him on the altar as a sacrifice to God. The actual death of Isaac could not have added to Abraham's experience in any way. He was fully obedient to God's command.

Abraham obeyed because he knew God had the right to demand anything from him. Abraham did not deserve one blessing, not even the blessing of a son, much less the rich promises God had made to him. But Abraham also knew that God would surely fulfill his promise, for God could not lie.

How it was possible Abraham did not know, although according to Hebrews 11:19 he believed that God could raise Isaac from the dead; and Abraham received Isaac from the dead as a figure of the resurrection of the bodies of those who are righteous in Christ.

The power of the example is incontrovertible. Abraham's faith was genuine because it resulted in an act of complete obedience. Faith resulted in works. Without faith such obedience was impossible, but because his faith was genuine, even this ultimate act of obedience was not too much.

So much is a living faith like its works that James as much as identifies the two. In the same way that the life of a peach tree pours into a grafted branch and inevitably brings forth peaches, so a living faith produces the fruit of good works as a part of the graft itself, though distinct from it. Jesus spoke of those grafted into him as resulting in the believer's being "in" Christ, but also Christ's being "in" the believer (John 15:4–5). Thus James can use faith and works interchangeably for true faith *is* works, and works *are* true faith. As a graft on a peach tree makes the grafted branch one with the tree, so does faith make a person one with Christ and Christ's life one with the life of a believer. That life produces fruit.

Genesis 22:1 says that God tried Abraham's faith. This does not mean that God tested Abraham to learn whether Abraham had faith, or even whether Abraham's faith was genuine. Abraham's faith, a gift of God, was tried, but through trial it was purified and perfected. His faith (and Abraham) emerged from the trial triumphant. The work Abraham did was obedience.

This truth requires some emphasis and explanation. It is possible for a man with dead faith to perform some apparent good works. He may regularly attend church, give to the poor, support Christian schools, bring a dinner to a family with a sick mother, and any number of other seemingly good works. But the performance of them means nothing as far as his faith is concerned and can mean only that they do not have the characteristics of any work that is truly good as defined by the Heidelberg Catechism. Good works are characterized by an inward holiness. They are done to God's glory and not according to men's imagination of what good works are. Good works proceed from a true faith and are done according to God's law.

Good works are obedience to God, an obedience that arises out of a true faith. James uses the illustration of obedience because obedience to God's commands is the supreme work in the life of a believer. As the illustrations of Abraham and Rahab show, they are good works of obedience when obedience seems hazardous and downright dangerous and from our perspective could lead to disaster. They are good works when there is no reason to believe that any good can come from them, but only harm to yourself and the cause of God. In other words, good works are done simply because the one who has faith believes that God's promises cannot fail, and no matter how impossible it may seem, obedience will be made right. Obedience is to refuse to join a godless labor union, which could lead to starvation for you and your family. Obedience is to refuse the mark of the beast even though refusal will result in slow death. Obedience is to pray to God alone even when the punishment is to be thrown into a den of lions. Obedience is characteristic of all the heroes of faith mentioned in Hebrews 11, whose lives and actions were by faith.

The federal visionists ought to read Hebrews 11. Perhaps they will see that a man with faith does what he does because faith produces good works, and not because a man is justified by faith and works.

Seest thou how faith wrought with his works, and by works was faith made perfect (2:22)

Faith is the subject of the sentence and is what must be emphasized.

The relation between faith and works is described in a way that gives the lie to all erroneous views. Some people claim that the Christian cannot do good works. Antinomians say that the necessity and reality of works in the life of the justified sinner are detrimental to the truth of justification by faith alone. There is no need for good works because Christ did all our good works for us. In James' day, too, the antinomians wanted no part of good works. Others say that justification is by faith and works. This is the position of Roman Catholicism, of all Arminianism, and of the federal vision.

James demolishes all of these erroneous views. By beginning the verse with the words, "Ye see," he means that the example of Abraham is so clear that anyone can see it without any difficulty. In Abraham, a man of outstanding faith, faith worked with works. If one does not see this, he is spiritually blind.

In the example of Abraham, faith was always on the foreground. It was always faith that was working. Not faith *and* works, but faith working *with* works. Nothing Abraham did was without faith.

Abraham's faith was not dead. He did not claim that faith was sufficient for him. Abraham did not claim a faith that never manifested itself in any way. His faith was genuine because works were its fruit.

Salvation or justification is not by faith and works, as two distinct and disconnected forces that cooperate in a joint venture to accomplish salvation. Faith works with works in such a way that faith is working when works are performed. That was the case with Abraham. He offered up his own son because he had faith.

"Wrought with" is in the imperfect tense, which indicates continuous action from the past to the present. Faith always works. There is no faith present in a man except it is accompanied by works. Where works are not present, faith is absent.

Such is the relation between faith and works because faith is the bond that unites the spiritually dead sinner to Christ. Just as a dead branch, when grafted into a living tree begins to bring forth fruit, so the dead sinner when grafted into Christ comes alive with the life of Christ and brings forth fruit. It is inevitable.

Lest there be some misunderstanding and some still dare to think that faith and works are two contributing causes to salvation and justification, the text continues, "and by works was faith made perfect."

The words "was made perfect" are one word in Greek (*eteleiōthe*, a verb form of the noun *telos*, which means goal or end), which can be translated as "attained its purpose" or "achieved its goal." Clearly the idea is that God attains his purpose in bestowing faith on the elect when faith produces good works, for good works are always to the glory of his grace. The elect are united to Christ by faith, and the life of Christ becomes their new and heavenly life. That life is one of holiness as God is holy. Holiness produces good works. Good works are to God's praise. So faith reaches its goal in good works.

In Ephesians 2:1–10 the apostle Paul emphatically stated that we are saved by grace through faith. That salvation by grace through faith is not of works. If it were of works, we could boast of our accomplishments. But it is of God. The apostle seems to anticipate the question, what place do good works have in our lives, if any? He answers, "For we are his workmanship, created in Christ Jesus unto [for the purpose of] good works, which God hath before ordained that we should walk in them" (v. 10).

And the scripture was fulfilled which saith, Abraham believed God, and it was imputed unto him for righteousness: and he was called the Friend of God (2:23)

James reiterates that faith saves, not works. This is so clearly stated that it is hard to see how anyone who is honest with the scriptures can deny that James speaks of faith as the means of salvation altogether apart from works and that works are the evidence of a genuine faith, for works proceed from faith as an apple proceeds from an apple tree. Works are not before salvation and the basis of it; works are the fruit of salvation and a part of it.

Some commentators have a problem with the words "and the scripture was fulfilled," but unnecessarily so. The scripture referred to is Genesis 15:6. God told Abraham that in spite of having no son, his seed would be as great as the stars in the heavens. Abraham believed that God's promise would surely be fulfilled. As Hebrews 11:9–16 make clear, this multitude of Abraham's descendants was possible only in the coming of Christ. Abraham's seed was Christ and all those who belong to Christ (Gal. 3:16, 29).

This promise to Abraham was made about thirty years before its fulfillment in Isaac. It was typically fulfilled on Mount Moriah when Abraham sacrificed Isaac. As they climbed the mountain, Isaac asked Abraham why they did not take a sacrificial animal.

Abraham responded, "My son, God will provide himself a lamb for a burnt offering" (Gen. 22:8). God indeed provided a ram for a burnt offering (v. 13) as a type of Christ whom God provided to take away the sins of those for whom he died. He was the Lamb of God who takes away the sin of the world (John 1:29).

James 2:23 has "believed" with the dative case of the word translated as "God" as the object of the verb. This construction is common in scripture with the verb *believe*. It indicates that faith puts one in fellowship with God and emphasizes that one who believes is already in God.[14] That faith was reckoned to Abraham for righteousness. Christ's perfect sacrifice paid for the sins of his people and earned for them the righteousness of God. Righteousness is perfect conformity to the law of God. The result is the justification of the sinner, so that although he remains a sinner until heaven, Christ's righteousness is imputed to him.

Imputation is the declaration of God that what Christ accomplished for the sinner is put on the account of the sinner. The righteousness that Christ earned is reckoned as belonging to the sinner. It is the marvelous work of God that raised Martin Luther to the freedom of the gospel from the bondage of Roman Catholic works-righteousness, and it is the glorious truth that gives the elect sinner the forgiveness of sins, the hope of everlasting blessedness, and the resurrection from the dead.

Thus Abraham's faith in God's promise was imputed to Abraham. Faith was imputed, for faith is the living power that unites the sinner to Christ and makes him one with Christ. That faith was a true faith, for believing God's promise of Christ, Abraham offered up his only son.

---

14 *Believe* with the preposition *eis* (into) emphasizes that faith puts one into fellowship with God and Christ. *Believe* with the object in the dative case emphasizes that fellowship is already a reality and that faith is part of salvation, a gift of God.

Two thoughts are bound up in this truth. The first is that Abraham's faith was his righteousness. Not by any works or any deeds of obedience was Abraham made righteous, but by faith alone. The second thought is that on Mount Moriah, when Abraham received Isaac back from the dead (Heb. 11:19) and saw that God provided the sacrificial victim—typically in the ram and finally in Christ—he received the assurance of his righteousness imputed to him by faith in the Christ who was to come.

The fruit of this imputed righteousness by faith was that Abraham was called "the Friend of God."

The idea of friendship between God and his people is one of the great truths of the scriptures. Friend of God in a unique way implies the covenant of grace. This is not strange, for the promise God made to Abraham and subsequently to his people was and is always and essentially the promise of friendship with God through Jesus Christ. The following truths are implied in this rich name for God's people.

The covenant that God established with his people in Christ is not, as some allege, a conditional pact or agreement. There is no friendship between those who agree to certain conditions to maintain an agreement between them. An agreement is only a cold, business-like transaction. Rather, the covenant is a living bond characterized by fellowship, love, and friendship.

The covenant between God and his people is realized through Christ when, on the basis of Christ's sacrifice, God's people are made the body of Christ in which God dwells. It is a covenant divinely established, divinely maintained, without any conditions, in which God through Christ takes his people into his covenantal life and they dwell in fellowship with God.

The chief characteristic of that bond is friendship: God and his people are friends. The very thought is overwhelming. The infinite God of all glory, all perfection, and all beauty, takes insignificant people, terrible sinners, into his covenantal life and makes them his friends. It is an astounding wonder of grace!

Friendship is between those who trust each other, believe each other, enjoy nothing so much as being with each other, and share together the most intimate thoughts one can have. God tells his people all about himself, all about his works, all about his purpose in saving them, and his people pour out their thoughts and desires to God. Things they would tell no one else, they tell to God. Their hopes, longings, sorrows, and fears—all are whispered in the ear of God. His people know that he hears and understands, that he is merciful and quick to forgive, that his purpose is to make them everlastingly happy, and that he loves them with an eternal and unchangeable love. There is nothing more blessed in this life or in the life to come than to be called the friend of God.

Ye see than how that by works a man is justified, and not by faith only (2:24)

Before going on to the example of Rahab, James concludes his example of Abraham. What James says in this verse is the heart of the argument, the point that needs to be made to refute those who deny the necessity and reality of good works.

By the words "ye see" James means you understand. It ought to be evident that a man is justified by works and not by faith only. Nothing can be more clear than the example of Abraham.

That justification is by faith that produces works is stated again here by "only." Not faith only, but faith that produces works is the only true faith. Not a faith by itself without works justifies. Such a faith is dead. Thus the apostle refutes the antinomians.

The example of Abraham settles the matter.

Because of the importance of the subject, a few words that deal particularly with the seeming contradiction between Paul and James are in order. The apparent contradiction comes from two statements, one written by Paul and the other by James. Paul wrote in Romans 4:5, "To him that worketh not, but believeth on him that justifieth the ungodly, his faith is counted for righteousness." James writes, "Was not Abraham our father justified by works?"

It ought to be evident from the outset that for one who believes that the author of the scriptures is the Holy Spirit, no contradiction exists, for the Spirit will not contradict himself.

It also ought to be evident that James does not deny that we are justified by faith. There are three evidences of this. First, his use of the example of Abraham, a man whose entire life was characterized by faith. Second, James says, "Seest thou how faith wrought with his works." Lest anyone should want to interpret that as meaning that faith *and works* justify, the apostle immediately puts that to rest by explaining what he means: "and by works was faith made perfect" (v. 22). The apostle means faith that justifies and insists that faith that justifies attains its goal in works. Third, verse 23 emphatically states that the truth that faith was made perfect by works is itself the fulfillment of what God said to Abraham, namely, that he was justified by faith only: "The scripture was fulfilled which saith, Abraham believed God, and it was imputed to him for righteousness."

Earlier in my exposition of Abraham's faith, I quoted Ephesians 2:10: "For we are his workmanship, created in Christ Jesus unto good works, which God hath before ordained that we should walk in them." This verse explains why salvation is by grace through faith and not of works.

God's purpose in saving his people is to glorify his name. He justifies them and gives them all the blessings of salvation to glorify himself. Works that we do for our salvation distract from God's glory. Paul added that our salvation makes us God's workmanship; we are his work of art, his poem, his magnificent painting, because we are created in Christ Jesus.

Then Paul added "unto good works." We are God's artistry because God's purpose in creating us in Christ Jesus is that we may do good works. It is good works, the fruit of justification, that glorifies God, in addition to the fact (but also because of the fact) that we are justified as sinners.

To seal this truth, Paul added that these good works and the power to walk in them are determined as part of our justification from all eternity: "which God hath before ordained that we should walk in them."

The Heidelberg Catechism puts it all together in a beautiful way.

> Since then we are redeemed from our misery by grace through Christ, without any merit of ours, why must we do good works?
>
> Because Christ, having redeemed us by his blood [justification], renews us also by his holy Spirit after his own image [sanctification], that with our whole life we may show ourselves thankful to God for his blessing, and that he may be glorified through us; then, also, that we ourselves may be assured of our faith by the fruits thereof, and by our godly walk may win our neighbors also to Christ."[15]

Several truths are included in this question and answer.

First, the Catechism speaks to believers who are justified by faith alone: Why must *we* do good works? Because we are redeemed and delivered by Christ's blood.

---

15 Heidelberg Catechism Q&A 86, in Schaff, *Creeds of Christendom*, 3:338.

Second, the truth of the necessity of good works is sharply affirmed. We *must* do good works. The antinomians, who deny the necessity of good works, are dead wrong and are guilty of a serious denial of one of God's works in the salvation of his people. That includes the antinomians concerning whom James writes and the antinomians who have throughout history plagued the church.

Third, we must do good works because by our good works we give thanks to God for all he has done for us. Good works are not the ground for justification, but the fruit of it.

Fourth, good works that proceed from our justification by faith alone have two necessary purposes. One is "that we ourselves may be assured of our faith by the fruits thereof." That is a powerful statement.

The negative is that should we refuse to do good works or neglect them or teach that they are unnecessary, we have no assurance of faith. That is, if we walk in sin, disregard obedience to God, and be careless and profane, we have no assurance of faith. How can God give us the assurance of his favor if we sin against him?

The positive teaching of the Catechism is that *because good works are the fruit of justification by faith,* we are assured of our faith that justifies by our good works.

Further, the works of faith are the manifestation of our justification by faith and is God's means of the witness and testimony of believers in the world: "that we…by our godly walk may win our neighbors also to Christ."

In these ways God is glorified and praised.

James, if only we are willing to understand him, explains it all. There is no conflict between Paul and James. There cannot be. There is only harmony to those "who have ears to hear what the Spirit saith to the churches."

Likewise also was not Rahab the harlot justified by works, when she had received the messengers, and had sent them out another way (2:25)

The connection between verse 25 and verses 21–24 is clear. "Likewise" indicates that a similar example can be found in Rahab, which, like the example of Abraham, proves the point that they were justified by works. The conjunction used here is the weaker adversative and means that although James uses a different example, the truth portrayed by it is the same as the truth established by the example of Abraham. "Also" indicates that yet another example from the Old Testament will establish the point without any doubt.

The example of Rahab is striking. In almost every instance where she appears in sacred scripture she is known as "the harlot." Scripture does not do this to remind us of her terrible sins—something like the old saying, "Forgiven but not forgotten." Rather, the point of her example is that while she also is proof of the truth that justification is by faith that produces works, her faith that produced works was very different from Abraham's faith. Not essentially different, but different in its working.

After reading of Abraham and the strength of his life of faith, the believer who reads of him may conclude, "Yes, I see; but Abraham's faith was so far beyond any faith found in me that I will never attain to it." God gives us another example, one we can identify with, for we are more like Rahab than we are like Abraham. If Rahab's faith produced works, the greatest of all sinners can put himself at Rahab's side and see in himself or herself the marvelous power of a true faith.

Abraham was born in the line of the covenant from which Christ came according to the flesh. Rahab was not only born outside covenantal lines, but she was also a descendant of Ham and Canaan and thus under the curse of God (Gen. 9:25).

Abraham was the father of believers, and he performed an act of faith that stood as the climax of a long life of faith. Rahab's act of faith stood at the beginning of a life of faith.

Abraham was all his life a God-fearing man. Rahab openly flaunted her terrible sins from the wall of Jericho, one of the most wicked cities in all Canaan. Rahab sold her body for money and despised that most sacred and intimate of all relationships for carnal pleasure and material gain.

The contrast is as sharp as it can be.

That Rahab had faith is stated in Hebrews 11:31: "By faith the harlot Rahab perished not with them that believed not, when she had received the spies with peace."

Israel was a small and insignificant nation with few weapons, and Jericho was a walled city, an impregnable fortress, the doorway to Canaan. Archeology has estimated the thickness of the wall to be sufficient to drive two chariots side by side on its top.

Israel was a nation in the center of which was the tabernacle with smoke arising daily from the altar of burnt offering. Jericho was a city wholly given over to sin, where a prostitute could live openly on the wall to commit whoredoms in the sight of all the inhabitants.

Rahab possessed living faith. Scripture does not tell us when God gave her faith and how she came to know the importance of the nation of Israel. She had heard, as had all Canaan, of Israel's miraculous deliverance from Egypt, of the wonders God performed at Sinai, of the manna and the quails with which Israel had been fed, and she knew of the tabernacle and sacrifices in the middle of the camp. Her faith told her that this nation was the people of God in the midst of which God lived. Somehow her faith was directed to Christ. She knew that deliverance from her sins could come only through the nation that offered typical sacrifices of the perfect sacrifice for sin. Faith always has as its object

Christ, God with us, who makes the perfect sacrifice for sin. Her confession was, "The LORD your God, he is God in heaven above, and in earth beneath" (Josh. 2:11).

God reached down to pluck this woman out of the sin and depravity of her native city to put her in the company of his church. He implanted in her heart a true, powerful, and active faith. She basically said what Ruth confessed somewhat later, "Thy people shall be my people, and thy God my God" (Ruth 1:16). Rahab abandoned Jericho and came to despise it. She left everything behind except her family, for whose life she entreated the spies. She cast her lot with Israel, confident that Jericho would be destroyed and Israel would inherit Canaan as God had promised, even when she was still a part of Jericho and had no assurance that Israel would defeat that mighty city.

Her faith was not the dead faith of one who only claims to have it. If that had been her faith, she probably would have told the spies that while she sympathized with their cause and even believed they occupied a favorable position as God's people among the nations, she could not risk her life and the lives of her family by assisting Israel. She would have said, "Let's wait and see." If she was spared in the coming battle, then she would cast her lot with the ones who were victorious in the struggle, but it was too much to expect her to invite such danger prior to the fall of the city.

Such reasoning would have been understandable. Jericho was invulnerable; the Israelites were only a wandering band of nomads. Jericho was rich and powerful; Israel was poor and property-less. Jericho had a trained army; Israel had no strong weapons or experience in battle. Jericho offered all the pleasures of sin; Israel resembled a tribe of ascetics.

Rahab was a whore from a godless city. What gave her the right to claim an inheritance among a holy people? Faith had to leap over incredible obstacles, and faith required Rahab to stake her life on what appeared to be humanly impossible.

But her faith was living. She showed that by her works. She received the spies. Scripture does not inform us how the spies came to her house. God in his providence led them to her dwelling on the wall. The language of Joshua suggests that she saw the spies coming over the plain and met them at the gates of the city to lead them to her house. She risked her life, hid the spies from the Jericho police, told the spies everything they wanted to know, and believing that Israel would be victorious in the struggle with Jericho, she exacted from them a promise that the nation would spare her and her family.

It is true that she lied to the men sent to inquire of her concerning the strangers that had entered her house, and lying is always wrong. Her faith, though so strong, was nevertheless imperfect, as ours so often is. Scripture, while never hesitating to speak openly of sin, mercifully emphasizes her faith not her sin.

She sent the spies "out another way." She let them down from the top of the wall by a rope, because it was impossible to escape the city through the gates.

So Rahab too was justified by works. That is, she was justified by her faith that came to manifestation in her works of faith. Never would she have done such daring things without the work of faith within her. Faith, against all human wisdom, sets its hope on God's promise and acts in keeping with that hope.

Her justification was obvious. When Jericho was destroyed by the miracle of the falling of the walls, the part of the wall on which her house stood did not fall. She was spared. She was incorporated into the nation of God's people and became a part of that nation whose God is the Lord. She was included among those who were the heirs of the promise and, wonder of wonders, became a mother of Christ (Matt. 1:5).

For as the body without the spirit is dead, so faith without works is dead also (2:26)

James sums up the entire discussion of the difference between dead faith and living faith by an analogy between faith and the human body. It is a powerful comparison that both sums up the whole subject and at the same time makes clear the difference between dead faith and living faith.

Scripture uses the word *spirit* in different ways. Its most common usage is a synonym for *soul*. That is the case in Genesis 2:7, where the breath (spirit) of life is identical with the soul: "Man became a living soul." Sometimes *spirit* is used to identify the aspect of the soul that puts a man in a relationship to God, enables him to know God, to love or to hate God, and to be morally responsible before God. This is the meaning in 1 Thessalonians 5:23: "The very God of peace sanctify you wholly; and I pray God your whole spirit and soul and body be preserved blameless unto the coming of our Lord Jesus Christ." Sometimes *spirit* is used to express the unique principle of life in man. All living creatures are given the gift of life, each with its own kind of life. The life of trees is a different life from the life of animals. Man's unique form of life is a rational and moral life that pervades the body and causes it to live. This is the meaning of the term in Ecclesiastes 12:7. In distinction from the body (a distinction made in Ecclesiastes), the spirit is the life that makes the body live in relation to God, to the creation, and to all the circumstances of life as God's representative in the world.

Without the spirit the body is a corpse. The body is so dead that its mouth cannot speak, its eyes cannot see, its brain cannot function in thinking and remembering, its heart does not beat, and its limbs are cold and motionless. It is useless, it is put into a grave, and it returns to the dust.

So it is with faith. If it is genuine, it imparts spiritual life to spirit, soul, and body. But that faith must be living, for dead faith is like a body without the spirit. Dead faith is as ugly, repulsive, useless, and vain as a body without a spirit. It cannot and does not function in any way. In contrast, living faith puts the one who possesses it in union with the living Christ of God. The life of Christ pervades a man's body so that it acts by the power of that faith. It speaks God's praises, knows God's favor and love, and lives in obedience to the will of God in all it does.

Such a powerful conclusion must by its very nature bring us all to self-examination. Is our faith a mere confession of what we think is the truth, while our lives show no evidence of spiritual life? Are we always seeking excuses for why the demands of God's word do not apply to us? Or is it rather that in spite of all evidence to the contrary, we believe that his promises cannot fail, and we live in obedience to whatever he demands of us?

It is all very sobering, as it must have been for the churches to which James addresses his letter.

JAMES 3

The Sinful Use of the Tongue

1. My brethren, be not many masters, knowing that we shall receive the greater condemnation.
2. For in many things we offend all. If any man offend not in word, the same is a perfect man, and able also to bridle the whole body.
3. Behold, we put bits in the horses' mouths, that they may obey us; and we turn about their whole body.
4. Behold also the ships, which though they be so great, and are driven of fierce winds, yet are they turned about with a very small helm, withersoever the governor listeth.
5. Even so the tongue is a little member, and boasteth great things. Behold, how great a matter a little fire kindleth!
6. And the tongue is a fire, a world of iniquity; so is the tongue among our members, that it defileth the whole body, and setteth on fire the course of nature; and it is set on fire of hell.
7. For every kind of beasts, and of birds, and of serpents, and of things in the sea, is tamed, and hath been tamed of mankind:
8. But the tongue can no man tame; it is an unruly evil, full of deadly poison.
9. Therewith bless we God, even the Father; and therewith curse we men, which are made after the similitude of God.

10. Out of the same mouth proceedeth blessing and cursing. My brethren, these things ought not so to be.

11. Doth a fountain send forth at the same place sweet water and bitter?

12. Can the fig tree, my brethren, bear olive berries? either a vine, figs? so can no fountain both yield salt water and fresh.

Having completed the main message of the epistle, James turns to the subject of the use of the tongue. There is the obvious connection with the preceding verses that living faith manifests itself in the good work of the proper use of the tongue.

One might ask, why turn to the use of the tongue? Are there not more important ways in which living faith becomes manifest? The answer is that the use of the tongue is perhaps the most important calling a child of God has. James points this out when he says, "In many things we offend all. If any man offend not in word, the same is a perfect man, and able also to bridle the whole body" (3:2).

The apostle's statement is a surprising assertion. Control of the tongue makes a man perfect, for control of the tongue means a man controls all the activities in which he engages in his life in the world.

James called attention to the importance of our use of the tongue in 1:26: "If any man among you seem to be religious, and bridleth not his tongue, but deceiveth his own heart, this man's religion is vain." That emphasizes what is described in greater detail in chapter 3:1–12.

God has saved his people so they may show forth his praise, and God's people show forth God's praise by speaking. They witness to their salvation and to the truth of God (Isa. 43:10).

My brethren, be not many masters, knowing that we shall receive the greater condemnation (3:1)

Here again James uses the earnest and warm address "my brethren." This address is fitting, because by it James acknowledges that to gain control of our tongues is a struggle in which he and all God's people engage and which lasts a lifetime.

While the old English translation "masters" was correct in the days of the translation of the Authorized Version, a better and more modern translation would be "teachers." The warning is that everyone addressed here who wants to be a teacher should not be one.

It is possible that teachers refer to those with the special gift of prophecy found in the early church among the gifts of the Spirit. It is also possible that James refers to teachers in the church, ministers and elders. But the text seems to indicate that the desire to teach was more widespread and not limited to those with special gifts or to those who held special offices in the church. It seems that many, if not most in the church, wanted to teach others, and few or none wanted to learn. Everyone expressed his idea of the truth and the Christian calling, and no one wanted to listen to anyone else. Everyone thought he had a corner on spiritual matters and that he was obligated to share his wisdom with others. The result was that no one had time to listen to what others said. People liked to hear themselves talk and always had something to say. Such activity apparently took place even in the worship services, for early in the epistle James warns the people to be "swift to hear, slow to speak" (1:19), and he addresses the problem of uncontrolled use of the tongue (1:26).

Their root sin was pride, which resulted in contention and strife among the brethren and nothing was done decently and in good order in the church (1 Cor. 14:40). The situation among them was similar to what prevailed in Corinth and which Paul addressed in 1 Corinthians 12.

The reason one ought to be extremely wary of always being a teacher and never a listener or learner is that when teachers instruct, they take on unique responsibilities, which if misused lead to condemnation. The Greek word translated as "condemnation" literally means judgment and has a wide connotation. It can refer to either a favorable judgment or a condemnatory judgment. The translators of the Authorized Version were correct.

If one aspires to be a teacher and takes upon himself the obligation to teach others, he must be very sure his teaching is in complete harmony with the word of God. If it is not, he uses his instruction to lead people astray. He could teach them a half truth or a lie and thus lead them on a road other than the road to heaven. He could instruct them in an activity that is contrary to God's law and thus bring upon people God's wrath. These are terrible and undesirable consequences.

The admonition is urgent. A minister assumes this responsibility every time he mounts the pulpit, or every time he is confronted with a pastoral situation in which he must point one of his sheep to the word of God. The fear he might give wrong advice is enough to make him hesitant to answer questions concerning the truth. He does not always have his mouth open to blurt out whatever enters his head. He quickly says, "I don't know" when that is appropriate.

An elder must be "apt to teach" (1 Tim. 3:2). Apt to teach does not mean glib of tongue and smooth in speech; it means to know what the word of God teaches and to be ready to apply it to those who need to be instructed.

A teacher in a Christian school ought to let these words weigh heavily on him or her. Teachers instruct covenant children who in their learning look up to their teachers as the fountains of all wisdom. What a great responsibility to teach the seed of the covenant the ways of the Lord and how grim is the teachers' punishment if they teach wrong ideas and say things that lead to sinful conduct.

The positive truth is that God's people are all prophets who in the communion of the saints are called to edify one another, to instruct their children and their fellow saints, to comfort the sorrowing, to admonish the wayward, and to bring a word in season. This is obligatory. But let each be sure that he brings the word of God, for his words have profound consequences in the lives of those whom he teaches.

The admonition is urgent and needed.

For in many things we offend all (3:2)

The connection between verse 1 and verse 2 is clear. We ought not to be too eager to assume the position of teachers, for those who teach others offend many more people than those who listen and learn, and to offend others brings greater condemnation than keeping still.

The reason for being careful in our speech is given in verse 2.

The translation of the Authorized Version is somewhat misleading. James does not mean that we offend everyone, but that we all offend with respect to many things. James makes the point strongly. He insists that offending others is characteristic of all people. The word he uses (*hapantes* not *pantest*) indicates that he refers to every single person. Not only are those who assume the role of teachers prone to offend, but everyone offends, adults and children, young people and old people, men and women, poor and wealthy. To offend others is characteristic of everyone, for all are sinners. James refers specifically to the members of the church, those who are saved and called to be holy, also in their speech. They offend by their speech and they cause others to stumble.

James makes the idea even stronger by adding "for in many things," which means in many ways. Offending by our speech is a constant danger, especially for those who teach others. We are called to use the wonderful gift of speech to show kindness, sympathy, encouragement, and happiness to our fellow saints and to show them and to help them walk the right way of God's word. Instead, we offend them. What we say is offensive to others because our motives for speaking are often wrong. We want to impress others with our knowledge, or we admonish others out of a holier-than-thou spirit. We speak before we really know what we are talking about, or we jabber about things we do not understand.

"Offend" can be used either transitively, in which case it means to cause one to stumble or fall, or intransitively, in which case it means to stumble, fall, or err. The context shows clearly that the word is to be understood transitively. By our speech we cause others to stumble or fall. We should teach them, but we teach them wrongly by our hasty speech or by sharp and cruel words, which rather than help those to whom we speak, hurt and grieve them.

In our relationships with fellow saints, we are to listen to others and to learn from them, and if we are compelled to speak, we are to be sure that our words are God's word. If we do that, we cannot go wrong. We must not interpret this admonition to mean that we should never speak of spiritual things and the joy of our salvation, never contribute in Bible study groups, and never admonish a wayward brother.

Further, if our conversation is always limited to earthly things and is always only about inanities, we also sin. We are God's witnesses especially in relation to the saints with whom we live. We must make use of the marvelous gift of speech God has given us. But let us be careful to speak the word of God.

If any man offend not in word, the same is a perfect man, and able also to bridle the whole body (3:2)

After his general statement about the moral state of affairs within the church and the proper use of our tongues in the fellowship of the church, James makes this startling statement. How surprising! To make proper use of the tongue is to make proper use of the whole body. We hardly ever consider the tongue to be as important as that.

Although the sentence is formulated as an if-clause, it is the truth. Anyone who can control his tongue is able to control his whole body. James uses the figure of a bridle, which makes the statement vivid and clear. With a bridle one controls a horse's mouth and controlling a horse's mouth, one can control the whole body of the horse. One who controls his tongue with a bridle controls his whole body.

The figure is apt and powerful, and sets the main theme for the passage that follows in verses 3–12.

Although the statement is general, James speaks to the members of the church. The hand that holds the reins of the tongue is the new man created by Christ through regeneration, but the old man of our sinful nature still interferes with the work of the new man in Christ and turns our tongues to the service of sin.

God gave Adam the gift of speech when he was created in paradise. When Adam named the animals, he was apparently capable of speaking a word that echoed the word of God in the animal. It was an echo because God's word was creative and powerful and formed the essence of each individual animal. When Adam repeated that word, though in a creaturely way, he spoke God's word, by means of which he expressed the wonders in the creation to the glory of God.

Sin corrupted man's ability to speak. After the fall all man's speech is used in the opposite way from which it was created. Instead of speaking God's word in his speech, man speaks Satan's word. He speaks only the lie and does everything in his power to contradict God's word. He does this in his instruction of his wife and children and in all his relationships with his fellowmen. His goal in his speech is not to glorify God but to glorify himself.

When a child of God is regenerated, the new man, created by God through Christ, is given control over the tongue, although he still possesses his old sinful nature that struggles against the new man in Christ to gain control of the tongue, because sinful man knows the truth of what the scriptures teach here—that control of the tongue means control of the whole body.

Thus man makes idols and teaches others to do likewise with him. He takes God's name in vain and refuses to use the Sabbath for calling on God's name. He controls institutions of learning so that his devilish lies can be promoted in the world and men can be taught to eat, drink, and be merry. He kills others with malicious gossiping and a backbiting tongue that extols himself at the expense of his fellowman. He tells dirty jokes and revels in pornography so that his adulterous impulses may be given free rein, and his body may be an instrument of fornication. He uses his tongue for deceit and thus advances himself and attains those things he covets. How powerful is the tongue! But the converted child of God is given the power of grace in the new man in Christ, who here in James' powerful figure is once again called to use the tongue to speak God's word in praise to God and for the advantage of his neighbor.

When a man controls his tongue and puts it in the service of God, he is able to put his whole body in the service of God. He is a "perfect man," which means that man attains the goal for which he was created. "Perfect" is a word similar in root to *telos,* which means end, goal, or purpose. How much we need God's work in us to use our tongues in the service of God and in love for our neighbor!

It may seem to be an exaggeration to claim that controlling the tongue enables one to control the whole body, but such is not the case. The truth of the apostle's statement is found in the difficulty of controlling the tongue. It is so desperately difficult to control the tongue that in comparison, the control of the body is relatively easy.

The use of the tongue is determined by the inward moral state of a man. James does not speak of only outward actions, the actions of the tongue, but he still has the distinction between living and dead faith in mind. Living faith connects one to Christ, from whom comes the new life of the regenerated man. This new life is in the deepest part of man's being, his heart. Everything the tongue speaks comes from the heart, as Jesus explained in Matthew 15:18–20. "Those things which proceed out of the mouth come forth from the heart; and they defile the man. For out of the heart proceed evil thoughts, murders, adulteries, fornications, thefts, false witness, blasphemies: these are things which defile a man: but to eat with unwashen hands defileth not a man." If the tongue is under the control of the inner man created by Christ Jesus, the whole man is under the control of this principle of regeneration.

Behold, we put bits in the horses' mouths, that they may obey us; and we turn about their whole body. Behold also the ships, which though they be so great, and are driven of fierce winds, yet are they turned about with a very small helm, whithersoever the governor listeth (3:3–4)

These verses are connected to the foregoing context and to verse 5. They are connected to verse 3 by demonstrating that it can be and is true that one who controls the tongue controls his whole body, just as one who controls a horse's mouth controls the entire beast, and just as one who controls the helm of the ship controls the entire ship. These verses are connected to verse 5 by the comparison of the smallness of the tongue with its tremendous power.

Thus there is a double comparison implied. The first comparison is between the small size of the tongue in relation to the human body and the bit in a horse's mouth in relation to the horse. Though the bit is only a small piece of iron, the horse is easily directed by it. If a horse or a team of horses is being driven by a farmer who is plowing a field, one senses the strength of the horses and knows that should they turn against the farmer, they could kill him. But the farmer controls the horse with the bit.

So also it is with a sailing ship. The ship is huge, with billowing sails reaching toward the sky, carrying a large load of cargo and many passengers. It may be caught in a fierce wind that creates waves fifteen or twenty feet high, but the smallness of the helm makes no difference, though its size is negligible in comparison to the size of the boat.

The second part of the comparison demonstrates James' assertion that the one who is able to control the tongue can also control the whole body. So is the tongue in relation to the body. If the tongue is guided by the new man in Christ, the whole body can be controlled by the tongue, so that the purpose of God is accomplished in that person. But when one's tongue is controlled by his evil nature, his whole body is used in the service of sin.

Even so the tongue is a little member, and boasteth great things (3:5)

Because James has his eye on those who claim to have faith but do not have living faith, he concentrates in this and the following verses on the evil use of the tongue. Hence boasting is to be taken in the evil sense. Even though the people of God surely use their tongues in the service of God, even they badly misuse their tongues. Every commandment is broken by the tongue. James sums it all up with the one word "boasteth."

James uses the literary device called apostrophe. He ascribes human qualities and actions to the tongue: it boasts. Though it is so small, it boasts of its huge accomplishments. Because it is controlled by a depraved nature, its accomplishments are evil.

We use our tongues to boast of our evil deeds and accomplishments. We boast as if our works do startlingly wonderful things. The artist boasts of his painting. The builder boasts of the house he has built. The minister boasts of his sermons and how he is able to move people by his preaching. The teacher boasts of the lives she has changed by her skillful teaching techniques. Parents boast of their children's prowess on the basketball court. Those engaged in industry and the development of technology boast of sending a spaceship to the moon and an unmanned vehicle to Mars to take pictures. Doctors boast of their surgical successes and the miracles of modern medicine. The tongue, though very small, boasts of mighty deeds. No mention is made of God who created man and gave him the power of speech.

Behold, how great a matter a little fire kindleth (3:5)

The apostle continues his comparison between the smallness of the tongue and great things, whether good or bad, that the tongue controls. What the tongue accomplishes is out of proportion to its size.

James emphasizes in verses 5–6 the evil of which the tongue is capable and the results of its wicked use. He sharply reprimands the saints in the churches to which he writes for the evil use of their tongues.

It is a reprimand the church always needs to hear because the evil of wagging tongues still is a great evil among the saints.

The righteous are God's covenantal people. God is their God and they are his people. Together they dwell in the fellowship of love. But fellowship is impossible without communication and conversation. God speaks to his people and they respond to him in prayers, praise, and adoration. God tells his people the secrets of his will (Ps. 25:14), and his people pour out their hearts to their God in earnest supplications and tell him of all their woes. Since covenantal fellowship requires conversation, God created man with a tongue with which to speak. What a great blessing comes to those who use their tongues aright! Centrally the Word is Christ, for he became flesh and dwelt among us (John 1:14). By the power of God's word Christ arose from the dead and by that word we are engrafted into Christ. In Christ we have conscious fellowship with God.

James compares the tongue to a fire.

It takes only a small spark from the campfire of a careless camper to start a forest fire that burns thousands of acres of forest, destroys houses, and kills people. It takes only a small match to start a blaze that can destroy millions of dollars of property. The destruction brought about in a fire is far out of proportion to the spark or small flame that started it. I have watched lightning strike the earth in a dry forest. Almost immediately a small spiral of smoke creeps upward from the spot. Within minutes a pile of dead twigs is ignited and a large fire begins. In a frantic effort to quench what was only a very small column of smoke, firefighters are called and equipment is brought in to extinguish the flames lest the fire destroys the entire forest. Nothing is quite as sad as seeing a beautiful forest of trees, shrubs, flowers, and animals made desolate by a fire. The fire leaves in its wake destruction, ruin, utter desolation, barren landscape, and the dead bodies of large and small animals. All signs of life are gone.

The tongue is a fire that destroys lives, reputations, and successes. One small moment of backbiting or slander can start a chain of events that destroys people's lives. I have witnessed it in the church. I have seen one small slanderous word drive people out of the church. I have seen families shattered by cruel gossip. A word or two spoken off-handedly and carelessly becomes a conflagration of mammoth proportions.

We are not even considering how false philosophies such as evolutionism sweep around the world, are defended by the false church, and corrupt the minds of millions. We have not even considered how hasty and false words start wars and revolutions with the terrible destruction they leave behind them. Who can even begin to add up the price in lives, cities, natural resources, and ruined countries paid by the nations in World War II—all started by the speeches of Adolph Hitler.

Who can imagine the terrible results of the words, spoken and written, of Lenin, Trotsky, and the leaders in the Russian revolution?

In James' emphasis on the evil of which the tongue is capable his comparison of the tongue with a fire is a fitting and powerful metaphor.

And the tongue is a fire, a world of iniquity: so is the tongue among our members, that it defileth the whole body (3:6)

The interpretation of "world of iniquity" hinges on the meaning of "world." The ordinary word for world (*cosmos*) is used here, and the use of the word is determined by the sentence in which it is used.

First, James writes of the power of the tongue "among our members." He refers to what he said in verse 2 that the bridling of the tongue will bring the whole body under control. Hence the "world" of the tongue is our bodily members.

Second, the tongue is a world "of iniquity," the literal meaning of which is unrighteousness. The reference is to the activity of the members of our body. In the world of the activities in our daily lives, the wrong use of the tongue is a power for evil. Every member of our bodies is used for perpetrating and committing unrighteousness.

That is a stinging indictment, but sadly it is true. We can

consider how true this is by a brief survey of the law of God.

The tongue breaks the first two commandments by all the false philosophies and heresies taught from the churches' pulpits and the schools' podiums. The antichrist described in Revelation 13 creates an image of himself that speaks (v. 15). Men violate the third commandment when they blaspheme and curse God or vainly use his name in jokes. The fourth commandment is broken by false worship of God as, for example, among Roman Catholics, Pentecostals, and those who peddle a false gospel. Spiritual desolation results when the tongue breaks these commandments.

The fifth commandment that requires submission to authority is broken by demagogues who stir up rebellion, revolution, anarchy, schism, and disobedience. By a gossiping tongue it is possible to kill a person in a more horrible way than murder and thus to break the sixth commandment. People are crucified on crosses of slander; darts more cruel than bullets enter the hearts of those slandered; cruel and mocking words destroy lives. It is almost impossible to overstate the corruption, fornication, and adultery inspired by lewd and filthy talk. Perverted sex is on everyone's tongue and leads only to the most abominable sins imaginable. Envious words can rob our neighbors or express our desires to rob them of their possessions. We need not speak of the ninth commandment when it above all others is dedicated to curb our wagging tongues. Covetousness comes to expression in a hundred ways in our speech and characterizes the language of the man who sets himself above his neighbor.

All the unrighteousness bound up in the heart of man comes to expression in the tongue's use. The tongue is indeed a world of iniquity. James sums it all up with the words "it defileth the whole body." The tongue corrupts all the activities of the body. Nothing we say or do escapes the evil the tongue has spoken.

And setteth on fire the course of nature; and it is set on fire of hell (3:6)

The phrase "the course of nature" has been variously interpreted. The word translated as "course" is the Greek word that means wheel. "Nature" is better translated as "beginning." The idea is that at birth the wheel of one's life begins to turn and continues to turn until death. The wheel of life is turned by the sin of the tongue. Our lives are determined by how others—parents, pastors, teachers, and fellowmen—use their tongues. In turn we influence the lives of others by how we use our tongues. If our lives are controlled by living faith, all these influences serve a good purpose, but within a wicked world the opposite is true. The use of the tongue is always evil, so that the entire life of man, set on its course by the tongue, is evil throughout. In other words, the evil of the world has its origin in the wrong use of the tongue.

James does not mean to imply that human depravity is not transmitted from parents to children. This also is true. But he speaks of the entire world of human life. Man's depraved nature is the fountain of the depravity, but the tongue determines how that depravity comes to expression in life.

The translation of the Greek word for hell is *gehenna*. The word was used for the valley of the son of Hinnom just south of the walls of Jerusalem, which was used for the worship of Molech, to which idol Judah sacrificed her children (2 Chron. 28:3; 33:6). Josiah declared the place unclean (2 Kings 23:10), and it was henceforth used as a place for the disposal of the offal from the temple and the city of Jerusalem. It was the city dump where all the trash and garbage of the city was burned. It became a stinking valley where the fire never went out. As such it became a symbol of hell as the place where the damned suffer everlasting punishment.

The devil and his hosts have their place of punishment in hell, and their purposes and works throughout the history of the world are of hellish origin. When the tongue is set on fire by hell, one's use of the tongue represents all that belongs to hell. It represents the cause of Satan and his foul hosts. It represents all the evil embodied in Satan, who by means of the tongue persuaded Eve and then Adam to eat of the forbidden tree, thus opening the gates to all the terrible destruction brought about by the tongue in the history of the world.

The fire brought about by the tongue is a burning, consuming, destroying, stinking, yellow, eerie, terrifying stench that originates in hell. In that awful fire we are caught up when our wagging tongues do their devilish work.

For every kind of beasts, and of birds, and of serpents, and of things in the sea, is tamed, and hath been tamed of mankind (3:7)

In verses 7–8 James speaks of the impossibility of controlling the tongue by any human power. Man is capable of taming any creature, but he cannot tame the tongue. James gives many examples of how the power of an evil tongue controls and directs men's lives and the course of history.

Interestingly, the different types of moving creatures are divided according to the divisions God formed in the creation week. "Beasts" are all walking creatures; "birds" are all creatures that fly; "serpents" are all creeping creatures; and "things in the sea" refer to fish and mammals that live in the oceans.

All these creatures have been tamed not in the sense that pets have been made of representatives of each kind of creature. Rather, man exercises lordship over every kind of creature in God's world to put it to man's use. Man is sufficiently powerful to put into his service creatures stronger than he. Nothing is able to escape his dominion.

The emphasis is unusually strong by repeating the idea: "is tamed, and hath been tamed." "Is tamed" is present tense and indicates continuous action. Man is still taming the creatures under his lordship. "Hath been tamed" is perfect tense and indicates that man has successfully put animals and all creatures to his use so that the present relationship between these creatures and man clearly shows man's lordship over them.

We need think only of the horse used for so many purposes in agriculture and forestry; of the elephant used in more primitive cultures to carry people and heavy loads; of the cobra bewitched by the flutes of man; of a dog obedient to his master's commands; of homing pigeons trained to return to their homes; of porpoises that entertain people with their willingness to obey commands from humans. James' assertion is not an exaggeration.

But the tongue can no man tame; it is an unruly evil, full of deadly poison (3:8)

The tongue is the exception; it cannot be tamed. Where in the world can one person be found who uses the tongue for the purpose God gave it to man? In the halls of academia? There false philosophies and evil ethics are openly taught. On the streets of the nation? One hears only cursing and blasphemy. In the halls of government? Lying is endemic and becomes a useful tool to deceive the people. In the church? Even there false teachers arise to spread their deadly heresies, and even the saints enjoy gossiping and tale-bearing, which is so harmful to the communion of saints.

In all the relationships of man to God and in all the relationships between man and man, the tongue is an unruly evil, a deadly poison. While "unruly" is a good translation of the Greek word (*akatastaton*), it also means restless. No one can control the tongue so that it is used only for good, but no one can cease to use it. To refrain from speaking is impossible. To vow to say no single word is beyond the scope of man's ability. He has to talk, for he lives in all the relationships of life that require speech. There are times when one should not talk; yet he does, and the talk is almost always bad. "I wish I had kept my mouth shut," someone says. Speech often does more harm than good. It often makes a bad situation worse. It creates trouble where no trouble formerly existed. The tongue not only wags incessantly, but when it wags, it does so in the service of sin.

The tongue is also a deadly poison. When the tongue wags, poison is spewed out as lava from a volcano or as the deadly poison from the fangs of a rattlesnake. The poison is truly deadly, because it kills people. It does not kill them physically, but the death that the tongue causes is more excruciating. It is able to ruin the life of a schoolgirl who perhaps does not dress as well as other girls and is the object of mockery, isolation, and taunting talk. It spoils, sometimes for one's whole life, the inner psychical life of an individual who has been browbeaten by a cruel parent. It makes a mouse out of a beautiful woman who is constantly verbally abused by a wicked husband. The sad tally of examples could go on forever, for the poison is there in every relationship of life.

What a powerful description of the tongue! It is no surprise that Solomon in his proverbs makes mention of the tongue over and over again.

Therewith bless we God, even the Father; and therewith curse we men, which are made after the similitude of God. Out of the same mouth proceedeth blessing and cursing. My brethren, these things ought not so to be. Doth a fountain send forth at the same place sweet water and bitter? Can the fig tree, my brethren, bear olive berries? either a vine, figs? so can no fountain both yield salt water and fresh (3:9–12)

Although James addresses the church, the descriptions of the dreadful power of the tongue apply to all men.

Beginning with verse 9, the power of an evil tongue is applied specifically to the people of God. Only they can be compared with a fountain that brings forth salt water and sweet. The evil that is present in the world is also found among the saints, but they have also the power of the life of Christ.

It must not be forgotten that James still speaks of the difference between dead faith and living faith. Dead faith is a caricature of living faith and looks somewhat similar to it. It leads a man to come to church and even to claim to believe in the truth being proclaimed in the church. But its falsity is evident in that it never produces good works. In contrast, living faith is the bond that unites the believer to Christ, so that the life of Christ flows into a man and manifests itself in good works. The difference between dead faith and living faith is now strikingly described in one's use of the tongue.

Verses 9–12 imply that a man may have dead faith and living faith at the same time. He can bless and curse. He can produce a fountain of good water and a stream of bitter water. He can produce good fruit and rotten fruit.

This is very strange, but true. You can hear a child of God sing fervently God's praises in church on the Lord's day as he sits next to you in the pew. But when you stand near him outside of church, you may hear him curse someone as he relates what that person did to him. You are inclined to ask, "Can this be the same person?" Then it comes to you sharply and as a dagger. You do the same in your home. You lead the family in devotions, but suddenly you speak evil of someone within the congregation and repeat a juicy bit of gossip that was told you by one of your fellow workers on the job.

Such contradictory activity can be explained only when we

consider that the child of God is a strange person. He has true faith and thus possesses the life of Christ in his heart, but he carries with him his old sinful and depraved nature, full of sin and corruption. In this sense these verses must be understood.

To bless means to speak well of. We use our tongues to speak well of God. We do so because we know and believe that he is God above all gods. He is the eternal one, the creator of heaven and earth and everything in them. In him is found all perfection and glory, and his attributes proclaim him as the infinite one.

He is also our Father. That means he loves us with an eternal and unchangeable love in Jesus Christ, for he loved us while we were yet sinners (Rom. 5:8). He determines in his counsel everything that happens in heaven and on earth, in order that all things may serve our salvation. He always does good to us and uses all the experiences and circumstances of our lives, over which he rules, to make them subservient to our final salvation. He takes us into glory that we may be with him. He assumes all responsibility for our total care in life, in death, and forever in the world to come.

Knowing and believing all this, it is impossible to do anything else but speak well of him. We bless him when we pray, and in our prayers we praise and honor him for who he is. We speak well of him when we join our voices with our fellow saints in songs of praise. We bless him when we confess his name to our families and friends and to the wicked world around us. He is our God and Father, and we can do nothing else but boast of him.

But with that same mouth and tongue we curse man. As blessing someone means speaking well of him, so cursing someone means to speak evil of him. We speak evil of a person when we tell others of his sins and faults, whether they are true or false. We speak evil of a person when we degrade him, attempt with our speech to ruin his reputation, or bring to his attention or the attention of others what a miserable person he is.

Underneath this discussion lies the ninth commandment. Our Lord also reminds us that to refrain from cursing and to speak well of others is an important part of our lives as citizens of the kingdom of heaven (Matt. 5:44).Whether it is a fellow saint or someone outside the church makes no essential difference. We are to curse no one. Yet sadly we not only curse the wicked outside the church, but we also curse those with whom we live in fellowship within the church, those who also confess God as their Father.

The clause "which are made after the similitude of God" emphasizes forcefully the anomaly of our double-tongued speech.

This text has been misused and misinterpreted. It has been used to prove that some remnants of the image of God that Adam possessed are still found in the wicked. This interpretation is pressed further to prove that some elements of good are still to be found in totally depraved man, and that the preservation of these remnants of good is due to God's universal grace.

However, scripture is clear that when man fell in Adam, he lost entirely the image of God. The scriptures maintain that since the fall of Adam and as universal punishment for the guilt of the fall, man is totally depraved (Rom. 3:9–19), dead in trespasses and sins (Eph. 2:1). Paul spoke of the restoration of the image in the people of God in Ephesians 4:23–24 and Colossians 3:10, which teach that the image of God is spiritual and consists of true knowledge of God, righteousness, and holiness.

Man continued to be man after he fell: he retained his rationality and morality. It was corrupted and badly weakened, and worst of all, it was put into the service of sin. Because he is rational and moral, able to distinguish between right and wrong, he remains capable of bearing an image. In paradise Adam was an image bearer only because he was created as a rational and moral creature. This rationality and mortality were not lost after the fall, although now, because man remains capable of bearing an image, he bears the image of the devil. Jesus tells the wicked Jews that they are not children of Abraham, but that they are children of their father the devil, whose works they do (John 8:44).

The text therefore does not teach that man still possesses the image of God, but that man is unique in all God's creation because he was created to be an image bearer. Although he lost the image, he is still capable of bearing God's image, if it is graciously restored to him. When you curse any man, James says, you curse one who could, if God is merciful to him, become an image bearer once again. You ought to be seeking his salvation, not cursing him.

Even worse, you curse those whom God blesses when you curse your fellow saints. You consign to hell those whom God has determined to take to heaven. You gloat over sins in others that God has forgiven. What a terrible sin this is!

There is a certain note of sadness in James' address "my brethren." After all, both he and those to whom he writes are saints in the church of Christ. They are all saved and belong to Christ's kingdom and have the royal law of liberty (1:25; 2:8) in their hearts. Yet they use the most powerful member of their bodies for such wicked goals and contradictory purposes. The admonition lays its finger on a grave weakness in the lives of the people of God and exposes a deadly sin of which they are guilty. God's people ought not to be doing these things.

A slightly different emphasis appears in the words "doth a fountain send forth at the same place sweet water and bitter?" In verse 10 the sin of being double-tongued is condemned. In this verse the spiritual impossibility of being double-tongued is defined: it is impossible for a fountain to produce two kinds of water.

Three elements constitute the figure. One is a spring of water deep under the ground. The second is the opening in the ground from which the water comes out. The third is the water that flows from the spring.

The point is that the quality of the water is determined by its source. If the source is pure, the water that flows through the opening in the ground will also be pure. If the source of the spring is in minerals or impurities of some kind, the water carries the characteristics of its source.

So it is with our mouths. The underground spring is the heart of a man. The opening through which the water comes is our mouths. The stream of water is the words a man speaks. If the heart is pure, the speech that comes from the mouth is also pure and sweet. If the heart is corrupt, the words a man speaks are also corrupt. But the heart cannot be both pure and corrupt at the same time, and neither can the words that come forth from it.

It may be that when he turns to his figures of plants (v. 12), James has in mind again the difference between living faith and dead faith; he appeals to the trees to make the point. "Can a fig tree, my brethren, bear olive berries? either a vine, figs? so can no fountain both yield salt water and fresh." Living faith grafts one into Christ, and the fruit it brings forth is not the strange fruit uncharacteristic of the nature of the plant, but fruit that bears the nature of the tree and can in turn produce a tree like that from which it came.

What is true in the world of God's inanimate creatures is also true in God's world of living plants. A tree or a vine produces fruit according to its nature. This rule in God's world is inviolable. The creation narrative tells us that this is God's order: "And the earth brought forth grass, and herb yielding seed after his kind, and the tree yielding fruit, whose seed was in itself, after its kind" (Gen. 1:12).

All would be confusion if a corn seed yielded a thistle and a plum pit yielded a watermelon. So it is in man. The spiritual nature of man determines the nature of the fruit.

Yet in the lives of the people of God, this very anomaly happens. Good speech and bad speech come from the same mouth. The only explanation is that in the regenerated Christian, sometimes his heart speaks, and sometimes his old nature speaks. This is precisely the struggle that goes on in the Christian, which Paul described in Romans 7:14–25.

However, the regenerated heart must have and does have the victory. It is true that in this life we bless and curse. But the victory of faith is complete already in this life. The one who does use his tongue wrongly, if he is regenerated, has the victory by confessing his sins before God, repenting of them, and by faith clinging to Christ in whom he is righteous. In his repentance he hates the misuse of his tongue and fights against this sin, and he daily strives to use his tongue aright.

Our calling is clear. We must remember what a powerful instrument the tongue is, and we must earnestly beseech God to give us the power to control this mighty member of our bodies so that it may be used for the welfare of our fellow saints and the glory of God. If we should through weakness fall into sin, we ought to hurry with our sins to the cross to confess them to Christ and to God and to seek forgiveness and renewed strength to fight against such atrocious sins and thus to overcome them through the strength of our Savior.

Two Wisdoms

13. Who is a wise man and endued with knowledge among you? let him shew out of a good conversation his works with meekness of wisdom.
14. But if ye have bitter envying and strife in your hearts, glory not, and lie not against the truth.
15. This wisdom descendeth not from above, but is earthly, sensual, devilish.

16. For where envying and strife is, there is confusion and every evil work.
17. But the wisdom that is from above is first pure, then peaceable, gentle, and easy to be entreated, full of mercy and good fruits, without partiality, and without hypocrisy.
18. And the fruit of righteousness is sown in peace of them that make peace.

Who is a wise man and endued with knowledge among you? (3:13)

This is a rhetorical question, for no answer is or can be given. The force of the question is that it calls attention to the fact that not everyone in the congregation has true wisdom. At the same time, it directly appeals to those who do have wisdom.

"Wisdom" and "knowledge" are nearly synonymous words. Wisdom is the spiritual ability to apply the truth of God's word to life with all its problems. Knowledge comes from a verb (*epistamai*) that means to put one's mind to something. It has come to mean experience. It is the knowledge that arises out of experience. The kind of knowledge that comes from experience certainly produces wisdom. Therefore, the phrase can be translated as "who is a wise man and experienced among you?"

This rhetorical question is loosely connected with the immediately foregoing description of the power and evil of our tongues. James asks, "Are there people in the congregations wise enough and with sufficient experience to use their tongues properly?" At the same time he also looks ahead and asks the question in connection with the whole lives of the individual members of the church. It is an important question that calls to their consciousness their own lives and callings in the world. Are our lives in all respects, including the use of our tongues, lives that manifest true wisdom that comes from experience in the Christian calling?

We must not forget that such penetrating questions still include the question of faith: is it true faith or counterfeit? That this question is still in James' mind is evident from the next sentence, in which James again reminds us that true faith produces good works.

Let him shew out of a good conversation his works with meekness of wisdom (3:13)

This statement is an admonition: let every wise and experienced person in the congregations demonstrate his wisdom and experience, and let him do so by his works, for his works will show not only that he is truly wise, but also that he is a man of genuine faith.

The word "conversation" is consistently used in the Authorized Version to translate a Greek word that means walk of life. "Good" is a translation of the Greek word (*kalos*) that means beautiful. However, beautiful in Greek thinking does not mean physically attractive, but ethically beautiful, that is, able to serve its purpose (*agathos*). For example, an apple is beautiful when it is not rotten, but crisp, juicy, and nourishing. Our lives are beautiful when they reflect God's purpose in saving us.

This life that a child of God is called to lead is possible when he is experienced in the many facets of life, has acquired by these experiences a knowledge of the moral pitfalls of sin, and has learned how to live in all life's circumstances to God's glory. Such a person is wise. He is a veteran in the battle of faith. He has wept with those who weep and has sung psalms with those who are happy. He understands the subtleties of the devil's temptations and how to resist them. He knows what it means to bring up children in the fear of the Lord and how to discipline them according to the scriptures. He hones by an active and busy life in Christ's kingdom the wisdom he received from God.

Such a person of true faith is called to manifest his wisdom and experience "in meekness of wisdom." The genitive "of wisdom" can be either a genitive of description or a genitive of source. If it is the former, the expression means a wise meekness: he must show his meekness wisely. If this is a genitive of source, the meaning is that he shows in his life meekness that has its source in wisdom. Although the meaning of the two is not greatly different, I prefer the genitive of source. The wisdom that a child of God possesses produces meekness when he shows his wisdom and experience.

Meekness is despised in today's world. A meek man will have grave difficulty getting a job. Not the meek man is held up as a role model, but the gifted sports figure, the man of wealth who is successful in business, the powerful figure who commands strong armed forces or who leads a nation. Meekness will not gain for one the presidency of the United States or even the office of state governor. Even in the church, the meek man is frequently not appreciated.

A man who is meek does not allow himself to be a doormat for others. He is not shy and shrinking. In some instances he may be bold and of considerable courage. Moses is described in the Bible as the meekest man who ever lived (Num. 12:3). Yet he was a man who could lead three million Israelites through a great, howling wilderness to the land of promise. He was courageous beyond anything known in the world when he had to take a stand against the rebellion, the criticism, and the opposition of his own people. He could be justly furious at Israel's sins, as he was when he threw the tables of the law to the ground in dismay over Israel's idol worship.

Meekness in one's relation to God manifests itself when a man, endowed with this priceless gift, is very careful that not he, but God alone receives all glory. Without hesitation he is willing to be pushed into the background if this would point his fellow saints and others to how great God is.

In relation to his fellow saints, he seeks the welfare of his neighbor and the spiritual good of the church, no matter what the cost to himself. He never carries in his heart hatred or envy for his brothers and sisters. He always aids in trouble and distress. He never seeks revenge or allows jealousy in his heart. He is also courageous in the defense of the faith: he is quick to anger when God's name is mocked or when God's truth is attacked. He is jealous for the Lord his God, as Elijah was in apostate Israel (1 Kings 19:10). He boldly contradicts sinners, no matter what the price is to himself personally.

This is the man who possesses meekness that is born in wisdom. What a blessing such a man is in the church!

But if ye have bitter envying and strife in your hearts, glory not, and lie not against the truth (3:14)

The Authorized Version does not quite convey the meaning of the Greek. The word (*zelos*) translated as "envying" means zeal. The word translated as "strife" comes from a word (*eritheia*) that means electioneering and comes closer to the English word *partisanship*.

The verse strongly suggests that these evil sins were common in the churches to which James writes, for the sentence is a first class condition. "If ye have" describes a condition of fact. The last part of the sentence, "glory not," is an imperative or admonition. The fact that an admonition is included strengthens the case for maintaining that zeal and partisanship were present in the congregations.

Zeal can have a good or a bad meaning. One may have zeal for the truth and for the cause of Christ. The word can also be used in a bad sense if the object of the zeal is contrary to the will of Christ.

The admonition of the text uncovers a sin in the congregations that is the direct opposite of "meekness of wisdom." The zeal against which the text warns is bitter zeal that puts bitter thoughts in one's heart. It is consuming energy that forces bad actions. For example, it is the zeal of the sect Jehovah's Witnesses. It is the zeal of a man seeking revenge as he stalks his victim. In the church it is hatred of one's fellow saint that not only detests the object of the zeal, but also embitters the one who lets such emotions characterize his life. Wrong zeal is born from envy and pride.

Electioneering or partisanship refers to a party spirit. It means to have a desire to advance oneself at almost any cost. One guilty of this sin tries to climb the ladder of success by trampling on others and exalting himself. He puts forth every effort to gain admirers and those who will side with him. He is quick to criticize others who stand in his way, and he is not averse to creating a party spirit in the church: those for him and those against him.

These things are sufficiently common in the church of Christ to make the admonition relevant and to prompt some serious self-examination.

The admonition is, "Glory not, and lie not against the truth."

One who is guilty of the sins mentioned here needs very much the warning not to boast, for boasting is the real essence of evil zeal and partisanship. One is interested in advancing himself, and he will surely boast of what he has done: how faithful he has been, how vigorous in the cause of Christ, and how untiring in the work of the gospel. He will want others than Christ to know how good he is, for his motives are to advance his reputation and standing.

"Lie not against the truth" can have two meanings. "Truth" can refer to the truth of the word of God. In that case the meaning would be do not contradict the truth that you claim to confess by your life. Do not demonstrate by boasting that you are uninterested in God's glory, for you seek your own glory and the praise of men.

The clause can also refer to the truth of your life and your spiritual condition. You are only a man, subject to all the infirmities of a creature. You are dependent for everything on God. And, much more, you are a sinner. If you have done any good at all in the church, your good is corrupted and polluted with sin, and insofar as it is useful in God's kingdom, it is good only because God works in you both to will and to do of his good pleasure (Phil. 2:13). This second meaning seems to be more in keeping with the entire context, and I prefer that.

How often are not congregations destroyed by men who act in a way condemned by James! How often are not denominations troubled endlessly by cases that have their origin in bitter zeal and partisanship. Almost always heresy arises in the church because a man is self-seeking and reveals his self-centeredness by trying to demonstrate his superior knowledge of scripture or his skills in leadership.

How blessed is the congregation where the saints strive together for the peace of Jerusalem, the welfare of their fellow saints, and the advancement of the cause of God's kingdom.

This wisdom descendeth not from above, but is earthly, sensual, devilish (3:15)

The statement in this verse implies that there are two kinds of wisdom: wisdom that comes from heaven and from God (James 1:5) and a counterfeit wisdom, an imitation, a caricature that belongs to this world. It is of the latter that James speaks to further elucidate the strong tendency in the church to engage in wicked zeal and partisanship that destroys the church. It is a wisdom found only in the world and within those in the church who have only dead faith.

The three adjectives that James uses to describe it emphasize that this wisdom from below is completely earthly. True wisdom is the spiritual ability to apply biblical principles to this life. The wisdom of which the text speaks is the ability to apply earthly goals, principles, and motives to a life contrary to the kingdom of heaven. This wisdom is "earthly" and belongs to the sinful life in the world, which is a life apart from God and heaven. This earthly wisdom is also "sensual." The better translation of the Greek word (a cognate of *psuchē*, which means soul) is "psychical." The psychical powers of the human soul include such powers as sensation and perception. These powers are emphasized in connection with this earthly wisdom because they speak of our relationships to the earthly creation and in isolation from any powers of the soul to know God and his truth. Further, such wisdom is "devilish." It is cunning, sly, and as deceitful as Satan himself. It is also devilish because it belongs to life apart from God in this world in which Satan now rules to attain his wicked purposes.

One can find such wisdom in wicked men who are able to use their natural abilities to attain success in this world and to acquire for themselves the things their hearts crave. This wisdom is also found in the world's books on how to become rich, how to influence people, how to bring up children, how to have successful marriages or satisfying sex lives, or how to run a large company. Shelves in bookstores are full of such "how-to" books. They tell us how worldly principles can bring worldly success according to the world's definition of success. But it is all wisdom apart from God.

For where envying and strife is, there is confusion and every evil work (3:16)

The connective "for" creates some problem in the *connection* between verses 15 and 16, because it seems to require that verse 16 be the reason for verse 15. This is probably correct, if one understands the relationship as meaning that because envying and strife result in confusion and every evil work, it is evident that envying and strife belong to earthly wisdom and not to wisdom that produces meekness.

The same two words used in verse 14, "envying" and "strife," are used here. Where these two sins are found in the congregations, there is confusion and every evil work. Confusion, disorderliness, turmoil, and unrest are the opposite of good order, which Paul required of the church in Corinth (1 Cor. 14:40). These can be found in consistory and council meetings, in congregational meetings, in relationships among the saints, and in worship services. It is not a good experience to be present in such a congregation, and preaching as well as the work of the church becomes next to impossible, for the Spirit is grieved.

"Evil work" accomplishes nothing. The New Testament uses three words (*phaulos, kakos,* and *ponēros*) for evil. *Phaulos* is used here and it means good for nothing, of no value, without possibility of anything worthwhile coming from it.

It can be objected that the word used here is rather weak in comparison with the horror of the sins of misplaced zeal and partisanship, but such is not the case. Confusion in the church results in an impossible situation: the church finds it difficult and even impossible to fulfill its Christ-given calling in the world. Such a church could just as well close its doors.

The possibility of such sins ought to be added incentive to seek the peace of Jerusalem (Ps. 122:6–9) and to strive earnestly for the unity of the Spirit (Eph. 4:1–3).

But the wisdom that is from above is first pure, then peaceable, gentle, and easy to be entreated (3:17)

I have explained the biblical concept of wisdom in connection with chapter 1:5–8. James speaks here of true wisdom from above that is to be sharply contrasted with earthly, sensual, and devilish wisdom. True wisdom is the gift of God, for if we lack it, we are to ask God for it. Centrally that wisdom is Christ (Prov. 8). It is then a gift that Christ merited for his people in his sufferings and death, and is graciously given to God's people by the Holy Spirit. Such wisdom is related primarily to our use of our tongues. They must be used wisely.

Wisdom is described by the use of many adjectives, for it takes many adjectives to describe it in all its riches and fullness.

The primary adjective is found in the expression "is first pure." "First" indicates that purity is most fundamental. Without pure wisdom, the other adjectives are impossible.

When the attribute of pure wisdom is connected to the use of the tongue, it is apparent that James refers to the inner principle of holiness in the believer that controls the tongue. The believer is still bothered greatly by his totally depraved nature. Sometimes that nature gets control of the tongue, and the tongue is then used to promote wisdom from below.

Although a man can be seen as wise by the kind of life he leads, wisdom from above is evident especially in the use of his tongue. In the company of God's people where he uses his tongue, his speech must be wise. Pure wisdom is such because the principle of the new man in Christ, which controls the tongue, is pure. The result is that the tongue is used to speak pure wisdom.

Purity is holiness. Wisdom from above is holy because it reflects God's speech in holy scripture. God's speech is always without fault, imperfection, and error. Wisdom found in us, coming from a pure heart, is also without fault, imperfection, and error, for it speaks the word of God.

It is a point that needs emphasis. Within the church of Christ many problems arise in the lives of the people of God: marital problems, problems with unruly children, mutual problems among the saints, problems in coping with sickness, suffering, sorrow, and other problems created by sin. Many, also within the church, attempt to solve these problems with human wisdom. They use psychological techniques that are intended to discover what makes a person act the way he does, counseling sessions in which a person subjects himself to psychical probing, and the latest books, of which there are hundreds, supposedly written by Christian counselors. True wisdom, however, is found only in the word of God, and ministers and elders in the church are fully equipped when they come to those with problems with the wise word of the scriptures.

True wisdom is also "peaceable." Wisdom that is pure brings peace. It brings peace to the troubled heart of the child of God who is disturbed by problems, and it also brings peace to the mutual relationships in which we are called to live. Nothing else can do that. Only God's word can bring peace to the troubled heart, not man's word.

Peace is the great gift of the grace of God, earned in the cross of Christ and given to God's people as their possession. The gift of peace cannot be found in the wicked. "There is no peace, saith the LORD, unto the wicked" (Isa. 48:22). Christ earned peace for his people by paying for their sins: "Having made peace through the blood of his cross, by him to reconcile all things unto himself" (Col. 1:20). Peace is therefore harmony with God. The heart of God and the hearts of the elect beat together. Peace is a blessing of covenantal fellowship with God. Wisdom from above creates peace, for those who have wisdom pursue peace.

True wisdom is also "gentle." Gentleness is a characteristic of a wise man that is closely related to serenity. The word comes from a verb (*eikō*) that means to yield. It is a characteristic of a wise man that he quickly yields to others. He yields to God first, for he knows that God, his heavenly Father, is in full control of his life and determines it in all its details. Yielding to God, he yields to others. He does not yield to others by permitting the glory of God to be disfigured or denied. He yields to others by refusing to insist on his own position or his notions regardless of any other considerations. He yields to others in the interests of peace.

Heavenly wisdom is also "easy to be entreated." A wise man with wisdom from Christ is approachable by anyone, be it a child, a poor man, or a man of little or no account. A wise man willingly and cheerfully is ready to do what is asked of him for the well-being of the church and the spiritual welfare of his fellow members. These three attributes—peaceable, gentle, and easy to be entreated—form one group.

All these things are contrary to our natural inclinations. Born out of selfishness and self-centeredness, we are quick to insist on our ideas and to defend with vigor our ways. We are quick to come to our own defense and to claim busyness as an excuse not to give help to others or to serve the church. All these tendencies breed arguments, confrontations, disputes, and disunity in the church, where there ought to be peace.

Full of mercy and good fruits, without partiality, and without hypocrisy

There is a second group of attributes that characterizes heavenly wisdom: they describe a wise man as "full of mercy and good fruits."

Mercy is a wonderful characteristic of the believer. A merciful child of God takes pity on others in misery, longs to be able to help them, and is not content until he has done what he can to relieve the suffering of others. A merciful person knows and has experienced the mercy of God toward him. In his abundant mercy God has seen the misery of his people, has freely given them Christ to deliver them, and makes them in Christ eternally happy and blessed. God does this to undeserving sinners according to his free purpose.

A wise man is full of good fruits and mercy. Good fruit is the expression of mercy. If one pities the suffering, he does something about it if his faith is genuine. God's mercy toward us carries on its tide an abundance of the good fruit of all the blessings of salvation. So the wise man possesses mercy that overflows in good fruits. It brings help and comfort to the miserable.

The word (*agathos*) translated as "good" means moral and ethical good. It is an expression of mercy that is according to the will and law of God. It is easy to interpret mercy as excusing of sin or overlooking in others what God despises. This is the position of many in our day. The execution of a murderer is viewed as cruel and unusual punishment that should be banned, even though God insists on it (Gen. 9:6). Mercy does not produce good fruit in a sinful world by excusing or overlooking sin, although it is done in the name of mercy.

Good fruit is a deed that serves the glory of God and the welfare of the saints.

"Without partiality" and "without hypocrisy" form a third group of attributes that characterize heavenly wisdom.

The one Greek word translated as "without partiality" means without judgment. The apostle considers this characteristic of a wise man to be as important as the other characteristics. One easily judges others. For example, he may say concerning a fellow member of the church, "Why should I help him? He brought his troubles on himself." Or, "He has ulterior motives in seeking my help; I don't trust him." Sometimes we even judge others by considering that one who should be the object of our concern has never showed mercy and love toward others. James condemns all evil judging of whatever sort it may be.

"Without hypocrisy" has the idea of genuineness. When one

is hypocritical, his outward conduct does not conform to his inner state of mind and heart. He appears outwardly pious and eager to do God's work, but inwardly he is grumbling and thinking to himself, "What a nuisance, what a pest this person is; what a miserable character to have to deal with." Such hypocrisy is not only abominable before God, but is also of no good in the church and is certainly not an expression of wisdom from above.

We are confronted in these verses with the characteristics of true wisdom. It is extremely difficult to be truly wise. We recall James' words, "If any of you lack wisdom, let him ask of God" (1:5).

And the fruit of righteousness is sown in peace of them that make peace (3:18)

The broader context in which this verse is found is, first, the general purpose of the entire letter James writes. James combats dead faith that is manifested in the church. There will always be those in the church who claim to have faith, but show no good works. Their faith is dead and without profit for the church. James' lengthy description of the tongue is intended to show how one with dead faith acts when he uses the tongue, and how a person with living faith uses the tongue.

Second, James concludes chapter 3 by contrasting a man who possesses wisdom from below and how he uses his tongue with a man who has wisdom from above and how he uses his tongue. Wisdom and proper use of the tongue characterize the man with true faith, but wisdom from below and an evil use of the tongue characterize a man with dead faith.

The conclusion of James' discussion of the tongue and its wise use contains a beautiful promise that ought to encourage God's people to make proper and wise use of their tongues.

The figure is of a farmer who goes to his field to sow seed. What grows is determined by the nature of the seed. If he sows wheat seed, he will have a harvest of wheat. If he sows thistles, he will have a harvest of thistles.

So in the church God's people are called to sow peace, and the harvest will be the wonderful fruit of righteousness.

The clause "of them that make peace" is three words in the Greek (*tois poiousin eirēnēn*). "Them that make" is one word, a participle in the dative case. In this context the dative case can be a dative of means or a dative of advantage. If it is the former, the translation ought to be "*by* them that make peace," that is, the fruit of righteousness is sown *by* them that make peace. If advantage is meant, the translation of the Authorized Version is correct: "*of* them that make peace." The meaning is that the fruit of righteousness benefits and blesses those who sow peace.

There is not a lot of difference in meaning between making "them that make" a dative of advantage or a dative of means. After all, the calling to make peace is the calling of the whole congregation. Every member must pray for the peace of Jerusalem (Ps. 122:6), and every member must strive to keep the unity of the Spirit in the bond of peace (Eph. 4:4). When each member seeks the peace of Jerusalem, the fruit of righteousness is the resulting blessedness of the entire congregation.

It is hard to know what the apostle has in mind here. My inclination is to accept the translation of the Authorized Version, but the other translation need not be excluded.

The wise man sows the seeds of peace when by a proper use of his tongue he brings peace to the congregation. When he works in the church in true wisdom, every word he speaks and every deed he performs are good seeds dropped into the soil of the church. They are seeds that will certainly bring forth fruit in harmony with the nature of the seed.

The fruit is righteousness. The meaning is not righteousness in the forensic sense, the imputed righteousness given in justification, but righteousness in the moral and ethical sense.

God is righteous in his own being. His righteousness is the attribute according to which all God's actions and deeds are in perfect harmony with his holiness. God created man in his own image, which included righteousness. Man possessed a nature that was holy, so that everything he did was in conformity with his holiness. When he lost the image through his sin, his entire nature became corrupt and totally depraved. Hence all man did and now does is contrary to the law of God; it is all unrighteous.

Righteousness is the moral and upright lives of those within the congregations as the fruit of the seeds of peace that are sown. This is an amazing statement and one that in the form it appears here is not frequently mentioned in scripture. The wise use of the tongue has many wonderful characteristics (v. 17). The fruit of that wise use of the tongue is peace. Peace in turn produces a righteous walk by the members of the churches.

We can see how this can be if we consider the opposite. Members in the congregations can and frequently do use their tongues for earthly wisdom, which is carnal, sensual, and devilish. The result is that the congregations are filled with discord, suspicion, distrust, enmity, strife, bitterness, and hatred. There is no good fruit in the sowing of such seeds. But a righteous walk by the members is the fruit of sowing the seeds of peace.

It all begins with the tongue. May we use our tongues for God's glory and the welfare of our fellow saints.

JAMES 4

Friendship with the World is Enmity with God

1. From whence come wars and fightings among you?
   come they not hence, even of your lusts that war in your
   members?
2. Ye lust, and have not: ye kill, and desire to have, and cannot obtain: ye fight and war, yet ye have not, because ye
   ask not.
3. Ye ask, and receive not, because ye ask amiss, that ye may
   consume it upon your lusts.
4. Ye adulterers and adulteresses, know ye not that the friendship of the world is enmity with God? whosoever therefore
   will be a friend of the world is the enemy of God.

James applies the possession of true faith to a new subject in
the first verses of chapter 4. Dead faith produces no fruit. Living
faith does. What kind of fruit does it produce? James will demonstrate this pointedly by applying the differences between these
two kinds of faith to the lives of the saints in the world.

The churches to which James writes were being torn to pieces
by strife and warfare. His emphasis on peace in the last verses of
chapter 3 indicates that. Now James turns specifically to the sin
of lack of peace in the churches. He analyzes this lack by pointing
first to its source and then by showing that at bottom is a spirit of
terrible worldliness that has crept into the churches.

The letter of James does not explicitly connect the possession of dead faith by some with the strife and bitterness that existed in the congregations, but this was probably the case. The inwardly corrupt life of dead faith surely leads to a mad pursuit of the things of this present time, to the exclusion of spiritual and heavenly things. The evil use of the tongue, itself an evidence of dead faith, brings about strife and war in the churches.

From whence come wars and fightings among you? come they not hence, even of your lusts that war in your members? Ye lust, and have not (4:1–2)

The words for "wars" and "fightings" are very strong, and both refer to pitched battles between two nations. The first word is a broad term for a war, and the latter is used for individual battles in a war, for example, World War II in distinction from the Battle of the Bulge. The use of these two strong words is sufficient to show what scripture thinks of the disputes, bickerings, charges, counter-charges, and quarrels so often found in the church. These disputes are the exact opposite of the peace that ought to be sown and that produces the fruit of righteousness.

As the sowing of peace results in congregations in which the members walk according to God's holy law, so lust results in fighting and strife.

While the Greek word (*hēdonē*) translated as "lusts" means pleasures, the Authorized Version's translation is correct, because the Greek text looks at the objects of lust rather than at lust itself. To lust is to crave something one does not have and may not have. Sometimes lust is used in a good sense to connote a strong desire for spiritual things, but much more frequently it is used to indicate a strong desire for those things that are contrary to God's word.

It is somewhat strange that James speaks of these lusts as warring "in your members." In the narrowest sense, the reference is to our bodies with its various members, but scripture uses the term in a broader sense as well. The term can also mean everything that belongs to the earthly side of our creation. It can therefore refer to our souls, as the power of our souls connect us with the physical creation around us, give us knowledge of it and dependence upon it, and give us the ability to make use of it. Paul spoke of "members" in this broader sense in Romans 7:23: "But I see another law in my members, warring against the law of my mind, and bringing me into captivity to the law of sin which is in my members."

The verb "war" means literally to carry on a campaign as a soldier. It includes all that belongs to a military campaign: the establishment of a base of operations, the camp in which soldiers lodge, the headquarters in which strategy is planned and from which commands issue, as well as the actual fighting. The earthly aspect of the soul uses the body to express itself, so when these lusts war in our members, they originate in our souls, express themselves in our bodies, and bring division and strife into the church.

Against what do these lusts make war? Do they war between themselves? Do they war against the church?

The answer is that these lusts that belong to the sinful and depraved nature war against the new man of regeneration, the principle of faith and holiness created by Christ's Spirit and by which the child of God in principle walks in true and living faith. It is a bitter, unrelenting battle that goes on within us.

Such an interpretation would agree with Paul's statement in Galatians 5:17: "For the flesh lusteth against the Spirit, and the Spirit against the flesh: and these are contrary the one to the other: so that ye cannot do the things that ye would." Paul also connected this internal and spiritual warfare with the same problem in the church that James addresses: "But if ye bite and devour one another, take heed that ye be not consumed one of another.

This I say then, Walk in the Spirit, and ye shall not fulfil the lust of the flesh" (vv. 15–16).

While James explains all this more fully in the verses that follow, I note here that the desire for pleasure is selfishness. This terrible sin is the reason one seeks personal advancement or indulgence in carnal pleasure at the expense of anything or anyone else. There is no love or concern for God, his word, or the church. Lust drowns everything else.

The strange part of it is that although the members of the church lust passionately for the things of this world and often struggle with unwavering commitment to attain their desires, they always fall short. This seems to be contrary to fact. A person who lusts after fornication can almost always attain his goal. A person who lusts after a beautiful house can usually have it, although he may have to go deeply into debt.

There are two reasons that it is possible to say, "Ye lust, and have not." The first is that many times God so determines the circumstances of a person's life that he cannot obtain that for which he lusts. He may passionately desire wealth, but God strikes him with cancer. The second reason one does not have those things for which he lusts is the nature of man: having them, man always wants more. He acquires a million dollars, but he is not satisfied. He has a home more than adequate for his needs, but he wants one larger and more beautiful. He has an excellent car, but he desires a new, larger, more powerful, and more expensive car. The more he has, the more he wants. He is never satisfied.

Ye kill, and desire to have, and cannot obtain (4:2)

It is somewhat difficult to explain why the clause "ye kill" is inserted here. It seems much too strong a word for the other words that James uses to describe the sins in the churches to which he writes. Commentators have suggested various solutions. One solution is to take an alternate reading that involves punctuation. It puts a period after the words "ye kill," separating these words from the rest of the text. Yet there is no evidence that actual murder was going on in the congregation. Others have suggested that the two expressions "ye kill" and "ye desire to have" must be taken together. Then the translation would be "ye murderously desire to have." This explanation is also unsatisfactory because it leaves the question, what is a murderous desire? Is it a desire that leads to murder? Is it a desire that even contemplates murder as the way to obtain one's desire? This too is highly unlikely.

It is better to take the expression as it stands, but to remember that killing does not always imply murder. Jesus reminds us that one who hates his brother has really committed murder (Matt. 5:21–24). One can and often does kill another person by a slanderous tongue, a sin to which James called attention in the preceding chapter. One can with his tongue ruin a man's reputation and bring such grief and misery to him and his family and make his life so wretched that he would prefer to die. To charge the saints to whom the letter is written with killing is not too strong a language, especially in light of the strong expression James uses to describe the wickedness of which the tongue is capable.

"Desire to have" means to be zealous for. The Greek word has a good connotation, but it also can be used to describe an evil desire. Paul used it in the bad sense in Romans 10:2, where he described his countrymen as having zeal, but not according to knowledge. To be zealous for something is to devote all one's efforts toward a certain goal because one considers it extremely important to obtain it. It is worth his time, his money, his energy, and his strongest efforts. It is a powerful word when it describes the object of our zeal to be ungodly.

The conclusion "ye cannot obtain" is directly parallel to "ye... have not" in the preceding clause.

Ye fight and war, yet ye have not, because ye ask not (4:2)

The apostle sums up what he said in verses 1 and 2. The same two words "fight" and "war" are repeated from verse 1. What is unique about this sentence is that there is an additional thought concerning the reasons for the fighting in the churches. It is as if James says, "Now we must ask why you do not acquire that for which you lust." The answer is, you do not pray. That is, you do not recognize God as the giver of everything you have. You do not live in conscious dependence on him.

Ye ask, and receive not, because ye ask amiss (4:3)

It seems contradictory that James says in verse 2, "Ye ask not," while here he affirms, "Ye ask." James is anticipating an objection from those to whom he writes. "But, James," they would respond, "we do pray." In awareness that those to whom he writes would come with the claim that they do pray, he responds, "Perhaps you do pray, but you ask amiss. That is your problem."

Here again James has the main theme of the epistle in mind. Those who had only dead faith went through the motions of prayer and left the impression with others that they prayed regularly. But one who truly prays can pray only by faith (Heb. 11:6). In the sense of the prayers that scripture requires and that proceed from living faith, these people with dead faith did not really pray at all.

"Amiss" in the Authorized Version is weaker than the Greek word (*kakos*), which means evil. "You ask evilly," James insists. Whether he had heard some of their prayers or whether the Holy Spirit who inspired the epistle determined that description of their prayers apart from James' own experience, we do not know. But the fact is that their petitionary prayers were wicked. They were displeasing in the sight of God. No wonder they did not receive what they asked.

If they really thought that God would answer their carnal prayers, this was an arrogant assumption that arose out of ignorance of what prayer is all about.

That ye may consume it upon your lusts (4:3)

What a sharp arrow James aims at our hearts with this expression!

The word translated as "lusts" is the same word as in verse 1, and can better be translated as "pleasures." The Greek word is in the dative case with the preposition *in*. Hence "in your pleasures" is the idea of the text.

This clause above can refer to one of two ideas. In connection with "ye ask amiss," it can mean that you ask and receive not, because you ask in order to consume it in your pleasures. If that is correct, the statement defines the purpose of your asking. The clause can also mean that you ask and receive not, because you "ask amiss" (evilly), that is, your asking is evil because your motive is to consume it in your pleasures. The second idea is what the text has in mind.

It is possible that one prays correctly from a formal point of view and may even ask for permissible things, but his motives are wrong. He asks for certain things from God only to seek his own pleasure in the world. The word "consumes" is very strong and means to squander by spending recklessly.

How frequently in prayer meetings I have heard prayers for a new house, for a safe trip on vacation, for a good grade on a looming exam, or for a better car. I know from personal experience that a person may even ask for an opportunity to serve in the office of elder or deacon—a seemingly proper prayer. But the motive is the enhancement of one's own pleasure, whether that is an increase in this world's goods or a higher position that will bring prestige. Outward correctness in prayer does not necessarily mean an inward, correct, spiritual motive. Our prayers can be and often are very carnal and selfish. James touches a raw nerve with his sharp condemnation of our prayers.

The positive, as scripture reminds us, is that when we pray we may and must ask for what will be for the advancement of the kingdom of our Lord Jesus Christ. And even then, we must recognize that we do not always know what advances God's kingdom and covenant, so that with our requests we learn to pray, "Thy will be done." What happens to us personally is of little account. The welfare of the kingdom of Christ is the important thing. So we must pray.

Ye adulterers and adulteresses (4:4)

It is evident from the whole passage, but particularly from this expression, that James is angry. No wonder, when one considers the seriousness of the sin. We do well to remember that the Holy Spirit is angry and condemns sin through James' writing.

Although some commentaries explain this expression as referring to literal adultery as the "pleasures" of which James speaks in verses 1–3, this is incorrect. It is true that those who professed faith and were living carnal lives were also guilty of adultery, but this is not what the text has in mind. Scripture frequently refers to sin, especially worldliness, as adultery. This was true in the old dispensation and it remains true in the new (Ezek. 16 and 23; Hosea 1–2). From a general viewpoint all men are guilty of adultery because of their sin in Adam. God established his covenant with Adam, which is pictured in marriage. Departure from God's precepts is a violation of God's covenant and therefore of marriage.

The text looks at our sins from the viewpoint that the church is the bride of Christ. She is married to Christ, and as Christ's bride she is called to live in faithfulness and holiness with her bridegroom. Such holiness presupposes an antithetical life of keeping oneself from the evils in this world. Therefore to make friends with the world is spiritual adultery.

James has been criticized for such sharp language, especially because in other places in the epistle he addresses the saints as brethren. But the sin of worldliness is found at large in the churches, especially in times of affluence, and scripture is insistent that the people of God must understand that materialism and worldliness are spiritual adultery.

Know ye not that the friendship of the world is enmity with God? whosoever therefore will be a friend of the world is the enemy of God (4:4)

Although at first glance it may seem as if the figure is changed from marriage to friendship, this is not so. Both are covenantal ideas. The relation between Christ and his people is a marriage relationship (Eph. 5:22–33), but that relationship is described as friendship. Abraham was called the friend of God. The covenant of grace is a bond of friendship between God and his elect people in Jesus Christ. The closeness of friendship is especially evident in the marriage relationship, and therefore friendship is a covenantal expression.

"Friendship" is a warm and intimate term. It is a bond of unity that binds two or more together psychologically. This bond is characterized by mutual love, respect, and happiness in the fellowship friends have. It includes the intimacy of sharing one's life, including one's thoughts, desires, joys, and sorrows. It is a willingness to do anything for a friend: "Greater love hath no man than this, that a man lay down his life for his friends" (John 15:13).

The relationship of friendship is also exclusive. While the relationship is exclusive between friends, this exclusivity is especially true of marriage. There is no room for a third party. No wife would tolerate her husband's saying to her, "I love so-and-so, but I love you more." This is what all those who teach a common love of God for mankind do. Those who attempt to hold in balance a universal love of God and a love for the elect speak of degrees of love: God loves all men, but he loves his people more.

God loves his people with a great and eternal love (Jer. 31:3). He loved them while they were yet sinners (Rom. 5:10). He loved them not because they were worthy of his love, but for his own sake (Deut. 7:6–8). God revealed his love for his people in the giving of his own Son to die for them (John 3:16; 1 John 4:16). In his love for his people he sovereignly takes them into the heavenly bond of marriage and makes them his friends.

In his love for us, God delights in us, rejoices in fellowship with us, and reveals to us all the secrets of his counsel and will (Gen. 18:17–19; Ps. 25:14), tells us all that is in his heart, and never does anything but the greatest good to us. We are thus the friends of God who are called to walk as God's friends in the world, to love him with our whole being, to rejoice in him, to bring to him our needs, our cares, our sorrows, and to find in him all blessedness for time and eternity.

The question the text addresses to the readers borders on divine puzzlement. "Is it actually true that you do not know that friendship with the world is enmity with God?" Friendship is exclusive. I cannot be a friend of two people who are themselves enemies and who hate each other. This is impossible.

The world is the enemy of God. It hates God with all its being. It seeks to destroy God and blot out his name from the creation. We cannot be a friend of God and a friend of the world.

If we are friends of the world, we seek the world's fellowship and find pleasure in sharing with the world its goals, treasures, and pleasures. We find joy in sharing the intimacies of friendship with those who hate God. This is impossible. If we are friends with the world, we become by that very fact enemies of God.

It appears as if present in the congregations were those who claimed to have faith, but did not have true faith and were worldly, carnal, and materialistic. Such conduct is a manifestation of dead faith. Such people are always present in the church of Christ. They are frequently antinomian: they want no part of the law, claim to need no law, and pay no attention to any law because they have faith.

Scripture gives a startling but powerful example of such spiritual adultery in 2 Chronicles 18 and 19. Jehoshaphat was a pious and godly king of Judah. Probably with the best of motives, Jehoshaphat made an alliance with Ahab, the ungodly king of the northern kingdom. On his return from Ahab, the prophet Jehu said to him, "Shouldest thou help the ungodly, and love them that hate the LORD? therefore is wrath upon thee from the LORD" (2 Chron. 19:2). And so it was, for Jehoshaphat's son married the daughter of Ahab. This wicked daughter, Queen Athaliah, killed all the royal seed and would have wiped out the line from which Christ came, except for the heroic rescue of one son by the wife of the good prophet Jehoiada (2 Chron. 22:11).

The text sharply calls all of us to self-examination. It defines in clear language the antithesis and our calling to live an antithetical life.

The Humility of Repentance

5. Do ye think that the scripture saith in vain, The spirit that dwelleth in us lusteth to envy?
6. But he giveth more grace. Wherefore he saith, God resisteth the proud, but giveth grace unto the humble.
7. Submit yourselves therefore to God. Resist the devil, and he will flee from you.

8. Draw nigh to God, and he will draw nigh to you. Cleanse your hands, ye sinners; and purify your hearts, ye double-minded.

9. Be afflicted, and mourn, and weep: let your laughter be turned to mourning, and your joy to heaviness.

10. Humble yourselves in the sight of the Lord, and he shall lift you up.

There is no question that verses 5–6 are very difficult to explain. The problems are three.

First, what is the precise scripture to which James refers in his question, "Do ye think that the scripture saith in vain?" It cannot refer to the next clause, for that clause is found nowhere in scripture. The reference must be to the last part of verse 6. But then, why are several other thoughts interjected without explanation?

Second, what is the meaning of "the spirit that dwelleth in us lusteth to envy?" The reference must be to the Holy Spirit, for he is said to dwell in us. But does the Holy Spirit lust to envy?

Third, what can be the relation between the last clause in verse 5 and the first clause in verse 6? There seems to be no connection between the Spirit that lusts to envy and he "giveth more grace."

These are the questions with which commentators struggle, and few agree on an interpretation. There is no need to enter into the many and varied interpretations, some of which are complex.

My interpretation follows Calvin for the most part.[1]

Two characteristics of James' epistle ought to be kept in mind as we seek to understand this passage. One is that James is profoundly rooted in the Old Testament scriptures and makes many passing and indirect references to the Old Testament, without specifically quoting them. Further, he writes to churches composed chiefly of Jews who are well acquainted with these scriptures.

---

1 Calvin, *Catholic Epistles*, 331–33.

In addition, it is a characteristic of James, very evident here, that he frequently jumps from one thought to another without clearly showing the connection between thoughts. It seems as if there is no connection, and yet, thinking about the meaning, one sees that the connection is real and important. So it is here.

The text is a powerful addition to James' scathing remarks about the impossibility of friends of God being friends of the world.

Do ye think that the scripture saith in vain? (4:5)

There can be no question that the scripture to which James refers is quoted in the last part of verse 6. The insertion of other thoughts between the reference to scripture and the actual quoting of scripture cannot alter that truth. The question is rhetorical, and James expects a negative answer to it: "You do not think that scripture speaks without purpose, do you?" To be "in vain" is to be meaningless, without significance, useless, and of no account.

One could get the impression that the scriptures do speak in vain, if he would judge by those in the congregations who claim to believe the scriptures, but whose conduct belies what the scriptures teach. These scriptures are the word of God, and God does not say anything that is meaningless or of no value. God always means what he says, whether we take his word seriously or not.

The spirit that dwelleth in us lusteth to envy (4:5)

The reference is certainly to the Holy Spirit as the Spirit of our Lord Jesus Christ. He is said to "dwell in us," an expression that cannot describe the human spirit, but is a common description in scripture of the Holy Spirit. Yet it is difficult to ascribe to the Holy Spirit lust toward envy.

"Lusteth to envy" can be interpreted as an adverbial expression. The rather strange expression "to envy" can have the meaning of enviously or jealously.[2] Then "lusteth" would be translated as "yearning for" in the good sense of the word. To apply jealousy to God is not foreign to scripture. The second commandment teaches as much.

Nevertheless, I prefer to take this entire sentence as another rhetorical question: "Does it seem to you that the scriptures say in vain? Does the Holy Spirit lust to envy?" Before James actually quotes the scripture, he is determined that those to whom he writes take seriously what scripture says. He says, "You know what the Holy Spirit says in the text I am about to quote. The Holy Spirit inspired the scriptures. You claim to believe the scriptures. Do you really believe that the way you live is supported by the scriptures? Here is what the scriptures say."

But he giveth more grace (4:6)

The interpretation above explains the following statement as well. The sentence is introduced by the adversative conjunction "but." The point is that it is wrong to say that the scriptures ascribe envious lusts to the Spirit. Who would dare to do that? Contrary to that, the scriptures say that the Holy Spirit gives more grace.

This is the answer to all antinomianism: the Spirit sanctifies (Rom. 8:1–10). The Holy Spirit is the Spirit of Christ who supplies the believer with an abundance of grace. John speaks of receiving out of Christ's fullness "grace for grace" (John 1:16). Grace comes to us as the waves on the shore of the ocean: one wave follows another. So God through the Spirit sends grace wave on wave, sufficient for every need. He does the opposite of what the people who received this letter were implying that he does.

---

2 Robertson, *Word Pictures in the New Testament,* 51.

Wherefore he saith, God resisteth the proud, but giveth grace unto the humble (4:6)

Now comes the scriptural passage to which the apostle calls attention in the first part of verse 5. While not a direct quotation, the reference is to Proverbs 3:34: "Surely he scorneth the scorners: but he giveth grace unto the lowly." Peter used the same words in 1 Peter 5:5.

The text uncovers the deep sin of pride in those who make friends with the world. The text does not say this in so many words, but the whole train of thought compels us to find this meaning in the apostle's argument. Nor is this truth difficult to understand. Not only is it true that pride underlies all sin, but here particularly, in the sin of worldliness, pride raises its head.

Pride is the ugly sin that makes a person set himself up as superior to others. Ultimately in pride a man considers himself superior to God, monstrous thought that it is. Pride was the sin of Adam and Eve in paradise. God had told them what was pleasing to him. Man said, in effect, "We will determine for ourselves what is right and wrong. God has no right to tell us." If one ascends to those heights of pride so that he sets himself above God, he has no difficulty setting himself above his fellowmen. Thus in the church he feigns faithfulness to the cause of Christ, while he actually makes friends with the world.

God resists those who do this. To resist means to set in battle array against. God fights against those who are proud. When men are proud in the absolute sense, God frustrates them at every turn of their way, leads them down paths at the end of which is destruction, and causes them to experience his curse and his wrath. The passage in Proverbs 3 to which James refers is preceded by a verse that speaks of God's curse on the house of the wicked and his blessing on the habitation of the just (v. 33).

Pride is also frequently found in the lives of God's people, for their sinful natures are full of pride. Although they are made humble in the work of regeneration, they must constantly fight the awful sin of pride that is always present with them. God resists them too when they act or speak proudly. He may turn his back to them when they enter his courts of prayer. He may chastise them in his anger. The Spirit withdraws from their consciousness, so that they no longer know God's favor. But God's resistance of his people is always to restore and save. He breaks their proud boasts and brings them low, so that they may again know his favor and love.

God gives grace to the humble. That grace is God's unmerited favor whereby we have friendship with God, enjoy the blessedness of being in his covenant, and know his favor and love.

Humility is an attribute of a Christian who lives out of the principle of regeneration. Our Lord was humble above all. Scripture repeatedly calls attention to his humility. He washed his disciples' feet (John 13:1–17). He humbled himself to the death of the cross for us (Phil. 2:6–8) so that we could be delivered from our vain boasting and all the sins that follows from it. The mind of Christ that led him to the cross must be in us (Phil. 2:1–5).

If humility characterizes our lives, we live in the profound consciousness of God's glory, in contrast with which we have no glory in our nothingness and unworthiness. We live moment by moment in humble dependence on God, knowing that we are saved by grace and receive all things only out of his hand, and in the church of Christ, we esteem others better than ourselves (Phil 2:3).

Humility is not false modesty that leads one to refuse to do anything of worth in the church and kingdom of Christ. Some are falsely modest when they refuse to serve in positions in the church to which they are appointed. They say they are not qualified, or they are afraid to accept these appointments because that would manifest pride. Others show false modesty by an outward show of piety, which is actually a cover for a proud heart. Still others claim that true humility is lack of assurance.

Humility is a profound consciousness of the greatness of God and a desire for his glory. It is an awareness of our own unworthiness and spiritual inability to do anything pleasing to God. Hence it is a conscious life of dependence on God and a willingness to serve him in whatever station and calling in life to which he calls us. A humble man says with Paul, "I can do all things through Christ which strengtheneth me" (Phil 4:13). It is an essential ingredient for friendship with God.

The main and controlling thought of James in verses 5–10 is still the implied admonition to be friends of God. In speaking of our calling to be friends of God, James is almost certainly thinking of what he said in 2:23 in his description of living faith: "The scripture was fulfilled which saith, Abraham believed God, and it was imputed unto him for righteousness: and he was called the Friend of God."

Friendship with God, the essence of the covenant between God and his people, is possible only when we live humbly with God. God is infinitely great and we are not only less than specks of dust, but also sinners. That we can be friends of God is an astonishing wonder that fills the soul of the child of God with awe.

In verses 7–10 James specifically defines the fruit of humility. He does so in a series of ten admonitions, which are sometimes called the ten commandments of James. Central to these admonitions is "draw nigh to God." To be a friend of God is to live in fellowship with him. This requires coming close to him.

The admonition to draw nigh to God is an antithetical calling. Negatively it means to resist the devil. Its positive calling is to submit to God. In this way verses 7–10 are connected to the warning in verse 4.

Submit yourselves therefore to God (4:7)

The Greek word (*hupotassō*) translated as "submit" means to arrange under or to arrange in order, as a company of soldiers arranges itself in ranks under its officer. Applied to our relationship to God, it means to arrange the whole of our lives in such a way that everything we do is in conformity with God's will. To submit to God is to submit to his commandments as the rule of our lives. To submit to God is also to submit to his will, whatever he may be pleased to send us in our lives. Sickness, suffering, trouble, disappointment, grief, and pain—all are sent by God. Only in the way of submitting to him can we experience friendship with God.

Resist the devil, and he will flee from you (4:7)

To resist the devil is the negative part of our antithetical calling. We cannot submit to God if we do not resist the devil. To resist him is to draw near to God. To fail to resist the devil is to be friends with the world, for the devil seeks to make us friends with the world, that we may be friends of him.

The name given to the devil in this passage is *diabolos*, that is, slanderer. To slander is to speak evil untruths about someone. The devil slandered the saints in Old Testament times. He came to God and slandered Job (Job 1:9–11; 2:4–5). He also slandered the saints who died and went to heaven. He claimed legal authority over them and said that they had no right to be in heaven because the blood of atonement had not been shed (Rev. 12:10).

What is worse, the devil slanders God to the men on the earth. He slandered God to Eve when he contradicted God's command not to eat of the forbidden tree, and he claimed that the command was rooted in God's fear that man would become like him (Gen. 3:4–5). He still slanders God. He does so when he attempts to persuade men that happiness comes from earthly treasures and carnal pleasures. He slanders God when he claims that God is not the creator of all things, but that things come into existence by blind chance. He is the great slanderer, and men are eager and willing to listen to his slanders.

The devil is a very powerful adversary. On his side he has millions of demons who do his bidding. He has vast power because of the high position he once held among the angels. He has persuaded the whole world to join him in his efforts to destroy the cause of God. He has access to our minds and wills through our sinful and depraved natures. He is utterly implacable in his opposition to God and his Christ, and to those who represent God's cause in the world. He is utterly ruthless in his attacks.

We are called to resist him at every turn of the way. This is a formidable task, for we are weak and frail, very much intent on following his suggestions and slanders, and inclined with the whole of our natures to be on his side in his opposition to God. We are totally unable to succeed in this calling to resist him. It is really a miracle that there is a church in this world that is faithful to God.

We must not forget that James speaks of true and living faith. True faith unites us to Christ and gives us the life of Christ. By that faith we believe that Christ did battle with Satan all his life and on the cross. In this battle he crushed the head of Satan and made him powerless. Faith in Christ believes that Christ did this for us, his people, and that by Christ's strength we are stronger than Satan.

The weapon we use as our faith comes to expression in our lives is the word of God, a powerful weapon that Satan cannot withstand. With that word Christ sent Satan scurrying away (Matt. 4:1–11). Paul referred to that word of God as every piece of our armor and even as our offensive weapons in our spiritual battle (Eph. 6:10–17). A true and living faith is the victory that overcomes the world (1 John 5:4). When we stand in our own strength, we stand in the pitiful strength of our sinful natures. When we stand in faith, we stand in the strength and power of Christ. Wielding the weapons of faith in the word of God, we can be sure Satan will be defeated. This is God's promise to us.

Such victory does not mean that Satan will not come again to test our spiritual mettle, but it does mean that when we face him with the word of God on our lips and in our minds, his temptations have no power. Even at death's door, when Satan would have us crumble in overwhelming doubt while he sneeringly reminds us of our many sins, we have scripture to ward off his fiendish lies.

When we fall into sin, as so often we do, we have the victory of the cross to which we flee in humble confession.

Draw nigh to God, and he will draw nigh to you (4:8)

The admonition with which verse 8 begins is the central admonition of this section. It is the positive side of our antithetical calling. It is the only way to be a friend of God.

In this expression and the admonitions that follow, the text indicates how deeply rooted in the Old Testament scriptures James and those to whom he writes were.

Adam drew near to God in Eden when he met God in the cool of the day (Gen. 1:28–30; 2:16–17; 3:8). But Adam could no longer do so when he disobeyed God's command. The patriarchs drew near to God in all their wanderings when they built altars to the Lord (Gen. 13:18). The patriarchs were conscious that their drawing near to God was possible only through the blood of atonement.

From Sinai until the captivity, drawing near to God meant going to the tabernacle and temple. The temple was the place God chose to dwell in the midst of his people, and to the temple

Israel came to draw near to God. But the Israelites could not come very close to God, because although sacrifices pointed ahead to the coming of Christ, sacrifices could not take away sin, and the Aaronitic priesthood, the holy place, the veil, and the altar of burnt offering kept them at arm's length from God.

Many psalms express the truth of drawing near to God. "When shall I come and appear before God?" (Ps. 42:2). Israel's joy was evident when they sang, "With joy I heard my friends exclaim, Come, let us in God's temple meet" (Psalter 348:1, a versification of Ps. 122:1). Sometimes it was with fear that they contemplated going to God: "LORD, who shall abide in thy tabernacle? who shall dwell in thy holy hill?" (Ps. 15:1). Sometimes the swelling throngs on their way to the temple would sing as they traveled, "How amiable are thy tabernacles, O LORD of hosts! My soul longeth, yea, even fainteth for the courts of the LORD: my heart and my flesh crieth out for the living God…They go from strength to strength, every one of them in Zion appeareth before God…For a day in thy courts is better than a thousand. I had rather be a doorkeeper in the house of my God, than to dwell in the tents of wickedness" (Ps. 84:1–9). How the Old Testament saints loved to sing of their longing to be in the presence of God!

All this was fulfilled in the new dispensation. Christ's body is the real temple of God (John 2:21). In Christ the fullness of the Godhead dwells bodily (Col. 1:19; 2:9), and the church is Christ's body (1 Cor. 12:27). We are now as close to God as it is possible to be.

To come to God is to enter into covenantal fellowship with God through Jesus Christ. God came to us in Christ and brought us through Christ's work into fellowship with him. It is now our calling to draw nigh to God, but to do so through Christ, to whom we belong.

To draw near to God is to enter into conscious fellowship

with God; to say with David, "I have set the LORD always before me: because he is at my right hand, I shall not be moved" (Ps. 16:8). We live and walk in the consciousness of his presence. We know and enjoy his favor and love. We live in complete dependence upon him, looking always to him for strength, comfort in our sorrows, help in temptations, and deliverance from evil. These times of being near to God are the best moments of our lives. They can and do come, sometimes in the quietness of our inner chambers, sometimes in the hustle and bustle of life, sometimes in his house, and sometimes in moments of intense grief and suffering.

We know God's favor and love, for when we draw nigh to him, he draws nigh to us. God has drawn nigh to us in the person of our Lord Jesus Christ. When we are commanded to come to Christ, we know that we cannot come to Christ unless God draws us (Matt. 11:28; John 6:37; 44–45). So that we may know the blessedness of being with God, he draws us to him through Christ in such a way that we draw nigh to God himself. And drawing nigh to him, then and only then do we enjoy God's favor and love.

Cleanse your hands, ye sinners; and purify your hearts, ye double-minded (4:8)

Although James calls the members of the churches to which he writes brethren, here he does not hesitate to call them "sinners." This may seem harsh to some, but it is entirely in keeping with the scathing condemnation of verse 4. To promote a false faith is a terrible sin, and the sin was found in those to whom the letter is written. The word "sinners" applies.

The terms "cleanse" and "purify" are Old Testament language, for Israel's laws and traditions included laws for cleansing: the washing of hands and sacrifices. (Matt. 15:2; Mark 7:2–3).

Though cleansing was a part of drawing near to God in the old dispensation, it remains fundamentally true in the new dispensation. The principle has not changed. The God of Israel was a holy God; sinners might not approach him, for sin cannot be tolerated in his sight. Washing the hands was a symbol of purification from sin in order to appear before God. Aaron and the priests had to wash their hands and their feet before they appeared before God (Ex. 30:19–21).

The second admonition in verse 8, to purify your hearts, refers to spiritual and inner cleansing. To have pure hearts is to be sanctified. The children of God are washed clean in the blood of Christ. That blood of Christ is the only cleansing power for sin, for the blood of Christ is the perfect sacrifice for sin.

The text does not mean to imply that sanctification is man's work. It is not and cannot be man's work. But it does mean that the sinner who desires to draw near to God must do so in the name of Christ, taking hold for himself of Christ's perfect sacrifice.

This was true already in the Old Testament. When the priests were commanded to wash their hands and their feet to appear in God's presence, they washed themselves in preparation for and in connection with the sacrifices they were to offer for their own sins and for the sins of the people. By clinging to the cross as their only hope of cleansing, God's people are commanded to fight against sin in their own lives by the power of the cross of Christ. Thus the command to cleanse their hearts is entirely appropriate.

A man's heart is the moral center of his entire nature, body and soul. The heart is the organic seed of man's nature as a whole: of soul, mind, will, and body. If the heart is pure, the entire man is pure; but if the heart is corrupt, the whole man is wicked.

The people of God are addressed as "double-minded" or literally as "double-souled." Actually this is impossible, for no man has two souls. But morally and practically it is exactly what ails us. We have two minds and two wills. We halt between two opinions. We love God and we love the world. We desire heaven's treasures, but we have not escaped the powerful attraction of earthly treasures. We enjoy the company of saints, but we seek also the companionship of sinners. We desire forgiveness of sins, but we cherish our sins and secretly hope God will not deliver us from such pleasurable activities. Paul expressed the same idea in Romans 7:7–24. "The good that I would I do not: but the evil that I would not, that I do" (v. 19).

However, we must not picture the situation as if two principles war in us with the outcome of the war uncertain. We must not view the struggle with double-mindedness as a hopeless battle. In Romans 7:22 Paul spoke of the victory that is surely ours. The principle of holiness in us is Christ in us by his Spirit. We have the victory through the power of the cross, and we gain the victory when we hold to that cross as our only help. The victory we experience is already in this life when we seek forgiveness for our sins and strength to love God by faith in Christ's perfect sacrifice. With this sacrifice of Christ as our only strength, we can and do draw nigh to God.

Be afflicted, and mourn, and weep: let your laughter be turned to mourning, and your joy to heaviness (4:9)

The three expressions "be afflicted," "mourn," and "weep" form a progression.

The word translated as "be afflicted" comes from a Greek word (*talaipōreō*) that means to feel wretched, afflicted, and miserable. This is the only passage in scripture where the word is found, although it is common in the Septuagint and in classical Greek. The Authorized Version has captured the meaning.

The Greek word (*pentheō*) translated as "mourn" usually refers to an inward state of sorrow that does not necessarily manifest itself outwardly. It frequently is used in connection with the loss of a loved one.

The Greek word (*klaiō*) translated as "weep" refers both in Greek and in English to an outward shedding of tears and wrenching sobs as a manifestation of an inward sorrow of heart before God for our sin.

James admonishes the saints to feel wretched, to mourn in sorrow over their sins, and to weep tears because of their sins against the most high majesty of God. There is only one way to go to the cross of Christ and find their holiness in it. It is the way of sorrow for sin and repentance.

It is always characteristic of people who possess dead faith outwardly to worship God and to confess the need of the cross. The scriptures, in contrast, speak of a broken spirit and a contrite heart. There is not in all scripture a more powerful description of God's disgust with outward worship than in Isaiah 1:10–15. God castigated Judah for outward lip service and told them in blazing fury that he wished they would quit their sacrifices, for the stink of them was unbearable, and that they should forget the celebration of their feast days, for he will pay no attention to them. If they pray, he would slam the door of heaven in their faces and not listen to them.

Still today God abhors formal worship. When we sing the songs of Zion and have no sense of the words we sing, when we pray and are thinking about earthly cares, when we listen to a sermon with only half an ear while our minds are actively engaged in enjoying the pleasures of the flesh, and when we reluctantly put money in the collection plate, such worship is worse than no worship at all.

How often did not the prophets berate Israel and Judah for the worship of lip service. That word of God is still applicable today. This is what James has in mind: we must come to God in the name of Christ; we must come to Christ with broken spirits and contrite hearts. The path to Calvary is wet with the tears of shame and contrition. The eyes that can see Calvary's cross are blurred with the tears of deep sorrow for sin. To abandon ourselves, to throw away the trash of all our works, and to fall naked and bleeding in abject grief—that is the way to the cross. There is no other way.

James does not mean that we may never be happy. Paul charged the Philippians to rejoice always (Phil. 4:4). The laughter of Christians is the outburst of joy that comes with knowing they are saved by grace, although they are wretched and unworthy sinners. Christians rejoice in the Lord. That kind of rejoicing comes only after sorrow and repentance.

There is no room for silly giggling, for ribald laughter, and for the joy found in the pleasures of sin. Solomon says that it is better to go to the house of mourning than to enter the halls of feasting (Eccl. 7:2).

The way to the cross is one of mourning, because only when we see ourselves as nothing can we see Christ as everything. To go to Christ, and through him to God, is to see that we have all things only in Christ our Lord and never in ourselves.

Humble yourselves in the sight of the Lord, and he shall lift you up (4:10)

The connection between this verse and the foregoing is obvious. To humble ourselves before the face of the Lord sums up the other admonitions that precede it. To draw nigh to God by cleansing our hands and purifying our hearts, to be afflicted and mourn and weep, to turn our laughter to mourning and our joy into heaviness—all these are aspects of humbling ourselves before God.

We must humble ourselves in the sight of the Lord. There is an outward humility that includes weeping. Some people are able to turn the tears off and on at will and give a vivid and per-suasive demonstration of their profound inner sorrow by copious weeping. But it means nothing. There are also tears of remorse, but these tears express only the sorrow that we have to suffer for the consequences of our sins, not sorrow for the sins themselves.

To humble ourselves in the sight of the Lord is to be con-sciously in his presence. In our spirits we consciously enter God's throne room in prayer. We come into the presence of the Lord. He is the creator of all and the sovereign ruler of his creation. He demands his creatures to obey him. But we have sinned against him. Daring to come to the sovereign Lord in all the glory of his holiness is an act of spiritual courage that is possible only in the name of our Christ. Before him we confess our sins. We express to him who knows the heart our anguish because of our sins. Our tears tell outwardly the story of the pain and wretchedness that we know because of the magnitude of the sins that we commit. There is no room in the presence of the living God for hypocrisy, outward shows of humility, tears that mean nothing, and pious protestations of our good intentions.

"He shall lift you up" draws a stirring picture. Entering God's presence, we fall on our faces in shame and consternation. We dare not lift up our heads (Luke 18:13). But the Lord, who knows our hearts, reaches down from his high and lofty seat on the throne of the universe and takes us by the shoulders to set us on our feet. He puts his hand under our chins and causes us to look into his face. There we see great and eternal love, compassion for us in our misery, and a firm determination to deliver us from our miserable condition.

God does this through Christ who has paid for all these sins of which we are so ashamed. He gives us his Spirit in our hearts to assure us that he loves us, has taken away all our sins through his blood, and is doing much to bring us to heaven where we will see him face to face. He calms our alarms and brings laughter instead of mourning. He does this already in this life, and will make it perfect when he takes us to heaven.

Another Warning against Speaking Evil

11. Speak not evil one of another, brethren. He that speaketh evil of his brother, and judgeth his brother, speaketh evil of the law, and judgeth the law: but if thou judge the law, thou art not a doer of the law, but a judge.
12. There is one lawgiver, who is able to save and to destroy: who art thou that judgest another?

As it characteristic of James' letter, the connection between these two verses is not easy to discover. It may be that James has finished the subject begun in 4:1, and now he turns to another subject. Yet there are some connections.

The first connection is between the admonition not to speak evil of our fellow saints and the lengthy description of the power of the tongue in 3:1–12. Verse 11 then warns once again against the evil use of our tongues. If this is so, we have reason to pause and consider how important James considers use of our tongues to be, if we truly have living faith.

It is also possible that James reaches back to his sharp condemnation of those in the churches who have made friends with the world and lost the friendship of God. If we are truly friends of God, we live in covenantal fellowship with him. To live in covenantal fellowship with God is to live in covenantal fellowship with our fellow saints. Speaking evil of them makes covenantal fellowship with them impossible.

There is also a possible connection with the immediately preceding verses. The humility required of us to draw nigh to God characterizes our relationships with fellow saints. Christ's humility is the mind that ought to be in us when we consider others better than ourselves (Phil 2:1–8).

Speak not evil one of another, brethren (4:11)

"Speak evil" is a translation of the Greek word *katalaleō*, which means speak against. The Authorized Version is a commentary on the word, although a correct one. The admonition with which the text warns the saints is the violation of the ninth commandment. To speak against someone is to run someone down, to degrade him in the minds of others, and to rob a person of his good name and reputation. It is to speak this way about someone whether what we say is rumor, truth, or slander. The ninth commandment makes no distinctions.

There is always a subtle and hidden motive behind our evil speaking. We speak evil of others in an attempt to make them small to make ourselves big. It is a wicked attempt to leave the impression that we are better than the one of whom we speak, and that we would never be guilty of such things as others do.

While the ninth commandment forbids us to commit this sin in our relationships to our neighbors, here the warning is limited to the church of Christ. Suddenly James switches his address by laying aside his charge that the members of the churches are composed of adulterers and adulteresses and speaks to them as brethren (and by implication the women as sisters). We must not think that in verse 4 of this chapter James speaks to one segment of the congregations that is guilty of the sins he condemns, but that here he speaks to another and better part of the churches. The preaching is never addressed to one part of the congregation. The people of God are all sinners and saints in their lives in the world. They are brethren who commit the sins of friendship with the world, and though they can be called spiritual adulterers, yet they are brethren. Such is the life of the Christian in the body of this death.

The church, in spite of its many sins, is the elect of God, redeemed in the blood of the cross, saved, sanctified, and destined to live in glory. It is the apple of God's eye, his beloved, his bride of whom God speaks only good. Shall we speak against those who shout, "If God be for us, who can be against us" (Rom. 8:31)? Shall we then speak evil against those of whom God speaks good? You say, "Yes, but they are such sinners." Yes, of course. Doesn't God know that better than we? But God speaks of them as they are in Christ, and so must we.

He that speaketh evil of his brother, and judgeth his brother (4:11)

James uses a hendiadys in this expression. He means that he that speaks evil of his brother also judges his brother.

The text does not mean that we may not condemn as wrong any conduct by fellow saints. In the next chapter James calls us to confess our faults to one another and to pray for one another, which implies that we are conscious of own sins and the sins of others (5:16).

Nor does James encourage us to overlook sin. This is a modern theory that refuses to speak of sin, but takes a good attitude toward the most awful sins, approves of them, and even encourages them. Parents will sometimes do this with their children, for they cannot think that their children can do wicked things. Especially in the church, sin is overlooked when heresy arises. Although we know that heresy is being taught in the church, we will not condemn it, for we think we must be tolerant of such doctrinal aberrations. True friendship is interpreted to mean covering up sin and excusing it. James has nothing of this in mind, or he would be breaking other admonitions in his epistle.

We judge our brethren when we speak against them. We pass sentence on an individual, and that sentence is always condemnatory. We judge that this one of whom we speak is a sinner who does not confess his sins. Our opinion is that the man (or woman) lies outside the pale of the redeemed. He or she is not of the household of faith, not a member of the family of God, not a member of the body of Christ. He or she is an unbeliever much worse than ourselves. It is all a deadly evil.

We would never want anyone to speak of us as we speak of others. We would desire someone to rush to our defense when he is a witness of such speech. And if what someone said is true, we would want them to say it to us, not to others.

We cannot judge, for if we speak against someone and thus judge him, we claim to know the heart, which is something we cannot know. Some in the church live outwardly exemplary lives, but they do not have true faith. Others fall into some grievous sin, but they repent in dust and ashes.

James echoes the words of our Lord, "Judge not, that ye be not judged" (Matt. 7:1).

Speaketh evil of the law, and judgeth the law (4:11)

One who speaks against his brother and thus judges his brother speaks evil against the law and judges the law.

What scripture says here may sound very strange. How can speaking against our fellow saints be speaking against God's law? We must remember that the text does not refer to bare law, but to what James calls "the perfect law of liberty" (1:25), the "royal law" (2:8), that is, the law of the kingdom of heaven, or "the law of liberty" (2:12). This is the law of God fulfilled by Christ's perfect work on the cross for his people, and therefore a law written in the hearts of God's people, so they are able to keep that law.

The law of God summons us as children of our Father in heaven to love him and to love those who are of the family in

Jesus Christ. To speak against fellow saints is to say that the law does not apply to us and is no good. By speaking against them we put them outside the family of God and speak against the law. If, for example, with our children in the car, we exceed the speed laws and justify our conduct, we teach them that we do not agree with the law or that the law does not apply to us. So when we speak against a fellow saint, we say that the law of God has no importance for us and does not apply to us.

When we speak evil against our fellow saints, we do even worse, for we speak evil against the law of liberty in our fellow saints. We condemn the work of Christ in fulfilling the law for our brothers and sisters and deny that we are bound by the law as Christ fulfilled it for us.

James has a way of making us squirm with shame as we hear what he has to say about our conduct.

But if thou judge the law, thou art not a doer of the law, but a judge (4:11)

The construction James uses underscores the truth that in judging the law, we are not doers of the law. The sentence is composed of the if-clause, "if thou judge the law," and the conclusion, "thou art not a doer of the law, but a judge." If the if-clause is true, and it is, the conclusion necessarily follows.

Those who judge others are sinners who put themselves above the law, for one who judges the law has superiority over it. They condemn in others what they condone in themselves. They see others' sins clearly but are blind to their own sins. One tries to cast the speck out of his brother's eye, while he does not know that he has a splinter in his own eye.

What James says here describes antinomianism. Antinomians, always a plague in the church, are against the law and speak against the law. They excuse their violation of the ninth commandment on the grounds that the law has no claim on them, for they are freely justified in Christ's blood. They are the ones in the church who have dead faith.

Yet let us not try to evade the accusation of the text, for we are all guilty of speaking against our fellow saints. It follows that we are not doers of the law, but judges. One cannot be a doer of the law and a judge at the same time, for one who judges the law claims the law does not apply to him. If he does not do that theologically, as an antinomian does, he does it by his violation of the law. Then he becomes a judge of the law and not a doer. One who lives out of true faith in Christ loves God's law and joyfully and willingly keeps it.

There is one lawgiver, who is able to save and to destroy (4:12)

One who judges another judges the law, and one who takes it upon himself to judge the law acts as a lawgiver. Only a lawgiver has the right to judge the law. Thus James drives home the seriousness of the sin of judging others. One who judges the law takes the place of God. God is the supreme lawgiver because he is the creator and sustainer of all things. He has the right to determine how every creature must glorify him. That determination of God is the law for every creature, including man.

God alone can save and destroy. He has the right to save whom he wills and to destroy whom he wills. Ordinarily we would expect a statement here that would read something like this: "He is the one who can reward those who keep the law and destroy those who break that law." But that would be only half of what the apostle says. All men break God's law and all men come under the divine sentence of destruction. This means that some are saved, even though they are lawbreakers. They are eternally chosen to be God's people and have been redeemed by Christ, for whom Christ paid the penalty for their lawbreaking. They are sovereignly called out of the darkness of sin and death into fellowship with God and everlasting life.

There is indirect proof here that God does not save those who are worthy of being saved because of something they did. The saved ones are those whom God for his name's sake determined to save. It is the right of the supreme lawgiver to save whom he wills and for reasons known only to him.

Who art thou that judgest another? (4:12)

This rhetorical question is emphatic, "Thou, who art thou that judge another?" Some manuscripts have "neighbor" instead of "another." Earlier James spoke of the mutual relationships among the saints and of brothers' judging other brothers. Although this is the emphasis of the text, it has broader implications. We are to love our neighbors as ourselves. We show our love for our neighbors by keeping the ninth commandment: "Thou shalt not bear false witness against thy neighbor." But if we cannot even keep the ninth commandment in our lives in the church with the family of God, how shall we ever keep it in relation to our neighbors?

James says, "Who do you think you are when you take it upon yourself to judge another?" The implied question is, "Do you think you are God?"

We must rid ourselves of this terrible sin within the company of the saints. We must exercise what is often called the judgment of love. We must judge our fellows saints to be children of God. Only when they sin and refuse to confess their sins, even after the discipline of the church, do we refrain from considering them brothers. But even then we may not speak evil of them, but should rather seek their repentance.

Living in Submission to God's Will

13. Go to now, ye that say, To-day or to-morrow we will go
    into such a city, and continue there a year, and buy and
    sell, and get gain:
14. Whereas ye know not what shall be on the morrow. For
    what is your life? It is even a vapour, that appeareth for a
    little time, and then vanisheth away.
15. For that ye ought to say, If the Lord will, we shall live, and
    do this, or that.
16. But now ye rejoice in your boastings: all such rejoicing is
    evil.
17. Therefore to him that knoweth to do good, and doeth it
    not, to him it is sin.

It is difficult if not impossible to find any connection between
this section and the preceding context. It seems as if James simply turns to another weakness in the congregations to which he
addresses his general theme of true and living faith versus dead faith.

This passage has a vivid character that makes us think that the
author is taking an example directly from the congregations. We
know from 2:1 and 5:1–6 that there were rich and poor in the
congregations. But it seems that the wealthy men were not the
benefactors that they should have been. This is clear from 5:1–6.
There may have been a class of Jewish merchants in the churches
to which James writes.

**Go to now, ye that say, To-day or to-morrow we will go into
such a city, and continue there a year, and buy and sell, and get
gain (4:13)**

James says, "Stop a moment in your busy lives and consider
what I have to say." With that he begins a new section.

Picture the scene. A wealthy Jewish merchant is in a room

with his family and explains his plans. A map is spread out on the table and his rings sparkle in the light as he stabs his finger at different places on the map. He and some other merchants are going on a trip. They will leave today or tomorrow, depending when the boat departs. He speaks with glowing eyes, "We will go to this city and then sail to that city. In each city we will stay a year and buy and sell and get gain. It will be a profitable trip and our wealth will be increased by 75 percent. The children will be able to buy toys and you, wife, can have that new dress you like so well. We may even be able to buy a bigger and more beautiful house."

How familiar this all is to our ears. A businessman is laying before his family his plans to enter into partnership with his friend, and after borrowing several hundred thousand dollars, he will enlarge his business, increase his profits, expand his sales force, and so accumulate enough money to enjoy the good things in life.

Or a man and his wife plan their future. "We can put away so much each month in savings. We will have so much coming from our pension plan and have so much in life insurance policies. We will be able to retire at sixty; the children will be all married, and we can spend our winters in Florida and our summers traveling overseas."

Or perhaps you are planning a vacation, and the maps are all spread out on the table. "We will leave tomorrow at 6:00 a.m. We will travel to Lincoln, Nebraska, and get a motel. We will arrive in Loveland the next day. Then we will spend a week in Rocky Mountain National Park and another week exploring Denver, Colorado Springs, and the mountains in the area. We will return via Yellowstone National Park and the Black Hills and travel rather leisurely, for we will have another week and a half before we arrive home."

It is all so familiar to us.

Whereas ye know not what shall be on the morrow. For what is your life? It is even a vapour, that appeareth for a little time, and then vanisheth away (4:14)

The trouble with our plans, when we make them in the way that the rich merchant made them, is that we think we are able to predict the future with certainty and that we can control what happens to us. We know that is not true, for we are reminded of it every day. But we live as if it were true.

In this verse James reminds us of the transitory nature of our lives. We are not even able to predict what will happen the next day of our lives—whether we will be stricken with a stroke or heart attack, or whether we will die. We do not know. It is not ours to decide. In a moment the whole character and circumstances of our lives may change so completely that we are never again the same.

James uses the figure of early morning mist on a spring or autumn day. It is visible as the eastern sky lightens. It may be very thick, so that we cannot see in it or beyond it. But when the sun rises, its heat burns the mist away, and it is gone. So are our lives: here one moment and gone the next. We do not know the moment we will die. We need not be old to die. We are here for a fleeting time, but we soon vanish, and our places are remembered no more.

Scripture speaks frequently of the passing existence of our lives. Solomon warned, "Boast not thyself of to-morrow; for thou knowest not what a day may bring forth (Prov. 27:1). Expressing it all is Moses' sad song in the wilderness, "Thou carriest them away as with a flood; they are as a sleep: in the morning they are like grass which groweth up. In the morning it flourisheth, and groweth up; in the evening it is cut down, and withereth" (Ps. 90:5–6). Psalm 103 echoes the same words: "For he knoweth our frame; he remembereth that we are dust. As for man, his days are as grass: as a flower of the field, so he flourisheth. For the wind passeth over it, and it is gone; and the place thereof shall know it no more" (vv. 14–16). Isaiah speaks with words echoed by Peter, "The voice said, Cry. And he said, What shall I cry? All flesh is grass, and all the goodliness therefore is as the flower of the field: The grass withereth, the flower fadeth: because the spirit of the LORD bloweth upon it: surely the people is grass. The grass withereth, the flower fadeth: but the word of our God shall stand forever" (Isa. 40:6–8; 1 Pet. 1:24–25).

When scripture emphasizes so strongly and in so many places the frailty of our lives, it is foolishness in the extreme to live as if we will live forever and are in control of all that will happen in the future. Yet such is our sin.

For that ye ought to say, If the Lord will, we shall live, and do this, or that (4:15)

While the sad description of the wealthy merchant is surely evidence of dead faith, now James informs us concerning the confession of a person with living faith who puts his trust and confidence in God.

The text is in the form of a third class condition, in which there is some doubt concerning the if-clause, "if the Lord wills." The doubt is not that perhaps the Lord does not will everything that happens to us; the doubt is the uncertainty of what the Lord wills.

The text certainly does not imply that it is sin to plan for the future. We cannot live without planning, and we are called to be good and faithful stewards in God's house. Stewardship implies that we plan now for tomorrow, although many of our plans for the future are born out of our affluence. The less we have, the more we live in the present.

The will of God is the same as his eternal counsel and plan

that he determined before the foundation of the world. That will of God has several characteristics that ought to be noted in connection with this admonition.

God's will is unchangeable. It is a determination that cannot be altered by God, by what man does, or by any other circumstances. God's will is not merely a dead plan or a blueprint stored for reference somewhere in heaven. It is God's living will. What God wills to do, he does. Nothing and no one, devils and powerful kings included, can resist his will. God's will is all-comprehensive. Everything that takes place in heaven, on earth, and in hell is according to his will. The moments and circumstances of our births and deaths are all determined. Every second, with every thought, every act, every step, is determined by God. Nothing comes by chance or some other power. Our whole lives are in God's hands. He is the sovereign Lord. The center and focal point of God's will is his purpose to glorify himself through Jesus Christ. Everything that happens in God's creation has meaning and significance only as it is related to Christ and is subservient to God's glory in Christ. Because Christ is the focal point of all God's will, the salvation of the church in Christ is included in that central decree of God to reveal himself in Christ. Everything that happens to God's people is for their salvation: "All things work together for good to them that love God, to them who are the called according to his purpose" (Rom. 8:28).

The believer, the one with true and living faith that binds him to Christ, makes this text of James a crucial qualification of all his plans. By faith the believer appropriates the truth concerning God's will, a truth so clearly taught by all scripture. By faith the believer takes hold of the truth that he belongs to Christ who is "before all things, and by him all things consist. And he is the head of the body, the church: who is the beginning, the firstborn from the dead" (Col. 1:17–18). Confessing this great truth as it affects the whole of his life, the believer prays, "Thy will be done." He joyfully and thankfully submits his will to God's will. He walks in the consciousness of his total dependence on his God. He says with Asaph, "Thou shalt guide me with thy counsel, and afterward receive me to glory" (Ps. 73:24).

We are always in danger of forgetting this. When our ways are easy to walk and we have relatively few problems or troubles, we easily forget God and trust in ourselves. But when God sends us afflictions, disappointments, and great sorrows, our immediate reactions are to rebel against God's will for us and to question his goodness. Either way we disobey the injunction of the text. Even if we finally and grudgingly submit to God's will in times of distress, thinking that we cannot do anything about the situation anyway and we might as well make the best of it, we also fail to obey God's word and to live out of living faith. A simple recognition of God's hand in everything that befalls us is not enough. We must submit to God's will humbly, joyfully, and thankfully, for scripture requires us to give "thanks always for all things unto God and the Father in the name of our Lord Jesus Christ" (Eph. 5:20).

It is possible to use this expression of James as a mantra: "If only," we think to ourselves, "we use this formula before we carry out our plans, the Lord will give us what we really want and for which we strive." It is also possible to become so accustomed to using the expression without really knowing or thinking about what we are saying. A dear saint, born in the Netherlands in the town of Bussum, once said to me, "If I am living and am well, I want to be buried in Bussum."

But when we live out of living faith in the consciousness that God directs the whole course of our lives, we are happy and able to submit to what the Lord gives us in this life.

But now ye rejoice in your boastings: all such rejoicing is evil (4:16)

To live as if the Lord does not control all our lives is to boast. That may not seem evident at first, but when we fail to live in the consciousness of our total dependence on God, we live as if we are in control of our lives and that we have the power to bring about everything we intend to do. So strong is this in us that we are sad, angry, bitterly disappointed, and rebellious when our plans are cancelled by God's providence.

Worse, we even rejoice in our boastings. We are glad when what we plan to do is actually accomplished. We have achieved our goals. We have seized control of our lives. We have accomplished great things. How strong and skilled we are. How shrewd we are in business. How well we have planned for the future.

How sad! Our lives are as a curling mist that disappears in a moment. Jesus' words concerning the rich fool come to our minds to haunt us, "I will say to my soul, Soul, thou hast much goods laid up for many years; take thine ease, eat, drink, and be merry. But God said unto him, Thou fool, this night thy soul shall be required of thee: then whose shall those things be, which thou hast provided?" (Luke 12:19–20).

Therefore to him that knoweth to do good, and doeth it not, to him it is sin (4:17)

It is clear that this verse is connected to the preceding verses. We know that our calling is to live every moment of our lives in the consciousness of our total dependence on God, and we are to do this willingly, joyfully and thankfully. God determines the pathways of our lives, and he does not give the plans of our lives into our hands. That is also reason for gratitude.

There are two points to be made. First, it is common to speak of sins of commission and sins of omission. The former are sins committed deliberately, knowing that they are wrong. The latter are failures to do what we are called to do. The text deals with sins of omission. Second, we have the antithetical calling to reject sin and to choose the right. From this viewpoint James may have in mind what he said in 4:1–4. To omit to do what we know is good is to do what we know is wrong. We are never morally neutral, standing between good and evil, but going neither way. In all moral questions, we do not straddle a fence and refuse to get off on either side. We do either the good or the bad; we cannot do both at the same time. We also do the good when we reject the bad, and do the evil when we reject the good.

It is somewhat surprising that not the word for moral goodness (*agathos*) but the word for beautiful (*kalos*) is used in the text. Yet even the Greek word for beautiful means not just outward attractiveness, but also inward soundness and a fitness to be used for the appointed purpose. When we do good, we accomplish God's purpose, for God works in us the ability to do good works so that he may be praised through us.

Further, it is not enough to refuse to do the evil. To live antithetically we must say no to all evil. To say no to evil is good, for it is what God requires. But it is not enough. It is impossible to say no to evil without anything else. We would leave moral vacuums in our lives if we only refrained from doing evil. A man who has living faith by which he is bound to Christ in living fellowship does good in the positive sense.

Not everyone knows how to do good in the same measure, for men do not know equally the good. One who is brought up and lives in the sphere of a church where the gospel is fully and faithfully proclaimed knows the good far better than an individual from an island in the South Pacific who has never heard the gospel. He also knows what the good is and that he must do it, as is clear from Romans 1:18–31. The closer one stands to the truth in all its fullness, the greater also is his responsibility. The responsibility to do the good is also commensurate with one's knowledge of the good (Matt. 11:20–24; Luke 12:47–48; John 15:22, 24).

Knowing the good means to know what the good is and to do it. Failure to do the good is as much a sin as doing evil. Failure to teach one's children the ways of God's covenant, to fail to pay the church budget or Christian school tuition, to fail to visit the sick, to fail to speak up when God's name is blasphemed—all these and many more failures to do the good are sins.

Our moral obligations are not fulfilled by obeying a long list of don'ts. The positive calling God gives us is to love the Lord our God and our neighbors as ourselves. This is the good purpose for which God has saved us. To fail in this calling is a sin of which every one of God's people is guilty.

JAMES 5

God's Judgment of the Rich

1. Go to now, ye rich men, weep and howl for your miseries that shall come upon you.
2. Your riches are corrupted, and your garments are motheaten.
3. Your gold and silver is cankered; and the rust of them shall be a witness against you, and shall eat your flesh as it were fire. Ye have heaped treasure together for the last days.
4. Behold, the hire of the labourers who have reaped down your fields, which is of you kept back by fraud, crieth: and the cries of them which have reaped are entered into the ears of the Lord of sabaoth.
5. Ye have lived in pleasure on the earth, and been wanton; ye have nourished your hearts, as in a day of slaughter.
6. Ye have condemned and killed the just; and he doth not resist you.

Go to now, ye rich men, weep and howl for your miseries that shall come upon you (5:1)

Many commentators say that James addresses only unbelieving rich people outside the churches.[1]

---

1 Calvin, *Catholic Epistles*, 342; Kistemaker, *Exposition of the Epistle of James*, 155; Lenski, *Interpretation of the...Epistle of James*, 155; Ross, *New International Commentary: Epistles of James and John*, 85.

Whether they are Jews or Gentiles is not easy to determine and makes little difference in the meaning of the text. The direct address of verse 1 is a figure of speech called apostrophe, in which a person or persons or some inanimate object not present is addressed. An example of this, of which there are many, especially in the Old Testament prophets, is Paul's words in 1 Corinthians 15:55: "O death, where is thy sting? O grave, where is thy victory?" The address is general. The rich may be outside the congregations, or there may be rich within the congregations who have dead faith. But there may be members of the congregations who do not live out of their living faith. Although James addresses rich unbelievers in general, this word of God is for the comfort of God's oppressed people, as verse 7 indicates.

There does not appear to be any connection between these verses and the preceding context. This powerful word of God takes a completely different turn. From sharp reprimands the apostle comes with words of comfort, for God's people suffer the indignities heaped on them by the wicked, especially when it comes in the form of economic oppression.

James begins his tirade against the rich with the same words he used in 4:13, where he spoke to those in the congregations who had dead faith. Here the phrase "go to now, ye rich men" has a slightly different meaning. James says, "Pay attention, you rich men, for I have some important words to say to you. Remember, your riches mean nothing, for judgment comes upon you from God who cares for his people."

Certainly the rich can be and are members of the church of Christ. This was true in the Old Testament when God made Abraham, Isaac, Jacob, and others very wealthy. Even in Jesus' days some rich were among those who believed on him. Joseph of Arimethea was an example. In 1 Corinthians 1:26–29 Paul laid down the rule that generally God does not give riches to his people or gather the rich to be a part of the church.

Riches are spiritually very dangerous. Jesus said, "It is easier for a camel to go through the eye of a needle, than for a rich man to enter the kingdom of God" (Mark 10:25). Paul warned against the deadly traps that confront the rich (1 Tim. 6:7–10).

James refers to rich Jews who had settled in all parts of the Mediterranean basin and established lucrative businesses. More particularly, James speaks of wealthy landowners who had large farms, many servants, and possessed an abundance of this world's goods.

These rich people are told to weep and howl for the miseries that will come upon them. "Weep" is a translation of the general word used in scripture to indicate audible weeping. The word (*ololuzontes*) translated as "howl" is used only here in scripture and is onomatopoetic.[2] The two words together can be translated as "weep by howling." The expression is indicative of hopeless despair. The rich are told to recognize their end, for it will fill them with despair.

The admonition to the rich to howl is the right thing for them to do, for their existences are bleak. The use of the present tense emphasizes that their miseries are coming upon them even while they live in luxury and plenty, and will surely continue throughout their lives and even beyond death. The rich are told to recognize that their riches give them no pleasure, that wealth can bring no happiness, and that riches usually mean grief and trouble. Jesus spoke of the "deceitfulness of riches" (Matt. 13:22). Riches promise happiness and release from worry, but this is a lie. How strange that we too are so often deceived into thinking that if only we had more money, all would be well.

---

2 It comes from *ololuzō*, which when pronounced sounds like howling.

The rich are called away from tables loaded with delicacies, new and expensive cars, huge mansions, and social lives among the cultured and famous. It is better that they howl in despair, for if only they would take seriously what their true lot and dismal future are, they would howl.

Your riches are corrupted, and your garments are motheaten (5:2)

The words used to describe the riches of the wealthy indicate that in the use of their riches the wealthy corrupt them. This is not necessarily true of all riches, for the things of this world are creatures God has created, and every creature of God is good. Riches can be sanctified by the word of God and prayer (1 Tim.4:3–5), but man's wicked use of them corrupts them. Such corruption is true of all earthly possessions. All earthly possessions mold, rust, and rot away; and clothes, no matter how expensive, are soon motheaten. They cannot and do not last. This is true because the curse of God is on these things, as the curse of God was on everything in Jericho, except what was dedicated to God in the tabernacle (Josh. 6:17–19). The curse of God and never his favor is always on the house of the wicked (Prov. 3:33).

The same corruption is experienced by the people who use riches to live riotously and luxuriously. The drunkard becomes a physical and mental wreck; the debaucher turns into a diseased corpse; the pleasure-crazed man changes into a stunned and cynical fool. All learn in one way or another that happiness does not come with wealth.

Only when one's wealth is used in the service of God and of the kingdom of Christ is it sanctified.

Your gold and silver is cankered; and the rust of them shall be a witness against you, and shall eat your flesh as it were fire. Ye have heaped treasure together for the last days (5:3)

Much the same as what James said in the previous verse is repeated here, but he adds some very ominous words: the rusted riches will be a testimony or witness against the rich. The figure is graphic. The reference is to the judgment day when the world has ended and all men stand before the great white throne to receive judgment for what they have done in the flesh. When that great day comes, each rich man will have a pile of all his treasures alongside of him. These treasures will be rusted, useless junk. But they will be a silent witness that condemns the man who possessed them, for on them he set his heart and it is all he has.

First, the riches will show what a fool the wealthy man was. The very things that were so important to him and that he spent his life acquiring are junk. His life was wasted and useless, and he was a fool who spent his life for vanity. Second, they will be a witness against him, for they will demonstrate vividly what all these rich things did to him—how they led him into the service of sin and were instruments of wickedness in his hands. Third, the Lord will ask him, "How did you use these gifts of God? Did you use them as part of God's creation intended for his glory?" The man will be like Achan, who stole for himself Jericho's treasures and was stoned with his family in the valley of Achor (Josh. 7:19–26). Finally, that heap of riches, now decayed and rusted, will be the immediate reason for the rich to answer the Lord's question, "How did you acquire these riches?" The answer is the subject of the next verse.

Behold, the hire of the labourers who have reaped down your fields, which is of you kept back by fraud, crieth: and the cries of them which have reaped are entered into the ears of the Lord of sabaoth (5:4)

In addition to the pile of junk that represents the rich man's wealth, other witnesses will be called to testify. These witnesses are the people of God who were laborers robbed of their just wages. When they were oppressed over the centuries, they cried out to God. Although God did not answer them immediately, God wrote down every cry in his book of remembrance. Christ now holds that book in his hands as the rich man tries to give an account of how he became so wealthy.

James uses personification, the figure of speech that gives human language or human activities to inanimate creatures. The hire of the laborers cries out. "Hire" means wages, what an employer pays his employees. The wages cry out because they are kept back by fraud. It is a powerful figure. The word for "crieth" means an inarticulate cry. The suffering of the laborers is so great they cannot give words to their anguish.

The wages that cry out justly belong to those whom the farmer hired to do his field work, especially the reaping, for it is then that the farmer makes his money, part of which belongs to his laborers.

The wages are kept back by fraud. When he hires laborers, an employer owes them wages that are sufficient to provide for all their needs, including the monies needed to support the church, to give to the poor, and to pay for the biblical education of the children. Those needs may include necessary medical attention and other needs that arise in the life of a family.

The meaning of wages kept back by fraud is not only that the laborers are not paid enough to support themselves and their families, but also that the employer uses various devices and tricks of the trade to hold back from them what they justly earned.

James refers to believers who suffer at the hands of their employers. What happens to these saints is common throughout the world. Those in positions of power have only one goal in mind: to increase their wealth. They use whatever means possible to attain that goal. It is so common in our world that almost everyone has experienced being the object of this kind of grasping and grabbing covetousness that has no regard for anyone's well-being. If starving people, broken homes, physical wrecks, and helpless people are left in the wake of the rich in their mad pursuits of wealth, the rich seem not even to notice.

There is a special suffering involved for the Christians. Because of their faith in Christ, they especially are the objects of the persecution of the rich. This very well may have been true in predominantly Jewish communities in James' day. The gospel had saved many Jews who worked for wealthy fellow Jews and were considered traitors to the Jewish religion. They were the objects of cruelty by their compatriots, and much of their suffering was due to their faith. The same is true of employers today that will not hire men who for conscience sake will not join a wicked labor union.

Probably no one other than their families hears their cries. But one does: the Lord of sabaoth. Their cries enter his ears.

The name of God, "Lord of sabaoth," has been interpreted in different ways.[3] The meaning most likely is that God is the sovereign ruler of all the creatures he has created. He who rules sovereignly over wicked and righteous and will surely right all wrong opens his ears to the agonizing cries of those who are oppressed. Vengeance will come.

Ye have lived in pleasure on the earth, and been wanton; ye have nourished your hearts, as in a day of slaughter (5:5)

One gets the impression (and this may well be James' point) that this verse describes one of the reasons the laborers do not receive a just wage: the rich are intent on spending their riches

---

3 For various meanings, see Herman Hoeksema, *Reformed Dogmatics*, 2nd ed., 2 vols. (Jenison, MI: Reformed Free Publishing Association, 2004) 1:102–3.

on themselves at the expense of the workers. James' description is painted against the background of laborers who can barely survive because they do not have even their daily needs. The wantonness of the rich farmers is at the expense of the just wages the poor should have received.

James uses two expressive words to describe these rich. To live in pleasure, according to the original Greek word, means to be gluttonous and a winebibber and to spend fortunes on clothes, new houses, beautiful cars, and pleasure toys. To be wanton means to surround oneself with everything money can buy, to live dissolutely in the mad pursuit of pleasure, and to wallow in luxury.

These words for the wicked wealthy carry with them the sting of a whiplash when we consider the way in which we live. We pay the church budget, tuition to the Christian schools, and generously support the causes of God's kingdom beyond what is required of us. This is all well and good. We have done what is our duty to do—barely. It is easy to shrug aside the teachings of scripture and politely excuse ourselves from the descriptions of a righteous man in his use of this earth's goods, but it is well from time to time to pause and put our lives under the sharp scrutiny of God's word.

The text is about our lives "on the earth." How do we live as pilgrims and strangers on the earth with our earthly possessions, especially when God is pleased to give us much?

We may even justly argue that the wealth we have accumulated has not been squeezed out of the bodies of those who work for us, for we have amply provided for them. It is good that we do so. But there still remain the luxurious lives we live.

I am old enough to know some of our fathers and mothers who emigrated from the Netherlands. I can vividly recall their stories—how the father of an elder in the church I served worked from 4:00 a.m. to dark for a dollar a day, and how pleased the family was when his wages were raised to $1.25. The worst of it was that the farmer and his laborers went to the same church.

In a striking expression, James charges the rich, "Ye have nourished your hearts, as in a day of slaughter." The picture is of a steer being fed grain in abundance so that it will be sleek and fat, ready for butchering. The butchering is the day of the death of the wicked and the final judgment when their covetousness, self-seeking, ruthless determination to gain ever more, and cruelty to those who worked for them will be fully exposed. They are preparing themselves for the slaughter, while they remain determinedly blind to their fate.

Because the text speaks of nourishing one's heart, it is possible that James has Isaiah 6:10 in mind. God commissioned Isaiah to be a prophet to Judah and commanded him to preach in such a way that "the heart of this people [becomes] fat." Isaiah's reference is to the truth expressed by Asaph in Psalm 73:18, where Asaph understood why the Lord continues to give the wicked so many good things of this world. His purpose is to set them on slippery places, so that they slide into destruction. Here the forceful statement means that God gives them riches on which they feed to ready them as cattle for the slaughter.

God sovereignly does this, but in such a way that their hardening in their sins is done in the way of their impenitence and refusal to obey God's commands.

Ye have condemned and killed the just; and he doth not resist you (5:6)

In the Authorized Version the first "and" is in italics, which means that the word does not appear in the original. Thus the text reads, "Ye have condemned, killed the righteous." This is forceful and may be translated in this way, "Ye have condemned, even worse, killed the righteous."

The righteous are God's people who are righteous in the blood of Christ and belong to their Savior. In a wicked world they represent the cause of God, the cause of the kingdom of heaven, the cause of a kingdom that opposes at every point the philosophies, the activities, and the wickedness of the world.

The condemnation of the righteous is literally true. The same condemnation takes place in thousands of places where the rich become wealthy at the expense of the laborers. In their enjoyment of the luxuries of life, they have no time to think about the poor, the destitute, the struggling laborers. They despise them, disdain to bother with them, consider them beneath their notice. They look on them as means of gaining more of this earth's possessions, to be brutally used to the last drop of blood, and then discarded thoughtlessly.

The wicked hear condemnation of their wickedness from the righteous and the wicked see the loyalties of these folk to God and to Christ. Because the wicked hate God and Christ, they are often especially brutal to those who confess the name of Christ.

Although it has happened repeatedly in the history of this weary world that landowners deliberately killed their help, the meaning of James is that the wicked take advantage of the righteous and kill them by starvation. Many in the Netherlands, although they worked for landowners who were members of the same churches they attended, died early deaths and suffered many illnesses and injuries because of indifferences to their plights by those for whom they worked.

Then is added the significant clause "and he doth not resist you." This is not stated in the form of an admonition, but as a statement of fact. It is apparent that the saints in James' day were obedient to the principles of the kingdom of heaven: resistance of any kind is always wrong.

This principle, so clearly laid down in scripture, is openly mocked. Lower classes of society riot to gain equal rights. Unions strike and commit mayhem against employers. Oppressed people in many lands become revolutionaries to gain their ends. Women who are persuaded by the feminist movement rebel against their husbands and employers to gain equal rights. The United States was born out of revolution against authority, and today's churches approve!

The tendency toward resistance is always present with us. We want our rights. We are quick to hit back if someone hits us. We readily seek vengeance on those who are the authors of real or supposed wrongs. Yet it is not revolution that scripture lays down as the calling of God's people. It is exactly the opposite. Jesus set down the principle with unmistakable clarity in the sermon on the mount (Matt. 5:38–44). Paul repeatedly reminded the people of God that they must show submission to all in authority (Rom. 13:1–7). Peter said the same thing in 1 Peter 2:13–15. These commands were spoken during times of cruel Roman emperors who persecuted the church. Both Paul and Peter applied the principle to employer-employee relationships. Paul did so in Ephesians 5:6–8, Colossians 3:22–25, and 1 Timothy 6:1. Peter specifically mentioned employees in 1 Peter 2:18–19. He added that the injunction not to resist applies when employers are froward, and is to be observed by us even when employers cause us to suffer. Scripture is clear on the point. The saints in James' day knew this and obeyed. They did not resist. Such is also our calling.

An Admonition to be Patient in Suffering

7. Be patient therefore, brethren, unto the coming of the Lord. Behold, the husbandman waiteth for the precious fruit of the earth, and hath long patience for it, until he receive the early and latter rain.

8. Be ye also patient; stablish your hearts: for the coming of the Lord draweth nigh.

9. Grudge not one against another, brethren, lest ye be condemned: behold, the judge standeth before the door.

10. Take, my brethren, the prophets, who have spoken in the name of the Lord, for an example of suffering affliction, and of patience.

11. Behold, we count them happy which endure. Ye have heard of the patience of Job, and have seen the end of the Lord; that the Lord is very pitiful, and of tender mercy.

Be patient therefore, brethren, unto the coming of the Lord. Behold, the husbandman waiteth for the precious fruit of the earth, and hath long patience for it, until he receive the early and latter rain (5:7)

This passage is the conclusion of James' outbreak of anger against the wealthy oppressors of God's people, but strikingly it is an admonition to the oppressed people of God. The admonition is not to organize and strike against such cruel oppressors to gain your rights. It is not to take every opportunity to slow down the work or sabotage your boss' fields and machinery. It is the opposite. It is in line with scripture's many admonitions to submit to our employers not only to the kind and gentle, but also to the harsh and unfair (1 Pet. 2:18). Be patient! That is the calling of the oppressed worker. Do not do anything harmful to your employer's place of business. Do not strike back and seek revenge. Do not grumble and complain and curse your cruel boss. How different is the calling of the people of God from what is common practice in the world, and how quickly wicked men, even in the church, will reject this admonition as madness.

The word translated as "be patient" means to be longsuffering. Longsuffering in scripture is an attribute of God, as in 2 Peter

3:9: "The Lord is not slack concerning his promise, as some men count slackness; but is longsuffering to us-ward." Longsuffering is the divine attribute according to which God, out of love for his people, endures the suffering through which his people must pass because it is necessary for their salvation. The Lord could deliver his people at any time, but knowing that suffering is necessary to save them, he endures their pain, even though he finds it painful.

The earthly illustration is of a doctor who must operate on his son to remove a cancerous tumor. He trembles at the thought of cutting into the flesh of his son, and he cringes at the thought of the pain and misery which must follow surgery, but he endures it, knowing that it is necessary if his son is to be restored to health. The father-doctor is longsuffering.

Here the attribute is applied to the people of God who must exercise the same attribute God shows to them. They are to endure the pain of suffering with patience and without complaint, and they are to do this because suffering is for their salvation.

This truth is taught everywhere in scripture, but clearly in Romans 8:17–18: "If children, then heirs; heirs of God, and joint-heirs with Christ; if so be that we suffer with him, that we may be also glorified together. For I reckon that the sufferings of this present time are not worthy to be compared with the glory which shall be revealed in us." Paul was bold in his words to the Corinthians, "Our light affliction, which is but for a moment, worketh for us a far more exceeding and eternal weight of glory" (2 Cor. 4:17).

This truth can be believed only by the power of faith, for suffering always seems to be contrary to anything we desire or hope for. Suffering a blessing? Even a necessary one? Yet such is the teaching of scripture. In that suffering we are to be longsuffering. We bear suffering willingly, knowing that it is a necessary part of our salvation.

We are to be longsuffering "unto the coming of the Lord." The coming of the Lord is the end of the world when Christ returns on the clouds of heaven. Scripture speaks of the coming of the Lord in different senses. Christ returned to his church to abide with her unto the end of the world when he came in his Spirit on Pentecost (John 14:16–18). Christ also comes to take his children to heaven with him when they die (vv. 1–4). The death of a believer is the end of the world for him and the vindication of his cause, for he goes to glory. His oppressors, when they die, go to hell.

The reference in James is to the end of all things when Christ returns. The admonition of the text and the statement "unto the coming of the Lord" mean that believers are to be longsuffering in their affliction *because* they know the Lord is coming again to deliver them. When the Lord comes to deliver them from all their afflictions, he will also publicly vindicate their righteous cause. He will publicly condemn their oppressors and show these cruel men the terrible sins they committed in causing suffering to his people. He will show them that in their persecution of the righteous, they were persecuting Christ. He will publicly testify that his poor, oppressed people will forever be made blessed, while their oppressors will be punished. Our longsuffering is possible because our Lord will make right all the wrong we endured.

The admonition is further explained in the rest of the verse: "Behold, the husbandman waiteth for the precious fruit of the earth, and hath long patience for it, until he receive the early and latter rain." Most commentators refer this expression to God's suffering people and interpret it as a strengthening of the admonition. We must be longsuffering in the same way that a farmer waits for the early and latter rain before he begins his harvest. But this explanation is incorrect. There are certain elements of the text that do not fit that explanation, such as the expression "the husbandman waiteth for the precious fruit of the earth." It can hardly be said of us in our waiting for the return of our Lord that we are waiting for the precious fruit of the earth.

The reference is to God who waits for the time of the harvest of his elect. The figure is powerful. In Palestine, before the development of herbicides and insecticides, the crops were in constant danger of being destroyed by drought, insects, or frost. The farmer was impatient to get his crops out of the field before disaster would strike. I well remember this impatience of the farmer when as a college student I worked on a ranch in Montana. The rancher grew spring wheat and winter wheat, oats, and barley. But the growing seasons were short at the five-thousand-foot altitude at which he farmed, and snow could come with the passing of August and the beginning of September. However, the grain was not ripe until at least the middle of September. When September came our boss would go into the fields every day and check the grain to see whether it was ready for harvesting. Usually he came back dejected because the grain was not yet ripe, so he watched the skies almost every moment, hoping that they would tell him that fair weather lay ahead for a bit longer.

The farmers in Palestine had to await the early and latter rains before they could harvest. The early rains came in what is our autumn. After the baking heat of summer, these early rains made the ground soft and workable so that the land could be tilled and the seed sown. After another period of relatively dry weather, in what is our spring, the latter rains would come. These were essential for the ripening of the grain. The farmer, eager to get his harvested crops in before disaster struck, could hardly wait for these latter rains that were so essential to a harvest.

What a beautiful picture of our longsuffering God. He is eager to take his suffering saints home to him. They endure great cruelty at the hands of their oppressors, and their cries for deliverance come up to him. Eagerly God awaits the day when he can take his saints home.

Scripture speaks in more than one place of the gathering of all the church as a harvest. Jesus referred to it in the parable of the tares in the field, and said, "Let both [tares and wheat] grow together until the harvest and in the time of harvest I will say to the reapers, Gather ye together first the tares, and bind them in bundles to burn them: but gather the wheat into my barn" (Matt 13:30). The same figure is found in Revelation 14:14–20.

God cannot come until the harvest is finished. The harvest is finished when the last elect is born and brought to faith in Christ, and when the whole body of Christ has filled the cup of suffering (Col. 1:24) and is fully prepared through suffering to go to glory. The Lord is not in any doubt that all his elect will be saved, for he is sovereign, but the text does show us God, eager and longing to take his church to himself. He can do this only when the harvest is ripe. It is a beautiful picture to comfort the anxious hearts of the people of God who cry out to the Lord of sabaoth to be avenged of their persecutors, but who do not see that deliverance coming when they expect it.

Be ye also patient; stablish your hearts: for the coming of the Lord draweth nigh (5:8)

It is appropriate that the attribute of longsuffering is applied to us here: "Be ye also patient." There is indeed good reason to be longsuffering when the Lord reveals what is his reason for his seeming delay. Too early a harvesting would mean no harvest at all, but useless and unripened grain. If Christ would return too early, all the elect could not go to glory, and if one does not go, none goes, for the church is an organism, a body, a whole.

The Bible does not teach Arminian theology that the saved are a mass of people unconnected to each other. If their salvation depends on their free will, no one can be sure whether a person will go to heaven, nor is there any time when Christ should return, for there is always the possibility that someone else will accept Christ. Such a view is hopeless and unworthy of God.

James adds to his admonition to be patient "stablish your hearts." This means to make firm and stable. To understand this one can describe the opposite: a heart not established. One with an unestablished heart is one who can never make up his mind and is always changing it. He vacillates from one position to another. He is not certain about anything. He limps between two opinions. Such a one is a miserable character, one with whom it is impossible to do anything of value. With regard to his suffering, sometimes he thinks he can endure it; other times he finds it impossible to submit to his cruel boss. With regard to his calling to commit his cause to the Lord for vengeance (Rom.12:21), sometimes he talks about doing this, but a moment later he is cursing his unfair employer and vowing to get even. When it comes to pondering the longsuffering of God, there are times when he is prepared to believe in God's long-suffering, but he often finds it so difficult that he mutters to himself, "God is unfair and cares not at all about what I have to endure."

To establish one's heart is to fix it firmly on one goal and not to swerve from it. The goal is faithfulness to the truth of the word of God. To hold fast to that truth may entail suffering for the cause of Christ, but the suffering child of God is willing to commit his way to the Lord and wait patiently for vengeance to come from heaven. The man of God does not waver from that position. He is willing to endure all for the sake of the salvation of the church.

The heart of man is his moral and ethical center and a microcosm of his entire nature. If his heart is established firmly in God's word, his mind and his will grasp and confess the truth, and his entire life is as God says it should be.

The reason these admonitions are urgent is that "the coming

of the Lord draweth nigh." The verb is the perfect tense of the Greek verb *enggizō*. The perfect indicates that the coming of Christ has already in the past come near and now remains near.

The people to whom this is written must have wondered whether the Lord would ever come back. The Lord had promised to come, but in the meantime their suffering continued unabated, and heaven seemed closed to their cries. Did the Lord hear? And if he heard, did he care? Would he never come? But the coming of deliverance is near.

In what sense is the end near? Since James wrote his epistle two thousand years have come and gone. But the truth of the nearness of the end stands. We must remember that "one day is with the Lord as a thousand years, and a thousand years as a day" (2 Pet. 3:8). From that perspective the coming of Christ is indeed near. It is near from the perspective of the Old Testament, which is the viewpoint from which James writes his epistle. The hope and longing of the Old Testament church has been fulfilled in the coming of Christ. The New Testament saints must understand this. The coming of Christ is near also because Christ's work on earth is finished. In his incarnation, death, resurrection, and exaltation, he accomplished all the work of the Father in the salvation of the church. There is nothing more to do. Further, Christ's coming is near because we live in the dispensation of Christ's coming. He is in the process of coming again to save his church. Every saint saved and taken to heaven brings him nearer.

That process of Christ's coming is so near that as he promised he is present by his Spirit and his word. When each saint dies and goes to glory, Christ is so near that we sense his presence at the side of the coffin of a fellow saint who went to glory. God is not unmindful of our suffering. He is very near to sustain us in our trials, for he is longsuffering and comes finally as quickly as he can. "Behold, I come quickly," Jesus says (Rev. 22:12).

Truly, our Lord's coming is near.

Grudge not one against another, brethren, lest ye be condemned (5:9)

The text presents some difficulties. The first is that this admonition seems to be out of place and totally separate from the main thought of verses 1–5. This difficulty is made worse by the fact that in verses 10–11 James seems to return to the theme of the Lord's imminent return.

The second difficulty lies in the meaning of the word (*stenazete*) translated as "grudge." Different translations have different opinions on what the word means. The Revised Version translates the word as "murmur"; the Revised Standard Version translates it as "grumble"; Philips translates the word as "make complaints"; the New English Bible has "blame trouble."

A common and plausible interpretation of grudging one another is constant complaining about and to one another because of the weaknesses and sins in the congregations. Under the pressures of persecution and in the agony of personal suffering, the saints tended to accuse one another of the imperfections and weaknesses that are found in an imperfect church on earth.

James admonishes them to stop doing that and rather to assist one another in the difficulties of life when persecution is their lot. If they do not stop this incessant criticism of each other, God will judge those who are so eager to judge others, and his judgment will be condemnation.

This is certainly a plausible explanation of the passage. The suddenness of the admonition that does not seem connected to the context is explained by James' tendency to do that in other places in his epistle and by the tenuous relation of this fault being brought on by the pressures of persecution.

However, I prefer to interpret this in a different way. I consider "grudge" to be better translated as "complain." The point of James is that the saints, hard-pressed and suffering under their oppressors, were accustomed to complaining about their situations to one another. This is easily understandable. Their way was not easy. They had barely enough to feed their families. Their work was hard, and their bosses were heartless. They came home at night exhausted. For their work they received only a bare subsistence. As the people spoke to each other on Sunday before and after the divine worship services, they compared stories, engaged in bitter complaints about their situations and measured the extent of suffering each family was forced to bear.

The reciprocal pronoun, translated in the text as "one against another," could better be translated as "to one another."[4] Complaining is contrary to the will of God. The Lord himself told us that we must "rejoice, and be exceedingly glad" when we are persecuted, because "so persecuted they the prophets which were before you" (Matt. 5:12). To speak evil of our oppressors is wrong, for again in the sermon on the mount our Lord told us, "Love your enemies, bless them that curse you, do good to them that hate you, and pray for them which despitefully use you, and persecute you" (v. 44).

To complain about the way the Lord is pleased to lead us is to reject the sure promises and teachings of his word. They tell us why suffering is a part of our salvation, and they assure us of the blessedness of that salvation given to us, for the fulfillment of which our suffering is necessary. The point is that complaining about our difficult ways in life and refusing to submit to the will of God is the same as despising our salvation. To be dissatisfied with the means to our salvation is to be dissatisfied with the salvation itself. The end is condemnation.

---

4 Admittedly the difficulty with this translation is that the construction *kat' allēlōn* with the genitive rarely if at all means to one another and more frequently means against one another. But the preposition *kata* with the genitive is literally "down from" and is a possible translation.

Behold, the judge standeth before the door (5:9)

The judge is Christ. He is pictured as standing at the door of the creation, ready to enter. He has his hand, so to speak, on the knob and is turning the knob in preparation for entering. He is as near as he can possibly be without actually being here.

This statement added so forcefully is meant to be a reason not to complain about our lot. The Judge is ready to appear. When he comes, as the God-appointed judge of all men who ever lived, he will judge righteously: he will judge the wicked persecutors of God's saints by sentencing them to everlasting destruction, and he will vindicate the cause of his people. Let them therefore wait just a little while and endure their suffering patiently. Our light afflictions are but for a moment, but they work an exceedingly great weight of eternal glory.

The perfect tense of the verb translated as "standeth" is an important touch to the verse.[5] It indicates that our Judge has taken up a position in front of the door and is now standing there.

Take, my brethren, the prophets, who have spoken in the name of the Lord, for an example of suffering affliction, and of patience (5:10)

To encourage the people of God in their sufferings, the text points us to the examples of the Old Testament prophets. They all spoke in the name of the Lord as God's ambassadors who represented God's word and will to men. They spoke with authority given them by God, who had called them to their office. Thus they spoke for God himself. They received from God the words they were told to speak and they were commanded to do this regardless of what men said or did (Jer. 1:7–10). For bringing the word of God they suffered affliction, but they were patient.

---

5 *Hestēken* is the perfect active indicative of *histēmi*.

Those who caused them suffering were often themselves from the nation of Israel, the old dispensational church. They were killed all the day long and accounted as sheep for the slaughter (Ps. 44:22; Rom. 8:36).

Some of the examples to which the text refers are striking. Jesus spoke of these prophets in Matthew 23:29–35, and Stephen referred to them in his defense before the Sanhedrin (Acts 7:52). Abel was the first martyr, killed by his brother because he condemned his brother Cain's wickedness (Gen. 4:2–8). Enoch was taken to heaven without dying because wicked men sought his life (Gen. 5:24, Heb. 11:5). Elijah was hated by Jezebel and Ahab and fled for his life (1 Kings 19:1–4). Micaiah spoke the word of the Lord to Ahab and was thrown into prison with a dry crust of bread and dirty water (1 Kings 22:19–27). Zechariah was killed by Joash in the courts of the temple because he condemned Joash's sins (2 Chron. 24:20–22). Jeremiah was accused of treason and thrown into a muddy pit (Jer. 38:4–6). John the Baptist was beheaded because he accused Herod of adultery (Matt. 14:3–12).

These examples are powerful. They are to be emulated. That the prophets faithfully spoke the word of God in spite of suffering are powerful examples to the saints to do the same. The word of God always condemns sin. In its condemnation of sin, the word of God arouses the anger of the sinner, and he turns in fury against the messenger from God whose word he brings.

The examples go beyond this, and James calls special attention to this. It is the fact that the prophets were longsuffering, the same word used in verse 7. The prophets were longsuffering; so must the saints be longsuffering in their afflictions. They must not return evil for evil, but must bear their sufferings patiently, knowing that it is the will of God that they suffer and that their Judge is standing at the door.

It is our tendency to push aside these powerful examples on the grounds that the men who thus suffered were men of towering faith and unswerving faithfulness. How can we, such weak and frail people, possibly possess the strength that the heroes of faith possessed? James answers this question in 5:17–18: they were as weak as we are; therefore we can by God's grace be as strong as they were.

Behold, we count them happy which endure (5:11)

A more literal translation will indicate how this phrase is to be interpreted: "Behold, we bless the ones who endure."

To endure means to bear up under. Affliction and suffering at the hands of the wicked is a great burden to carry. It seems sometimes as if the burden is too heavy, and we sink beneath its heaviness. Endurance is the spiritual gift that enables us to continue to walk our pilgrim's way, though it be a struggle. It means to avoid being crushed under the load of suffering and to avoid being reduced to a sad and despicable mass of whining, complaining, and groaning people.

Verse 11 looks back to the example in verse 10 of the prophets' endurance. These men are cheering us on by their examples as we run the race of our lives, and their examples are our encouragement (Heb. 12:1–3). Verse 11 also observes that we bless, or speak well of, those who endured. They were the objects of God's favor. God turned their tears into laughter and their sorrows into joy. He lifted the load of their afflictions and gave them a crown of life. God speaks well of them; so do we

We know their blessedness, for they speak of it on the pages of Holy Writ. We see how God has blessed them, and we ourselves bless them as well. Why then should we groan under the burden of afflictions when we bless those who did the same before us?

Ye have heard of the patience of Job, and have seen the end of the Lord; that the Lord is very pitiful, and of tender mercy (5:11)

Those to whom James writes were acquainted with the history of Job, and they had heard of Job's patience. This would seem to imply that their pastors preached to them from the book of Job and had called attention to Job's patience in his afflictions. That the Holy Spirit in inspiring this letter of James should pick the example of Job from all the examples of longsuffering ought not to surprise us. Job's patience was astounding.

Few suffer as much as Job did. He suffered at the hands of his enemies far more than the poor in the churches to which James writes were suffering. Job's enemies were not only the Chaldeans and the Sabeans, but also Satan who was determined to destroy him. Though a wealthy man, he lost everything he possessed: his flocks, cattle, camels, and donkeys. He lost his entire family with the exception of his wife. He was stripped of his health and given an almost intolerable and painful burden of terrible boils. In addition, his three friends viciously accused him of great sins, and his wife advised him to curse God and die because she despised him. He was mocked by children and despised by those who formerly had praised him and sought his judgment. He was ignored by his servants and considered an outcast (Job 19:13–19).

Yet he endured. He bore up under it all. It is true that Job said some wrong things. He cursed the day of his birth and wished he had never come into the world. He questioned God's ways and wondered aloud why he could not receive an answer from God that would explain why God sent such afflictions upon him. His despondency and grief were palpable, and he spoke of his sorrow frequently. He bore the burden of his sufferings patiently. He did not contradict his wife or rail against her when she advised him to curse God and die. Although he had some sharp words of defense against his three friends, he did not speak evil of them or to them and return their accusations with similar charges. He did not allow the friends to destroy his good conscience when they accused him of sins, but he confessed, in one of the most beautiful and stirring confessions in scripture, the name of his Redeemer and the hope of being vindicated by him in the resurrection (a redeemer, among other things, vindicated the cause of another (Job 19:25–27).

Most importantly, he never charged God foolishly or said anything accusatory of God. It is true, he pleaded with God to tell him the reason he suffered so dreadfully, but when God refused, he accepted that. He never for one moment denied God's sovereignty in all his sufferings and God's goodness to him. He confessed, "Naked came I out of my mother's womb, and naked shall I return thither: the LORD gave, and the LORD hath taken away; blessed be the name of the LORD" (Job 1:21).

When God spoke to Job and reminded him forcefully that even in suffering Job had no right to summon God into the witness box and give an account of what he had done, Job humbled himself before God and confessed his wrong.

The people of God knew all this and received it as an example of patient endurance in suffering.

They also knew "the end of the Lord." "End" in scripture often means goal and purpose. They knew the purpose of the Lord in sending these afflictions. That purpose is defined in the expression "the Lord is very pitiful, and of tender mercy." This is God's sole purpose.

It is true that that purpose was made known to Job by restoring his wealth and family, but the purpose of God must not be defined as God's desire to give Job more than he ever had before. Job's restored wealth was the means to show that the Lord is pitiful and of tender mercy, that is, the Lord is filled with pity toward his suffering people.

"Pitiful" and "tender mercy" are nearly synonymous. Pitiful means literally of many bowels. The ancients considered the bowels to be the seat of all tender emotions. The word is used often in scripture to indicate these tender emotions, especially such feelings as compassion, sympathy, and mercy. The translation of the Authorized Version captures the sense: "very pitiful." Job's history teaches the saints who must suffer trials and bear burdens that the Lord does not send sufferings arbitrarily, nor that he is cold and indifferent to the sufferings of his people, but that he pities them very much and has compassion on them in all the difficulties of their way.

The second word (*eleos*) translated as "tender mercy" means mercy in action or mercy displayed.

Job could not have experienced fully that pity and mercy of God when he sat on an ash pile and scraped himself with clinkers. But they were there nonetheless. They were revealed in God's preserving Job in his suffering and preventing him from doing anything sinful: denying God, giving himself up to despair, cursing God for doing what he did, and such like things. God's mercy and pity were revealed in his being near to Job and giving him grace to make a good confession and to cling to the hope of his Redeemer and the resurrection of his Redeemer from the dead. That was pity and mercy indeed. God also showed Job that pity when he gave Job twice as much as he had ever possessed. At the end of Job's lengthy trial, God restored Job's riches as a vindication of the rightness of Job's cause before his three friends. These riches were a visible token of the blessedness of heaven, of which they were a picture. The Lord demonstrated his pity and mercy in remarkable ways.

Knowing and seeing these evidences of the Lord's pity and

mercy, the suffering saints ought to take good courage and bear up under their burdens of suffering. We are no longer in the old dispensation, and God no longer shows mercy and pity toward us by giving us earthly possessions, for in Job's time such possessions were typically pictures of spiritual blessings. But Job received spiritual blessings as well, and the chief of these blessings was God's vindication of Job's cause before his enemies. In the end the purpose of the Lord in our sufferings is the public vindication of our cause and our inheritance of the kingdom of heaven.

The Oath

12. But above all things, my brethren, swear not, neither by heaven, neither by the earth, neither by any other oath: but let your yea be yea; and your nay, nay lest ye fall into condemnation.

But above all things, my brethren, swear not, neither by heaven, neither by the earth, neither by any other oath: but let your yea be yea; and your nay, nay; lest ye fall into condemnation (5:12)

Again we are confronted with the relation between this verse and its context. There is no apparent connection other than the mild adversative "but." Many commentators conclude that there is no connection. Although the connection is somewhat elusive, the connective seems to indicate that a connection exists.

If we remember that the purpose of James' epistle is to distinguish sharply between dead faith and living faith, and if we remember that the congregations were composed primarily of Jews who had strong tendencies to swear oaths by all sorts of things (Matt. 5:33–37) and practices of keeping some oaths and not others, depending on the things by which they swore their oaths, it is not unreasonable to conclude that James warns against this practice in the context of faith. Perhaps the oath was still common among converted Jews and was sometimes used as a means to escape persecution by their employers. This may be the reason that "above all things" is added. The use of oaths and of failing to keep some of them may have been a part of the tradition of the fathers against which Jesus spoke.

Some groups and sects in the history of the church from the sixteenth-century Reformation to the present have interpreted these words as a command not to use the oath at all under any circumstances. This, however, is a mistake. Scripture gives examples of saints who swore oaths, and our Lord did not object to being put under oath by Caiaphas (Matt. 26:63–64).

There is a wanton use of the oath among God's people, especially children who are quick to say to their classmates, "Cross my heart and hope to die," and such like oaths. Most often these oaths are an effort to cover up something sinful that the oath-taker has done. There are also sinful oaths such as Peter took when he was confronted by the accusation that he was one of Christ's disciples and denied that he even knew Christ (Matt. 26:72).

Oaths are permissible, but only under definite circumstances. In a world in which people lie all the time, the magistrate must require an oath to ensure that a witness tells the truth. One may be required to take an oath when the good name of his neighbor is at stake. Consistories are sometimes compelled to put someone under oath when two members come with diametrically opposite statements concerning a matter, and when the truth cannot be determined.

Usually oaths are easily taken when one's yea is not yea and when one's nay is not nay. The text speaks directly to that underlying problem: people do not speak the truth. Sometimes they lie outright; sometimes they twist the truth; sometimes they speak a partial truth; or sometimes they keep silence and plead ignorance when they do not wish to speak the truth.

Thus Jesus' words in Matthew 5:33–37 and James' words here admonish the members of the church always to speak the truth. Then there is no need for oaths. This necessity of speaking the truth is rooted in the ninth commandment. Scripture never approves of the lie. Some have argued that the circumstances under which a lie is spoken determines the rightness or wrongness of the lie, but scripture makes no such distinction, and the whole effort to condone a lie ends in relative ethics. Scripture does record lies told by people of God but never condones these lies.

The frequency with which the epistle speaks of judgment and condemnation is worth noting. Constantly we are reminded of the condemnation that falls on those who do not walk in the way God has ordained. Put into the context of the theme of the letter, this takes on added significance. Those whose faith is dead and whose lives give evidence of this dead faith will surely be condemned. Dead faith means nothing at all. Only a true and living faith that binds us to Christ saves. Those who boast of their dead faith must never think they will escape condemnation. To speak the truth always is an important evidence of living faith that trusts that obedience to God is right, no matter the consequences. Living faith believes that God is able to turn evil to good and bless us in spite of the catastrophes that seem imminent in telling the truth.

The child of God must speak the truth always.

Spiritual Help in Trouble

13. Is any among you afflicted? let him pray. Is any merry? let him sing psalms.
14. Is any sick among you? Let him call for the elders of the church; and let them pray over him, anointing him with oil in the name of the Lord:

15. And the prayer of faith shall save the sick, and the Lord shall raise him up; and if he have committed sins, they shall be forgiven him.

Once again it seems as if James begins an entirely different subject without any apparent connection with the preceding context. This is probably not true, although James does not make the connection explicit.

In general, the context has spoken of difficult times for the people of God. As Jews who had been brought to faith in Christ by the power of the gospel, they were branded as traitors by their fellow Jews and called apostates from the religion of their fathers. They suffered for this, especially if they worked for wealthy fellow Jews. Their lives of joy and peace in the faith of the gospel were mixed with the anguish of suffering.

The believer has times of deep sorrow in life, as well as times of great joy. In this passage the church receives some instruction as to how the saints must react to the joys in their lives and the griefs that are always mixed with joys.

Is any among you afflicted? let him pray (5:13)

In the following series of questions this question is first because the saints to whom this is written undoubtedly experienced more afflictions than joys.

The Greek word (*kakopathei*) translated as "afflicted" literally means to suffer evil. The evil referred to is not sin. The idea is not that the people suffer the consequences of sin, but that they suffer evil at the hands of their oppressors.

At the same time, there is no reason that this word cannot be taken in a broader sense to include all the ills that befall the children of God: sickness, life's problems and disappointments, sorrow over the loss of loved ones, pain, and suffering. The results are loneliness, doubt, fear, perplexity, anguish of soul, and the grief that attends us in our lives in the valley of the shadow of death. Scripture speaks repeatedly, especially in the psalms, of the sufferings of the people of God. Never do the scriptures promise a believer a life of ease and tranquility, unalloyed joy, and happiness. The life of one who follows Jesus can better be described, according to our Lord, as a life of self-denial and cross-bearing (Matt. 16:24). Those who preach prosperity are false prophets who lead their hearers to hell.

What is the solution to our suffering?

The wicked have answers. No man ought to suffer, they say. Everyone has a right to happiness. The Declaration of Independence of the United States says that every man is endowed with certain inalienable rights that include life, liberty, and the pursuit of happiness.

When one does not find happiness, he drowns his sorrows in drink and and tries to escape them with drugs. Another goes to a psychiatrist to have his psyche explored and to discover the reasons for his unhappiness. Yet another takes various pills. Still another reads books to learn from misguided preachers how to be happy in life.

But the reason for sorrow in the midst of the sufferings of life is spiritual, for which there is no earthly cure.

The solution, James says, is prayer. Many, even in the church, find this simplistic and unrealistic, but scripture knows no other way. Pray! It is as simple as that. It is as difficult as that.

Prayer is a great blessing, a privilege given by grace on the basis of the merits of Christ's cross. The wicked do not have the right to pray, for the only way to God is through our mediator, Jesus Christ, who prepared the way for us into God's sanctuary.

Prayer is conversation with God in covenantal fellowship with him. That is its wonder. The infinitely great and glorious God through Jesus Christ condescends to us and carries us into his presence. He speaks to us through the scriptures, and we respond to his word by speaking to him. Prayer is the God-ordained way to keep us in fellowship with him in all of life and life's circumstances. Prayer is the means to cast all our cares on God, to seek him in our distresses, and to find comfort in sorrows, strength in our weaknesses, joys in distresses, peace in the turmoil of our doubts and fears.

This is the solution to our afflictions. Prayer is not a magic wand that removes our afflictions. It is not a guarantee that suffering will be taken away and sickness healed, but prayer leads us to God's word and to God himself revealed in his word, where all life's sorrows and afflictions are put into their proper spiritual perspective. Kneeling humbly before the throne of God's grace, we see how he averts all evil in our lives or turns it to our profit. We come to understand that he will never send trials that are more than we can bear, but will always provide the way of escape (1 Cor. 10:13). We are told in life's darkest hours, "My grace is sufficient for thee: for my strength is made perfect in weakness" (2 Cor. 12:9). We are urged to enter God's hallowed courts with boldness, "for we have not an high priest which cannot be touched with the feeling of our infirmities; but was in all points tempted like as we are, yet without sin. Let us therefore come boldly unto the throne of grace, that we may obtain mercy, and find grace to help in time of need" (Heb. 4:15–16).

So often prayer does not satisfy us, and we think it is ineffective because we consider prayer a shortcut to get what we want. But prayer is not a spiritual shopping center to which we go with lists of our desires. In God's hallowed courts we learn not what we want but what God wants, and we learn that we want what God wants.

Prayer is the way of peace in afflictions.

Is any merry? let him sing psalms (5:13)

If there are times of anguish and distress in the life of a child of God, there are also times of joy: the marriage of two covenant people, the birth of a covenant child, the deliverance from pain, the godly walk of one's children, and those times when even in our afflictions we know and experience the nearness of God.

These are reasons for true joy. The world also speaks of its joy that supposedly is found in drinking parties, fornication, and riches. It is a meaningless and totally superficial merriment expressed in silly laughter, ribald jokes, senseless mockery of others, and in earthly pleasures. It is usually an effort to cover up an anguished and fear-stricken soul that knows only the wrath of God. Even jokes are often laughter over life's tragedies: disobedient children, weak husbands, inane teenagers, and more.

Christians are often accused of being long faced, boring, unhappy people who walk around with scowls on their faces and recklessly charge others with sin whenever they are having a bit of fun. This is not true; it is a lie born out of jealousy. Laughter and fun have a legitimate place in the lives of the children of God. In fact, we are commanded to rejoice always (Phil. 4:4).

The joy of the Christian is found in his assurance that God loves him and that all is well, no matter what the circumstances of life may be. His joy is in his delight in the fellowship of fellow saints who share their happiness in the Lord. His joy is the pleasure of receiving God's good gifts. Christian happiness arises from a heart that is contented, at peace with God and man, and filled with serenity. It is not determined by the outward circumstances of life, for one can be happy in pain, at the side of an open grave, and in facing great problems. It is the fruit of joyful appropriation of the great truths of scripture.

The scriptures repeatedly summon God's people to be happy and joyful in life. They are to be joyful even when God's judgments come on the earth (Ps. 48:11; 97:8, 12). Isaiah called the daughter of Zion and those who mourned her destruction to rejoice (Isa. 40:9; 52:9; 66:10; and many other passages). Zechariah found Christ's entry into Jerusalem a great reason for joy (Zech. 9:9). Jesus admonished his disciples to rejoice in persecution (Matt. 5:12). Paul spoke of God's people as "sorrowful, yet always rejoicing" (2 Cor. 6:10). Peter spoke of the saints' rejoicing in their inheritance even when they were in fiery trials (1 Pet. 1:6–8).

What are we to do when we are happy? Sing psalms!

The word translated as "psalms" can refer to the Hebrew psalter. It means to pluck on a stringed instrument to make music. It also means to sing praises to God, and this is the meaning here. The church sang in its worship in the New Testament, and their book of songs was the Hebrew psalter.

The church has always sung praises to God. We have in scripture songs of Miriam, Deborah and Barak, Hannah, Habakkuk, Mary, Elizabeth, and Simeon. The passover feast ended with a song (Matt. 26:30), which was usually Psalms 116–18.

Singing is a gift of the Holy Spirit and it must be done with understanding and from the heart. The psalms are particularly important because in singing them, we confess the truth as God has revealed it. We pour out our hearts to God on high, tell of the joy of his deliverance of us from all our woes, and praise and bless his holy name. In other words, to sing psalms when we are happy is to express that our joy is in our God. Psalms are our delight, for they lift us out of sorrow to God's dwelling place and out of distress into the joy of salvation.

Is any sick among you? let him call for the elders of the church (5:14)

While we are to pray when we are afflicted and sing psalms when we are happy, there are times when afflictions are so overwhelming and our hearts are so crushed by the agony of suffering that we cannot pray. Every child of God knows such times. What then are we to do? We are to call the elders of the church.

There is much controversy in the church concerning the meaning of this passage. It is common among Pentecostal writers to appeal to this text in support of faith healing. It is not my intent to enter this controversy here. Much has been written on the question, and the claim of Pentecostalism that miracles of healing are still a part of the church's ministry has been frequently refuted.[6]

The controversy turns on the meaning of the word "sick." Pentecostalism insists that the word means physical sickness, and it often does. But the meaning can also refer to spiritual sickness, and that is undoubtedly the meaning here.[7] The noun form refers to spiritual weakness (Rom. 6:19; 8:26; 1 Cor. 2:3; 2 Cor.11:30; 12:5, 9; Heb. 4:15; 5:2; 7:28; 11:34). In many of these passages the word is translated as "infirmities." The verb form is used in Romans 8:3; 14:1–2, 21; 2 Corinthians 11:29; 13:9; and other places.

It is clear from the context that the reference in James is to spiritual sickness, resulting in the inability to pray. Verse 13 obviously refers to spiritual weaknesses or strengths, and the context following verse 14 speaks of sins to be forgiven. Further, we have here the absolute promise of God that our sicknesses will be healed, something scripture never promises when it refers to physical afflictions. Not even the apostle Paul could perform a miracle on himself, even though he prayed three times to be delivered from the thorn in his flesh (2 Cor. 12:7–9).

---

6 See F. D. Bruner, *A Theology of the Holy Spirit* (Grand Rapids, MI: Wm. B. Eerdmans Publishing Co., 1970); B. B. Warfield, *Miracle: Yesterday and Today* (Grand Rapids, MI: Wm. B. Eerdmans Publishing Co., 1984); David Engelsma, *Try the Spirits* (South Holland, IL: Evangelism Committee of the South Holland Protestant Reformed Church, 1987).

7 The Greek word is *astheneia*, which comes from the Greek word *sthenos* plus the alpha privans. It thus means lacking in strength.

The fact that "sick" refers to spiritual sickness does not preclude the close relation between spiritual sickness and physical sickness. All sickness is the result of the entrance of sin into the world. Sometimes specific physical diseases such as HIV, syphilis, and cirrhosis are directly traceable to sins. God frequently sends physical sicknesses to his people to chastise them and to restore them to spiritual health. Yet we must not try to understand the Most High, who does what pleases him. Many people of God who lead spiritually weak lives are not given much chastisement as far as we or they can see. Many spiritually strong saints suffer the severest of physical trials for no apparent spiritual reason. God's answer to Job, when he wanted to know the reason for his great suffering was simply, "Job, it is none of your business. I am God; I do what pleases me; I am never under any obligation to be summoned into your court to justify what I do."

Spiritual sickness is not unusual. It can come to a person after days, months, or years of suffering. It can come when God's people do not live out of faith. It can also come as a direct result of a particular spiritual failure to be faithful to God's commands in our lives. When it does come upon a person, the reason is frequently that in his consciousness it seems that God abandoned him. How frequently does not the psalmist speak of God's being afar off? God is deaf to our cries; he, as it were (in a powerful metaphor), is asleep when he ought to be awake. In times of such abandonment heaven's door seems to be closed, and we cannot pray.

What then are we called to do?

Call the elders of the church. The admonition presupposes that early in its existence the New Testament church was organized with officebearers, among whom were elders. These elders functioned in the office to which they had been called and for which they were qualified.

Although the minister of a congregation is also an elder, there is a distinction made between those who preached in the congregations and those who ruled. The conclusion is that while the minister may if necessary attend to problems of spiritually weak sheep, it is his main calling to preach the word, and the main calling of the ruling elders is to minister to the sick. The elders are responsible for the spiritual health of the congregation, for they hold the office of oversight of the flock. They are to be summoned when someone is so burdened with crushing affliction that he or she finds prayer impossible.

Let it not be forgotten that this is an admonition, a command of the scriptures. To neglect to do this is wrong. One may not be so confident of his own strength or so embarrassed by his own weakness that he refuses to call the elders. When the elders come, Christ comes, for he is the one who works through all the office-bearers to accomplish the salvation of the people of God.

And let them pray over him, anointing him with oil in the name of the Lord (5:14)

The duty of officebearers is to be intercessors who stand before God in the place of those who cannot pray. Contrary to Rome, the believer ordinarily needs no intercessor other than Christ, for the believer holds the office of prophet, priest, and king. However, the text speaks of unusual circumstances in which the believer needs an intercessor because he cannot go to God through Christ.

The elders must pray in the name of the Lord.

The question is sometimes raised whether the reference is to God or to Christ. Ordinarily we pray in the name of Christ, for in him alone we have access to God and from him we receive all things. There is no reason that this cannot be the meaning here.

The elders must pray that the person for whom they pray is brought to God. This means they must have knowledge of the spiritual reason for a saint's inability to pray. If they truly watch over the flock, they usually know the reason. But the sick person must be ready to tell the elders enough so that they know what specific need to bring to God. Yet the elders must not assume the role of medical doctor and advise the person with regard to medical ailments, something ministers and elders are frequently tempted to do. Nor must elders psychoanalyze the parishioner. While perhaps on occasion confession is good for the soul, a minister must not attempt to lead a parishioner to confess his sins to the elders. One must confess his sins to God. Elders must be content with an awareness of the spiritual reason for one's inability to pray. Nothing more needs be done. Prayer is enough.

The text emphasizes the importance and power of prayer. It is presented in the text as the one and only solution to life's problems. When elders are intercessors, they bring the troubled child of God to him in their prayers, and God hears elders who pray for the sick.

The phrase is added that the sick one must be anointed with oil. This injunction is not to be taken literally. James constantly makes references to Old Testament practices (4:8). Oil is a sign of the Holy Spirit. It was used in the consecration of prophets, priests, and kings. Here the anointing with oil indicates a prayer for the Holy Spirit to return to this sick person so that he may function again in his office of believer. It is a beautiful way of putting a profound spiritual truth.

And the prayer of faith shall save the sick, and the Lord shall raise him up (5:15)

A prayer of faith is uniquely a prayer of a believer. In this case the reference is to the elders whose prayers must be prayers of faith. Faith is the bond that unites the child of God to Christ and thus becomes the means whereby Christ and his blessings become his possession. When prayer is made in faith it is a spontaneous reaching out to Christ in whom alone is salvation. It is a prayer that believes that Christ will give everything needed to save the sick sinner.

That prayer will be heard and God will save the sick. The word translated as "sick" is not the one used in verse 14, but it means the weary one. It is used in the New Testament here and in Hebrews 12:3: "Consider him that endured such contradiction of sinners against himself, lest ye be wearied and faint in your minds." It seems that the word refers to one who cannot pray because the cares and afflictions of life have wearied him and exhausted his spiritual strength. When the prayers of elders are answered, he will receive strength from God to go on in his pilgrim journey no matter what the difficulties may be.

And if he have committed sins, they shall be forgiven him (5:15)

The clause is a condition of probability. The sick Christian is not necessarily one who has committed a sin that lies behind his spiritual sickness, but the possibility and perhaps even the probability is that he has. Unconfessed sin will bring on through a bad conscience the loss of the consciousness of God's favor and love, and consequently such spiritual turmoil that one cannot pray.

Elders must remember this when they are called to minister to the sick. They may not and need not know what sin or sins lie behind the sickness, if indeed such is the case, but they must take this into account, and when praying for the sick, pray for the forgiveness of sins as well. This prayer is always appropriate, for we all are always in need of forgiveness. The elders may therefore pray this prayer for forgiveness without implying that an individual sick person has some unconfessed sin that makes him spiritually sick. The Holy Spirit is a superb Christian counselor and pastor. The Holy Spirit gives elders guidelines in their work that cannot be found anywhere else, and which are almost always contradicted by counselors, worldly or Christian.

When an elder prays for the sick sinner, the Lord will hear that prayer and forgive the one for whom the elder prays. The elder must assure the sick one in whose place he prays that God has forgiven him. The Lord will restore such a person.

Prayer for Fellow Saints

16. Confess your faults one to another, and pray one for another, that ye may be healed. The effectual fervent prayer of a righteous man availeth much.
17. Elias was a man subject to like passions as we are, and he prayed earnestly that it might not rain: and it rained not on the earth by the space of three years and six months.
18. And he prayed again, and the heaven gave rain, and the earth brought forth her fruit.
19. Brethren, if any of you do err from the truth, and one convert him;
20. Let him know, that he which converteth the sinner from the error of his ways, shall save a soul from death, and shall hide a multitude of sins.

The connection between this passage and the preceding is made explicit by "therefore," a conjunction in the Greek but omitted in the Authorized Version. Verses 16–20 are a conclusion to what has preceded. The order is this: we are to sing psalms when we are happy; we are to pray when we cannot sing psalms because of great sadness; we are to call the elders of the church when we cannot pray.

The members of the church also have similar responsibilities between themselves as they live together in the church of Christ. They are responsibilities that when carried out will avoid the dangers of sadness and inability to pray. The heart of these responsibilities is stated in the admonition, "Confess your faults one to another, and pray one for another."

Confess your faults one to another, and pray for one another, that ye may be healed (5:16)

This admonition arises out of the truth that the church is the body of Christ in which the saints live in mutual dependence on Christ and on each other. Their concern for God's salvation is never selfish concern for their own spiritual well-being, but is concern for the spiritual welfare of the entire church. This concern is strongest in the local congregation, but it extends to the denomination of which one is a part and to the whole catholic church of Christ. The nearer we stand to our fellow saints, the more pressing is the admonition. Our concern for the cause of God everywhere is that the church, under the constant pressures of the enemy, may be preserved and prosper.

There are many kinds of sins in the church of Christ, for none of us has attained perfection. We each have personal sins; congregations have congregational sins; and denominations have denominational sins. These sins are real and powerful, and they affect the spiritual condition of the individual saints and of the churches of which they are a part. Denominational sins destroy and tear apart churches, families, and friends and create bitterness, distrust, and strife. The Spirit is grieved, prayer goes unanswered, sin disrupts the work of the church, and the whole body of Christ suffers.

Hence the admonition is urgent. We must confess our sins to one another and pray for one another. To confess our sins to one another does not mean that each member of the church has to confess all his sins to everyone else in the church. This is not only unnecessary, but impossible as well. We cannot get on with the work of the church if we are obligated always to confess every sin to everyone else. Rather, in the fellowship of the saints, and knowing that all our fellow saints are sinners, we assume without any doubt that each child of God confesses his own sins to God in the quiet of his closet, that each family confesses its sins to God in family devotions, and that each congregation confesses its corporate sins in congregational worship.

To confess our sins to one another means that we acknowledge in our confessions that we are incapable of doing any good and are saved by grace alone.

There are always those in the church who attempt to present themselves as better than other saints. They deny that they, with the lowliest of the low, are unworthy sinners who depend utterly on the cross.

When an officebearer or individual saint must point out a sin in a fellow saint, he or she does so reluctantly, confessing his own sins and going with the sinner to the foot of the cross, but never simply sending him there.

When we harm others with our sins, we readily confess this to them. Our natural inclination is to justify ourselves and angrily react against those who admonish us. Rather, as James warns the churches to whom he writes, we must be willing to confess our faults.

In this way the wounds created by sin are healed. Sin always creates wounds in the church. Sin is divisive in the unity of the body. Sin creates antagonisms and bitterness among the saints. This is in the nature of sin, for it creates chasms between us and God. God has bridged that chasm and come to us in mercy with the forgiveness of sins through the work of Christ. When our sins create chasms between saints and between us and those against whom we have sinned, the sins must be removed for unity to be restored.

Confession of sin is the wonder of the removal of sin and the restoration of unity. When we confess our sins to God, he forgives, and peace with him is restored. When confession is made between saints, sin disappears and unity is again the joyful blessing of the saints.

To the admonition to confess our faults to one another is appended the admonition to pray for one another. This is so crucial in the church that it must be repeatedly emphasized. It is common for the saints to pray for those whose pathways in life are difficult because of sickness, pain, infirmity accompanying old age, and temptations in life that are destructive. This is good. But the admonition is broader. The admonition includes prayers for the congregations to which we belong and that are for the spiritual well-being of the congregations: prayers for the spiritual growth of the congregations, for faithfulness to the truth, and for escape from the clutches of materialism. Such prayers are to be made for the aged, for the parents of families, for the young people who constitute the church of tomorrow, and for the children and their need of covenantal instruction.

These prayers are made on the Lord's day in the worship of prayer, but they also need to be made by the members for each other and the congregation as a whole. These prayers bring healing in the congregation when they are prayers of faith. Our prayers must be made in the confidence that they will be heard. Hebrews 11:6 explains this: "But without faith it is impossible to please him: for he that cometh to God must believe that he is, and that he is a rewarder of them that diligently seek him." God promises to hear these prayers and to answer them.

The effectual fervent prayer of a righteous man availeth much (5:16)

With this statement of fact James begins the last section of his epistle. Verse 17 is connected to verse 16 and is an illustration meant to encourage us to pray for each other. The example of

Elijah and verses 19–20 are assurances that our prayers for each other are heard and answered by God and that the truth of them applies to all prayer.

This powerful statement in verse 16 emphasizes that the prayers of which James speaks are prayers "of a righteous man." A righteous man is justified by the atoning work of Christ and has by the power of faith appropriated that righteousness to himself. He comes to God boldly because he knows he is without sin in God's sight and is a son of God. The church of Christ is composed of such righteous men, and James calls attention to this fact to remind us that the church is what it is because of Christ's work.

Only those in the church who are aware of their righteousness make powerful prayers. They do not attempt to earn their own righteousness by their works or boast of their superior holiness, but they humbly confess that they are damnworthy sinners made righteous by the work of their Savior. Their prayers have power because their reliance is on Christ and not on themselves. The spiritual welfare and strength of the congregations depend upon Christ's work alone.

The scriptures teach repeatedly that God uses the prayers of his people to give each of us and the church as a whole the blessings of Christ. Spiritual healing comes only in the way of prayer, as does the assurance of the forgiveness of sins. This is always the rule (1 John 1:8–10).

Prayer is not the condition we fulfill to attain what we ask. That would make our prayers our work and a part of salvation that is dependent on us and our spiritual prowess. From God's viewpoint in his counsel he established an unbreakable connection between our prayers and the blessings we receive. As he works out his counsel, he works prayers within us and uses these prayers to bless us.

From our perspective prayer is an obligation, a spiritual necessity, and we are admonished, indeed urged, to make prayer an important part of our lives. The reason for this unbreakable tie between prayer and blessing is so that we will be conscious of God's grace as it is worked out in our lives. We are not robots that perform acts in response to the pressing of different buttons. We are rational and moral creatures who fully enjoy God's blessings. That full enjoyment comes only through the prayers that God works in us and that we make.

This truth is emphasized by the expression "effectual fervent" that modifies prayer. In the Greek this is one word (*energoumenē*) that is the root of the word *energy*. The word is in the passive, so that it could be translated as "the energized prayer of a righteous man." The meaning is that the prayer of a righteous man has power because it is energized by the Holy Spirit in the heart of that righteous man. The spiritual energy of our prayers is worked by the Holy Spirit. The importance of this can be seen from the fact that this also determines the contents of our prayers.

Sometimes this verse is appealed to as proof that any prayer we make is guaranteed a favorable answer no matter what its content may be. If only we pray energetically enough, God will give us whatever we ask. But this is not the teaching of this text or of any other passage in scripture. Many of our prayers are carnal and concerned with earthly things that our covetous hearts crave. These prayers are not energized by the Holy Spirit, but are born in our own sinful lusts.

The righteous man may know what prayers are energized by the Spirit by finding in scripture the requirements and content of true prayer. Scripture teaches us how to pray and what is to be the content of our prayers. The Holy Spirit never works in us apart from the objective word of the Bible. This is true also in the prayers of a righteous man.

The words (*polu ischuei*) translated as "availeth much" mean much strength. The expression looks at prayer from a human viewpoint. God has ordained all things, including our prayers and their answers. Never do our prayers cause God to do something he has not determined to do, nor do they prevent God from doing something that he has not planned in his counsel. If our prayers could change the mind of God, and if the motto "prayer changes things" means that prayer alters God's plan, I would never dare to pray again. We simply do not know what is best for us. We are little children, and God is our heavenly Father. It is important to understand that God answers our prayers and brings to pass those things for which we pray because of the unbreakable tie between prayer and God's works in his church.

Scripture provides examples of prayers that can accomplish the humanly impossible. Jacob through prayer prevailed over God himself and received the blessing of the promise (Gen. 32:24–31; Hos. 12:3–5). Christ spoke of faith that can move mountains (Matt. 17:20). Christ heard the prayer of the Syrophenecian woman, for she had faith greater than was found in Israel (Mark 7:24–30).

Elias was a man subject to like passions as we are (5:17)

The illustration of Elijah is an apt and telling illustration.

The saints to whom James writes and we who find in scripture our guide might be inclined to say that Elijah's example is of little value, for the spiritual strength of this mighty servant of God so far surpassed our weak and wavering faith that his example does not matter much to us who struggle with prayer and hardly dare to trust its power. But scripture considers it important that we understand that Elijah had no special power or spiritual strength that we do not have. But Elijah was a man like us in all things. He too was weak and easily discouraged. We need only picture him under the juniper tree south of Judah, where he tried to resign from his office of prophet (1 Kings 19:4–7). If Elijah was as weak as we are, the summit of his faith is attainable also when we pray.

And he prayed earnestly that it might not rain: and it rained not on the earth by the space of three years and six months (5:17)

Elijah announced on the steps of the palace in Samaria that no rain would fall on the land, except by his word. And so it happened.

We must be careful to understand this prayer of Elijah.

First, there is no record in 1 Kings 17 that Elijah prayed for the drought, although he announced it. That he prayed for the drought is confirmed by James.

Second, Elijah did not pray for drought out of a spirit of vindictiveness or anger regarding the northern kingdom. He had no pleasure in seeing the drought take its toll: the pastures filled with the bloated carcasses of cows and sheep; the emaciation of those who could find no food; the crying of starving babies. His concern was the spiritual condition of the northern kingdom. Ahab sat on the throne, and his wife Jezebel persuaded her spineless husband to make the worship of Baal the official religion. Elijah was concerned that the northern kingdom was lost and considered drought to be a means by which Israel might be restored to the true worship of God. Elijah's prayer was the prayer of a righteous man.

Third, Elijah considered the possibility of this judgment of God a means to bring the nation to repentance because his prayer was according to scripture. God had said that if Israel turned away from the worship of God, "thy heaven that is over thy head shall be brass, and the earth that is under thee shall be iron" (Deut. 28:23).

Finally, although God had said such terrible conditions would come as his judgment on Israel's apostasy, the drought came in answer to Elijah's prayer. It was truly the energized prayer of a righteous man that had power with God.

And he prayed again, and the heaven gave rain, and the earth brought forth her fruit (5:18)

Elijah knew that it was the will of God to send rain after the drought of three and a half years (1 Kings 18:1). God said that Elijah was to show himself to Ahab because "I will send rain upon the earth." Yet the rain did not come until Elijah prayed. In fact, he had to pray seven times before a cloud as big as a man's hand appeared in the western sky (vv. 42–45). From God's viewpoint both the rain and the prayer of Elijah were fixed in his counsel. From Elijah's viewpoint, his prayer was necessary to bring the rain. God always works in this way, so that we may experience in our lives his marvelous works. The unbreakable bond between prayer and God's answer to prayer is underscored. Without the prayer of Elijah rain would not have come.

Such is the power of prayer, and such is the certainty of prayer's being answered.

Brethren, if any of you do err from the truth, and one convert him (5:19)

The two verses with which James concludes his epistle belong to the entire section begun in verse 16. He still speaks to the members of the congregations concerning their mutual responsibilities toward each other in the church of Christ.

More particularly, it is not always true that those who sin are ready and spiritually able to confess their sins, as verse 16 admonishes them to do. In the event that sin is unconfessed, the members have a responsibility to go to the sinner and point out the error of his way.

The construction of verse 19 is a third class condition, in which the if-clause expresses some hesitancy about the fact. Both verbs are controlled by that hesitancy. If it should happen that someone in the congregation errs from the truth, and if it should happen that another saint converts him, let him know.

To "err from the truth" is to teach false doctrine. One who does so is a heretic. Although surely the sin of teaching false doctrine is meant, the application is broader than that. The truth of God can never be separated from our walk. If we teach false doctrine, it will manifest itself in how we live. The opposite is also true. A wicked walk is slander of God's truth, for God requires holiness and righteousness in everything we do.

To err doctrinally from the truth is serious. God is in himself the truth. He has revealed his truth in Jesus Christ, who is the way, the truth, and the life. The confession of the truth by the church and its members is the measuring stick by which the saints' love for God can be measured. If we are careless about the truth and indifferent toward it, if we overlook aberrations and tolerate untruths about God and Christ, and if we consider the truth to be of so little importance that we never condemn heresy, we do not love God. If we love our wives, we will at any cost defend their good names to anyone who slanders them; whereas, apparently, we do not have that kind of love for the God of heaven and earth and for his Christ. We consider the truth to be merely intellectual, as we would consider a geometric theorem. If we love God, we will be quick to defend his truth at any cost.

So also is the case with a godly walk. To err from the path of right is to discredit the God who has saved us. A child who is knowingly and deliberately disobedient to his parents' commands does not think much of his parents. Love for one's parents is the fountain of obedience.

In the church, where all the members of the church are prone to sin, we easily lose the right way.[8] It happens all the time. Many times the one who errs becomes aware of it, is ashamed of his conduct, and confesses his sin before God. But sometimes that does not happen. He needs to be told by his fellow saints.

Belonging to the if-clause is the statement "and one convert him." Although this is part of the probability suggested by the third class condition, the apostle refers to those in the congregation that are aware of the sin of a fellow saint and have the obligation to convert him. Undoubtedly, the uncertainly of it rests in reluctance to perform our obligations. We find it much easier to speak of the sin to others and together to shake our heads at the horror of it. Or we may be reluctant to go to our brother because we are unsure of how we will be received, or we may be aware of our sins and be so ashamed of them that we dare not point out sin to an erring brother.

Paul in a similar passage pointed out that we have this calling. "Brethren, if a man be overtaken in a fault, ye which are spiritual, restore such an one in the spirit of meekness; considering thyself, lest thou also be tempted. (Gal. 6:1). This passage also tells us how we are to convert our erring brother. We are not to do so by assuming a better-than-thou attitude. We are not to do so by sharp and condemnatory statements. We are to do so in a spirit of meekness, which accompanies all those who know how easy it is to fall.

The text speaks of converting our erring brother. To convert an erring brother means to turn him around spiritually, to turn him about so that instead of walking the way to destruction, he walks in the opposite direction toward heaven. It means to bring

---

8 The word *planēthē* is in the passive voice. Some commentators therefore have translated this word as "are led astray." But the passive can be a deponent form: though passive in voice, its meaning is active.

the sinner to the consciousness of his sin, to instill in his heart sorrow for his sin, and to lead him to the cross, where alone he can find forgiveness.

Only God can convert the sinner. We can with effort put a drunk on the wagon; we can, though it is difficult, rehabilitate a drug addict; we can bring together a battling husband and wife. But these are all outward alterations in conduct only, not conversions. Conversion is a matter of the heart, and only God by his Spirit can reach into the heart of the sinner and turn him around.

Nevertheless, we are said to convert the sinner. The meaning is that God is pleased to use us in his work of conversion. There is only one power of conversion to which the Spirit ties himself, and that is the word of God. No well-written book by a psychologist is able to do such a great work. Because it is God's work through his Spirit, the only power to bring conversion is God's power. That power is found in the scriptures.

This is the reason it takes no training, no special gifts, no abilities to counsel to convert the sinner. Any member in the church can convert the sinner if he comes only with the word of God. The word of God can do what no human can do. One who converts the sinner is himself a sinner, who comes with the word and is used by God to bring about true conversion.

Let him know, that he which converteth the sinner from the error of his way, shall save a soul from death, and shall hide a multitude of sins (5:20)

The one who converts an erring brother performs a wonderful work.

The conditional sentence begun in the previous verse is a condition of possibility or probability because all the efforts of a child of God to convert a sinner from his error may end in failure. Only God can convert a sinner, and it may not be God's will to do this. God determines whom he saves by his decree of sovereign election realized in the cross of Jesus Christ. The child of God, if his efforts appear unsuccessful, must remember that he is only an instrument in God's hand and that God always accomplishes his purpose, for his word never returns void (Isa. 55:8–11). Verse 20 is as an incentive for each saint to go to an erring brother. It is his obligation, and if he fulfills his obligation, he saves a soul from death and covers a multitude of sins.

The clauses "shall save a soul from death, and shall hide a multitude of sins" are not to be interpreted to mean that a child of God who converts a sinner has done a meritorious deed that attracts and pleases God in heaven and that will surely be rewarded. This is Roman Catholic works-righteousness. When a child of God turns a sinner from the error of his way, he does not do this to gain favor with God; he is not even conscious that he is performing a good work. Rather, such a one who brings the word to an erring brother loves God's church and knows that a sinner puts a spot on the church and threatens the church's well-being. Further, he loves his fellow saints and longs to have them walk in holiness. His motive is only that God's people may be saved.

The erring person is called a "sinner." The general word for sin is used here, the word so often employed in scripture to include all sins and to define their basic character. The word means one who misses the mark.

The sinner, if converted, leaves the path on which he is walking, a path that has as its destination hell. When he is converted, he once again walks the pathway defined by the law of God, the destination of which is heaven. This is a wonderful event in the life of the church. In Luke 15 our Lord repeatedly emphasized in three parables that even the angels in heaven rejoice and that it is an occasion for the church to rejoice as well.

Further, the child of God who is used by God to convert a

sinner covers a multitude of sins. The plural is used because one sin, left unchecked, produces other sins in the sinner, as well as in the congregation. That these sins are covered means that if the sin is secret (as such sins sometimes are), the conversion of the sinner keeps the sins from the knowledge of the congregation. Jesus speaks of this in Matthew 18:15.

James also means that the sin is covered in the sight of God and Christ. God forgives sin, for to restore a sinner to the path of holiness involves confession of sin and repentance. God forgives; Christ forgives; the unity of the church is restored; and the sinner walks in the joy of forgiveness. The sin is so covered that it is gone; it exists no longer.

This is the concluding verse of James' epistle, and a proper conclusion it is.

OTHER RFPA PUBLICATIONS
BY THE AUTHOR

Contending for the Faith: The Rise of Heresy and the Development of the Truth

For Thy Truth's Sake: A Doctrinal History of the Protestant Reformed Churches

God's Everlasting Covenant of Grace

Justified unto Liberty: Commentary on Galatians

Mysteries of the Kingdom: An Exposition of Jesus' Parables

A Pilgrim's Manual: Commentary on 1 Peter

Portraits of Faithful Saints

Ready to Give an Answer: A Catechism of Reformed Distinctives (coauthor with Herman Hoeksema)

We and Our Children: The Reformed Doctrine of Infant Baptism

When You Pray: Scripture's Teaching on Prayer